ACCLAIM FOR TRAVELERS' TALES BOOKS
BY AND FOR WOMEN

Women in the Wild
"A spiritual, moving and totally female book to take you around the world and back." —*Mademoiselle*

A Woman's Path
"A sensitive exploration of women's lives that have been unexpectedly and spiritually touched by travel experiences...highly recommended."
—*Library Journal*

A Woman's World
"Packed with stories of courage and confidence, independence and introspection; if they don't inspire you to pack your bags and set out into the world, I can't imagine what would." —*Self Magazine*

A Woman's Passion for Travel
"This collection is sometimes sexy, sometimes scary, sometimes philosophical and always entertaining." —*San Francisco Examiner*

Sand in My Bra and Other Misadventures
"Travel stories bursting with exuberant candor and crackling humor, sure to leave readers feeling that to not have an adventure to remember is a great loss indeed." —*Publishers Weekly*

A Woman's Europe
"Many women believe it's not safe to travel, certainly not alone. These stories will inspire them to overcome that hesitation and find a way to visit places they've only dreamed of." —*The Globe and Mail*

Gutsy Women
"Packed with instructive and inspiring travel vignettes and tips."
—*The Boston Globe*

TRAVELERS' TALES

THE
BEST
WOMEN'S TRAVEL
WRITING
2007

TRUE STORIES
FROM AROUND THE WORLD

TRAVELERS' TALES

THE BEST WOMEN'S TRAVEL WRITING

2007

TRUE STORIES FROM AROUND THE WORLD

Edited by

LUCY MCCAULEY

Travelers' Tales
Palo Alto

Art Direction: Stefan Gutermuth
Interior design and page layout: Melanie Haage using the fonts
    Nicolas Cochin, Ex Ponto and Granjon.

ISBN 1-932361-49-9
ISSN 1553-054X

First Edition
Printed in the United States
10 9 8 7 6 5 4 3 2 1

For my parents, Elizabeth (Elisita)
and Clayburn L. McCauley

I am going away to an unknown country where I shall have no past and no name, and where I shall be reborn again with a new face and an untried heart.

—COLLETTE

Table of Contents

Introduction

*W*hy do we return to places where we've been before? What propels us to move away from our familiar orbits to revisit the landscape of memory? Is it that we hope to recapture a previous experience from an earlier time? Do we return out of a lingering sense of incompletion or to rewrite the past somehow, hoping to uncover a hidden layer that might enable us to craft a new ending to our story? Or do we return simply to know a place more deeply and fully?

I was thinking about that idea of return last spring when my husband and I revisited the place where we'd honeymooned six years before, in Tübingen, southern Germany. This time we'd added a new travel companion—our young daughter, Hannah—and as we walked the streets of that medieval university town, I felt acutely attuned to the layers of experience conjured like specters by our act of return. I was aware of how we inevitably return to a place as different people from who we'd been before, and how that in turn changes the place for us even as the place itself has undergone its own transformations. How that palimpsest of experience alters the way a place shows itself to us.

My husband's own return held several such layers: long before our honeymoon, he had spent four years in Germany as a student. His return, this time with Hannah and me, was through the lens of a youth grown to adult middle age; single young man to family man. I had first come to Germany as a bride, and now I was a mother. Yet for both of us there was the added layer of a particular period in between, when my husband and I had separated when Hannah was a year old. This trip marked our return not just to Germany but to each other as well. And the occasion was appropriately laden with another mantle of significance: the couple with whom we'd stayed during our honeymoon (the man a friend from Charles's student days) was at last getting married after many years together. My husband would be best man. Layer upon layer of return.

We walked the stone streets of Tübingen, viewing the same sites we'd seen on our honeymoon. Much remained physically the same: the medieval castle that crowned the old part of the city; the Neckar River edged with lilacs and chrysanthemums; the geraniums that burst forth in fuchsia and orange from window boxes; the solitary tower where the poet Friedrich Hölderlin had lived after he went mad, in a round room overlooking the roiling river. On the Neckar bridge we posed for a photo, as we had on our last trip, and this time we lifted our daughter high between us like a prize.

Yet time, even a short six years, had changed our experience of the place—and not just because we'd added an extra (small) pair of legs to our excursions. We walked again up the wide expanse of hill that stood at the edge of town, every inch covered by yellow buttercups through which Hannah ran, laughing; through which my husband and I walked hand-in-hand, just as we had on our earlier visit. But this time, walking up that slope, our daughter galloping ahead, I felt our fingers fitting together differently somehow, nestled into a deeper understanding—the hard-won kind, like the centuries of experience etched into the stone and mortar of the town itself. To regain our footing together as a couple, we'd had to excavate and re-lay the foundation of who we were to one another and of who we wished to be ourselves, as individuals. On this return to Germany, our hands fit together differently because we fit together differently.

As we walked up the hill, I thought about part of the

reading we had chosen for our wedding years before, from T.S. Eliot's *Four Quartets:* "And the end of all our exploring / Will be to arrive where we started / And know the place for the first time." Perhaps that captures one reason why we return to the places we've been before. Not simply to know the past or our past selves again, but out of a deep and impossibly complex desire to know the place—and ourselves—anew. That is how it felt to return to the place of our honeymoon. That is how it felt to return to each other. We had begun our life together only to end it a few years later. And now we had begun again.

In the accounts of journeys in this volume of *The Best Women's Travel Writing* we are confronted, through a diverse range of voices, with this enigma of return. Many of these authors do this through memoir—Diana Cohen, Laurie Covens, Suzanne Kratzig, and Lonia Winchester all write about travel through the lens of their personal pasts, in places as far-flung as Israel, Thailand, Africa, and Poland, respectively. Other writers—such as Francesca DeStefano, Diane Johnson, Tehila Lieberman, and Carmen Semler— write about a physical revisitation to a place, recapturing it through older, more experienced eyes, bodies, and inter-pretations. Other selections in this book recount returns of writers to places and experiences through the simple yet profound act of retelling the journey in prose.

I hope that as you turn the pages of this volume, you'll find again places that had been lost to the realm of mem-ory-even as you discover here new places for the first time. As T.S. Eliot wrote (again in the Four Quartets): "The end is where we start from." May you find in these stories an ending that lifts a veil onto some new beginning, opening a doorway to your own return.

—Lucy McCauley
Somerville, Massachusetts

ᔕ᠍ ᔕ᠍ ᔕ᠍

Flirting in Paris

She found the ultimate cure for existential despair.

R ain shrouds the Bastille Farmers Market in Paris and I'm flirting with a tall, chain-smoking ruffian who looks like he hasn't slept in a week. He broods over asparagus while making smoldering eye contact. Even though he's a stranger, his glances imply intimacy. Something along the lines of "I have a magnifying glass into your soul. I wish to nibble your ear."

His rumpled profile appeals to me. I telegraph my thoughts to him while considering cauliflower. "We share a beautiful, tortured existence. I'll trifle with your arm hair."

I'm not a brazen hussy, just an average Sunday shopper enjoying the frisson of flirtation. The art of coquetry is integral to everyday life in France. In fact, flirting is as much a part of the culture as eating stinky cheese after dinner.

My late twenties brought a meltdown of cosmic proportions. Despondency pervaded every corner of my being. Occasional acting gigs in my adopted hometown of Hollywood worsened my despair. I was too old to be a starlet and too cynical to lie about my age.

In a supposedly near-breakthrough role, I played a stewardess with a speech impediment opposite Jim Carrey in *Ace Ventura: When Nature Calls*. My part consisted of one word. "Peanuts?" I said, dropping the "t" and lisping the "s" as I offered the snack. I booked a ticket to Paris the day the royalty payment arrived.

I traded Los Angeles strip malls for the esthetic pleasure of the Place Saint Sulpice. Strolling aimlessly along the Seine, I struggled to recover my identity. I lingered at cafes and strayed deeper into nothingness. Poodle adoption became a consideration. Albert Camus's quote perfectly illustrated my state of mind: "Nobody realizes that some people expend tremendous energy merely to be normal."

Normalcy in Paris would mean learning the language. I enrolled in a free French course at the Sorbonne. On day one, a handsome, affable guy, Jean David, introduced himself as my teacher. The program used cultural references, rather than traditional grammar lessons, as tools. Jean David would screen an extract from a Truffaut film, then have the class interpret the dialogue. In the darkened room his attention turned to me. He shot playful looks that said, "There are many vineyards in my family. I have homes scattered across France, Switzerland, and Spain. I could have done anything I wanted in life, but I chose to enlighten others. I want to make love to you on this desk."

After a few days I warmed to the game. Feeling genuinely coquettish, I reciprocated Jean David's gazes: "I have angel's breath and a willing mouth. I cook a mean shrimp gumbo. You are a naughty boy and I like it."

Immersion in Parisian life helped erase the humiliating auditions that were the fabric of my former existence. The promise of connection fueled my bicycle rides to class. Jean David and I flirted every day for six weeks. I naturally expected he would ask me on a date when the course ended. For our class party, I prepared an apricot tart, hoping to impress him with my culinary skills.

The fête was in full swing when a beautiful curly-haired girl appeared and Jean David presented her as *"ma petite amie*, Isabelle." My French was honed enough to understand this meant girlfriend. I was dismayed. How could he have led me on? Did he lead me on? He'd only provoked me with his eyes.

As he left, he offered me a long, expressive stare, one that said, "It is such a pity we won't make love, but I will always long for you." Meantime, Isabelle threw me a look that said, "I am skinnier than you and wear much nicer underwear." I slunk out of the party, empty tart pan in tow.

The secret glances that Jean David and I shared flashed before me as I lugubriously pedaled away from the Sorbonne. Something illusory, yet very real, had happened. Our ocular encounters weren't meaningless, they roused and inspired. I rode by a baguette-toting businessman who was exiting a boulangerie. With utmost formality, he electrified me with a sincere "I'd like to be a bicycle seat in my next life" look. My face reddened as I biked on. Then a cultural epiphany struck. American men flirt as a means to an end: to get laid. The French flirt because it is part of *"la vie*," a chance to transform an ordinary moment into a profound acknowledgment of elusive potential. Wow. Being anonymously objectified could be fun.

Armed with my new understanding, I cultivated the thrill of locking eyes across the sidewalk with a stranger and wallowing in the unknown. Such communication

suited me more than one-sided conversations with preen-
ing, wannabe actors.

An unexpected exchange occurred at a hospital emergency room where I'd accompanied a friend with a broken
ankle. As she waited to receive treatment, a disheveled
paramedic entered, wheeling a bloodied body on a gurney.
He turned to me and slowed his pace. His drawn out look
said, "I am worn, battered, and need attention. Love me."
I returned with "I want to give you a warm bath and
a foot massage. I get your needs. I'm wearing pink lacy
culottes." The healing power of random connection out-
weighed my nihilistic tendencies and I actually started to
feel happy. But I feared relinquishing my mask of angst,
worried I might not attract as much flirt potential.

On an overcast afternoon when the Parisian clouds hung
dramatically low, I hopped a bus along the Boulevard Saint
Germain. The sandy-haired driver established eye contact
with a frisky ogle in his rear-view mirror. One that said,
"My Ile St. Louis apartment is lined with books by obscure
architects."

Clinging to my damaged persona, I demurely responded
with "the Ile St. Louis is too touristy." But he was persistent. He penetrated me with "my place is next to Bertillon
and the view, magnificent." Always a sucker for good ice
cream and a stunning panorama, I cracked a smile and sent
a "chocolate is my flavor, what's yours?" look. I decided to
flirt with abandon. My stop was next: I'd never see him
again.

His return grin sent me reeling with such intensity that
my internal dialogue was hushed. Of the many memories
I have of Paris, this one remains in the forefront. As I
descended the bus, I whirled around and for that moment,
enjoyed the sheer connection: the two of us strangers, radi-
ating intangible delight in the other.

As the doors closed I was tempted to write down his bus number, or run ahead to the next stop and board again. But the actress Anouk Aimee's words were a reminder to love and lose: "It's so much better to desire than to have." I felt immense joy as he drove away, marveling at how my mediocre day changed into one of pure elation.

♪♫ ♪♫ ♪♫

Kayla Allen, a PEN USA Emerging Voices Rosenthal Fellow, lives with her family in Nice, France and Shreveport, Louisiana. She is at work on her first novel, Rapture Dummy, *a fictional account of her years as a child evangelist ventriloquist.*

✍ ✍ ✍

Cupolas of Alghero

When the pull of the journey feels
too great, say *andiamo*!

The silhouette of Alghero rises from the Mediterranean. My husband, Ed, and I are walking toward town just after noon, when sunlight slips straight through the clean water, rippling the white bottom of the sea with ribbons of light.

"*Limpida*," he says, "*chiara*." Limpid, clear, the slow tide pushing light in bright arcs across the sandy floor. Alghero, nominally an Italian town on the western edge of Sardinia, has colorful geometric-tiled cupolas, Catalan street names, Arabic flourishes in the cuisine. I feel a sudden attraction to Spain, to exotic Moorish courtyards, fountains that soothed those desert invaders, to the memory of a Latin man who once whispered to me, "Please, share my darkness in Barcelona." A desire for some fierce, unnameable, dour, and dignified essence of Spain. I imagine walking there, along a whitewashed wall, peeling an orange, a book of Lorca's poems in my pocket.

"I'd like to taste the last drop," I say, a non sequitur.

Ed is not bothered by non sequiturs. He just picks up on the word *taste*. "We're going to a trattoria where they specialize in lobster with tomatoes and onions. Sounds delicious—*aragosta all'algherese*—lobster from these waters cooked in the style of Alghero." He consults a piece of paper where he has written an address. "And yes, I know what you mean."

"What if we didn't go home? What if we just kept traveling? The European writers always had their *wanderjahr*, their year of wandering in their youth. I'd like one of those, even at this late date."

"Probably better now than when you were young. Where do you want to go?"

"How far *are* we from Spain?"

"I must mention that I have a job." He points to a hump of land. "Neptune's Grotto—we'll take a boat out there after lunch. I would like to go to Morocco," he adds.

"Greece was the first foreign place I ever wanted to see and I've never been." A map of the world unscrolls in my mind, the one I looked at when I was ten in a small town in Georgia. Bright flags line the sides of the maps, and the countries are saffron, lavender, rose, and mint according to their altitude and geology. Sweden. Poland. The Basque country. India. Then I shift into an explosion of images: I'm threading my way through the spice bazaar in Istanbul, assaulted by hot scents rising from sacks of fenugreek, turmeric, gnarly roots, and dried seeds; we're leaning on the railing of a slow boat when a crocodile splats its tail in the murky green waters of the Nile; Ed is shaking out a picnic cloth as I look into the green dips and curves of the valley punctuated with cromlechs and dolmens; I'm driving past a marsh, russet in the autumn light, and I recognize the barrier island off the coast of Georgia, one of the Golden Isles, where I spent summer vacations as a child.

That archipelago was the first place I ever longed for. During the rainy winter months of my childhood, sometimes mercurial sensations of the island came to me in a rush—humid, salty air catches in my hair, the saw palmettos clatter in the torrid breezes of August, and my hand sweats in our cook Willie Bell's hand as we walk toward a low ridge, where she will lower a crab trap baited with "high" meat into black water. I ached *not* to be in Miss Golf's first-grade classroom, where the floors smelled of pine oil and sawdust and the little letters followed the big letters in colored chalk around the room. I wanted the firm feel of Willie Bell's hand, the horror of rotting raw meat in the crab trap, sunrises on the beach, and the long walk back to the house on the crushed oyster shell path.

At six, that sensation was a tide, a rhythm, a hurt, a joy. This powerful *first* sensation of a place I have come to know well because I've kept it all my life, just as I've kept square thumbnails and insomnia. One of my favorite writers, Freya Stark, acknowledged a similar feeling in *The Valley of the Assassins*: "It shone clearly distinct in the evening light, an impressive sight to the pilgrim. I contemplated it with the feelings due to an object that still has the power to make one travel so far." Her *it* being anything that pulls us hard enough so that we take the passport from the drawer, pack the minimum, and head out the door with an instinct as sure as that of an ancient huntress with quiver and bow.

The urge to travel feels magnetic. Two of my favorite words are linked: *departure time*. And travel whets the emotions, turns upside down the memory bank, and the golden coins scatter. How my mother would have loved the mansard apartment we borrowed from a friend in Paris. Will I be lucky enough to show pieces of the great world to my grandchild? I'm longing to hold his hand when he first steps into a gondola. I've seen his freedom burst upon him on hikes in California. Arms out, he runs forward. I recognize the surge.

Sardinia—the real name: Sardegna. I have wanted to come here since I read D.H. Lawrence's *Sea and Sardinia* years ago in a blank hotel room in Zurich. "It is a small, stony, hen-scratched place of poor people," I read. And, "In we roll, into Orosei, a dilapidated, sun-smitten, god-forsaken little town not far from the sea. We descend to the piazza." *We descend to the piazza.* Yes, that's the sentence I liked. I underlined "sun-smitten" in my paperback book, and as I fell asleep, the noise of Zurich traffic below became these waves I see right now lapping the sea wall.

We have a few days. I will look at all the Moorish tiles. Sample the hard pecorino and goat cheeses. Climb around in the prehistoric village. I will not buy one of the million coral necklaces in the shops. We'll look for wild medlar and myrtle, asphodel and capers on the hillsides.

Ed shades his eyes with the guidebook. He points. "The boat can drop us out there—see the white crescent beach—after we see the grotto of fabulous stalactites. Let's eat," he says. "*Andiamo.*" Let's go.

Travel pushes my boundaries. Seemingly self-indulgent, travel paradoxically obliterates me-me-me, because very quickly—*prestissimo*—the own-little-self is unlocked from the present and released to move through layers of time. It is not 2006 all over the world. So who are you in a place where 1950 or 1920 is about to arrive? Or where the guide says, "We're not talking about A.D. today. Everything from now on is B.C." I remember the child who came out of a thatched shack deep in the back roads of Nicaragua. She ran to touch the car, her arms thrown up in wonder. She would have looked at the headlights turn on and off all night. You are released also because you are insignificant to the life of the new place. When you travel, you become invisible, if you want. I do want. I like to be the observer. What makes these people who they are? Could I feel at home here? No one expects you to have the stack of papers back by Tuesday, or to check messages, or to fertilize the geraniums, or to sit full of dread in the waiting room at the proctologist's office. When traveling, you have the delectable possibility of not understanding a word of what is said to you. Language becomes simply a musical background for watching bicycles zoom along a canal, calling for nothing from you. Even better, if you speak the language, you catch nuances and make more contact with people.

Travel releases spontaneity. You become a godlike creature full of choice, free to visit the stately pleasure domes, make love in the morning, sketch a bell tower. Read a history of Byzantium, stare for one hour at the face of Leonardo da Vinci's *Madonna dei fusi*. You open, as in childhood, and—for a time—receive this world. There's the visceral aspect, too—the huntress who is free. Free to go, free to return home bringing memories to lay on the hearth.

A year after those, yes, sun-smitten days in Sardinia, we are going off to Spain; then we have a list of places in the world we would like to call home, at least for a while. At twenty, it's easy to sling on the backpack and take off. Later, you may find the responsibilities that the years layer onto our bodies and souls to be hard to impossible to escape. You have to wrench your circumstances to get out from under them. And my home lulls me. The yellow roses on the table, creamy ironed sheets with my mother's monogram, rabbit with fennel baking in the oven, guests about to arrive, my cat Sister purring against my foot, a sunroom full of books. These profound comforts—the joys of *home*. I'm elated when the Yesterday, Today, Tomorrow starts to bloom, when Ed loads the iron table from the consignment shop on top of the car, and when we cook with good friends—Brunswick stew, cornbread, coconut pie.

The thrown-off remark, *I want to taste the last drop*, will go down in my column of the book kept by the heavenly scribe. How did one sentence send me off into an intense five years of boarding planes, buses, trains, ships? The dream of a travel year became compromised by a complicated life. But the trips, arranged by season, become in my mind a single year in the world.

A series of events sharpened my sense of *carpe diem*, making me edgy to go. First a friend's heart attack, then my mother's death, then the stunning horror of breast cancer in nine, *nine*, of my closest friends. Two died. Other less drastic forces began to press. Teaching often swamped my writing. I longed for time. Unscheduled time, dream time, quiet time. Not just summers, when it took a month to recover from the exhausting academic year. *Quit*, I thought.

"You could be dead by evening," I read in Proust. Well, I know that. A potato chip truck can flatten you at any given stoplight—this happened to one friend—but knowledge sometimes slides off and sometimes scores a direct hit. The synergy of our decision to travel sent out sine waves. All fall I looked at maps, saying incredulously, "I always meant to go to Scotland." I read *The White Nile*, *Journey into Cyprus*, the poems of Hikmet, *Mornings in Mexico*, and all the Victorian women travelers who crossed Patagonia or Kaffirland, and refused to lift their skirts over mudholes in central Africa. From Colette I copied in my yellow notebook,...*nothing can equal the savor of that which has been seen, and truly seen*, and also her evocative sentence, *I'm leaving tonight for Limousin*.

In our *carpe diem* state of mind, we decide to take a big risk and live by our wits. Travel will be tied to a bigger word, *freedom*. We resign from our teaching jobs to work as full-time writers and to explore new possibilities. Are you crazy? Giving up two tenured university jobs in the Bay Area? Ed turned in his resignation on Valentine's Day and came home with three dozen yellow roses. We're giddy, then scared, then giddy. Imagine—*time*.

Everything I pick up seems to lure me away. Everything I do in my daily life begins to feel like striking wet matches.

The need to travel is a mysterious force. A desire to *go* runs through me equally with an intense desire to *stay* at home. An equal and opposite thermodynamic principle. When I travel, I think of home and what it means. At home I'm dreaming of catching trains at night in the gray light of Old Europe, or pushing open shutters to see Florence awaken. The balance just slightly tips in the direction of the airport.

I'm looking out my study window at San Francisco Bay, the blue framed by stands of eucalyptus trees. The wind, I imagine, blew across Asia, then across Hawai'i, bringing—if I could smell deeply enough—a trace of plumeria perfume. The western sun makes a grandiose exit in the smeared lavender-pink sky—a Mrs. Gotrocks gold orb sinking behind sacred Mount Tamalpais. The bay water, running into the ocean! Washing all the miraculous places.

With the force of an earthquake, a wild certainty forms in the center of my forehead. Time. To go. Time. Just go.

I asked an impulsive question, What if we did not go home, what if we kept traveling? Should you not listen well to the questions you ask out of nowhere? Only in looking back do you find those crumbs you dropped that marked your way forward.

❧ ❧ ❧

Frances Mayes is the author of the bestselling memoirs, Under the Tuscan Sun *and* Bella Tuscany, *in addition to two illustrated books, several works of poetry, and the novel* Swan. *Her latest work,* A Year in the World: Journeys of a Passionate Traveler, *from which this excerpt was drawn, further chronicles her love of exploration and the importance of travel. She and her husband divide their time between homes in California and Cortona, Italy.*

ஆ ஆ ஆ

A.K. Phone Home

A daughter tries to stay connected in Bolivia.

In theory, I'm a grownup. Crow's feet, mortgage payments, shattered illusions . . . name the badge of adulthood, and I'm probably sporting it. Still, I've never met another thirty-six-year-old whose parents expect daily communiqués from wherever she happens to be. And where I happen to be, quite often, is the boonies—if not the official, geographic Middle of Nowhere, then damned close. A reporter on (and addict of) all things eco, I gravitate toward places that require long lists of shots, days' worth of supplies, and a liberal definition of the word *toilet*. So checking in from the road is rarely easy—but then again, neither is dealing with a search party that's been dispatched by the world's most overprotective father.

Not that posse preemption is my only reward for checking in: I always manage to get the breaking news from home, regardless of where I am. (And really, why let a little Venezuelan rainforest stand between you and the knowledge that your niece just made her first poo poo in the potty?) Also, to the best of my knowledge, I'm serving concurrent terms as customer of the year at Telefónica, Thaitel, and Cingular. But of all my rewards for checking in, the strangest by far came last year.

I had just spent a week in Chile's Atacama desert, where I had contracted an acute case of brain wither. (If "oooooh, pretty!" is the only thought you can muster for seven solid days, your neurons justifiably check out.) So I failed to perform due diligence on the next leg of my trip—a three-day drive to Potosi, Bolivia, via the Gran Salar de Uyuni. In fact, only after I had been picked up at the Bolivian border—and four-wheeled several hours past it—did I think to ask the driver, Paulino, when we might be able to stop and use a phone or internet connection. At which point I had to wonder whether I had missed my calling as a stand-up; the joke killed. Except, of course, that it wasn't a joke.

If you've been to the area in question, you may be laughing, too. One look at the emptiness that stretches from the Chilean desert to the Bolivian salt flats, and any sane person would realize that the road is hardly paved with DSL. In fact, the road is hardly *paved*. All I can say in my defense is that I have a history of finding improbably placed internet cafés.

Had I prepared my parents for a three-day communication blackout (a feat I'd somehow managed in the past), well then, fine. But once a call is expected and doesn't come, I'm automatically presumed maimed, violated, or dead—and on a good imagination day, some combination of the three. So with much contrition for my abysmal planning—and many apologies for my family's quirks—I impressed upon Paulino the dire need to find a phone. Failure was not an option, unless we were prepared to deal with the Bolivian air force squadron that my father would inevitably persuade to look for us.

Whether sparked by empathy (like my dad, Paulino is an overprotective Latin father) or the extreme desire to shut me up, a light bulb suddenly went off. There was, Paulino now remembered, a borax refinery within a couple of hours' drive, and he had a friend there who might let me make a call. Of course, the phone's usefulness remained to be seen, as the connection was notoriously fickle, and routinely went out for days, if not weeks, at a time. But being the proverbial beggars—and therefore not choosers—we headed to the refinery. And while I was afraid to ask how far out of our way it was, I can safely say that the place isn't exactly on the standard "Wonders of Bolivia" tour.

Nonetheless, we eventually arrived, whereupon we were greeted by the most bewildered-looking guard I'd ever seen. No one but the resident employees and their visiting family members had turned up at the gate during his tenure. Luckily, I seemed sufficiently pathetic and desperate to gain entry, and thus became the first idiot tourist to visit the refinery—let alone use the phone—on his watch.

Now then. With all due respect to Hercules…forget killing a poisonous, nine-headed hydra—or kidnapping an underworld guard dog of indeterminate headcount. I'd like to see him place a non-operator-assisted collect call to the States from a Bolivian borax refinery where the only semblance of an instruction is written in Quechua and Aymara, and the Soviet-era phone has a severe anti-2 disposition. Yes, the very numeral without which I couldn't reach either my parents in Tucson (area code 520), or my husband in New York (area code 212), was the one that the phone found most objectionable. Every so often, a 2 did squeak through—when Paulino and I would simultaneously lean on the button to a count of 100, say. But by then, the line would cut out, and we'd have to start the twenty-step, Muzak-intensive process over. The first time a call actually went through, my incredibly confused husband rejected the charges, at which point *hari-kari* was beginning to seem a reasonable solution. Finally, however, I got through to his office again—and this time, he caught on. He accepted the charges and promised he'd call my parents immediately to attest to my ongoing pulse.

During the hour and a half required to achieve this victory, word of my presence spread throughout the refinery. Though the question of what the hell I was doing there fueled plenty of chatter, even more buzz-worthy was the observation that I had arrived in a jeep. A practically empty, Uyuni-bound jeep. One that could accommodate oh, let's say, the wife of one of the workers, the couple's three kids, and any attendant baggage. Coincidentally, just such a family was waiting for us when we exited the main building. Señora Lidia, her ten-year-old son, Gabriel, her four year-old son, Eloy, and her baby daughter, Nilda, had all been visiting for the week, and needed to return to Uyuni soon anyway. Conveniently, my record-breaking phone session had given them ample opportunity to pack up and be ready for immediate departure.

At first I had no idea what was going on, as Sra. Lidia took her proposal straight to Paulino, who was now standing at a bit of a distance from me. When I noticed his strained expression, however, I went over to investigate and caught the tail end of her ride-hitching request. She was hoping to travel one less time than was absolutely necessary on the dread *volqueta*, Spanish for "death wish." Or close enough. The word actually refers to the infamously ill-fated dump trucks that provide cheap, if harrowing, passage to countless Bolivians, who have no choice but to pile on and pray. The rosary beads get especially busy during the rainy season, when—in the hierarchy of likely outcomes—getting drenched in the open-air seating is second only to getting stuck (or overturned) in the mud. And while these conditions are hardly ideal for anyone, they're especially tough on a woman who's got a two-day trek to make with a stuffed-up little girl and a couple of fidgety boys.

Initially, Paulino gave Sra. Lidia the party line: Basically, "This is a tourism vehicle with a private passenger, and as much as I'd like to help you out, lady, I hope you'll understand that I can't." He had apparently deemed my neurotic phone quest a sign of general uptightness—and assumed there was no way I'd want to spend the next two days with a family of strangers. But he couldn't have been farther off. Though I had little credibility at that point, I did my best to convince him that I'm usually quite laid-back (true), and that nothing would make me happier than to offer these people a ride (also true).

I wish I could say that my motives were purely altruistic. But there was plenty of opportunism mixed in. How many times had I walked or driven by a so-called *cholita* (one of the bowler hat-wearing, stripy bundle-schlepping, Quechua- or Aymara-speaking indigenous Andean women) and wished I knew anything more about her than the painfully obvious? So here was my chance.

Paulino's worries duly assuaged, we all piled into the jeep. And though what followed was hardly the sweeping cultural revelation I might stupidly have imagined, it was something even better: a good, old-fashioned family road trip…with a few unusual twists, not least of which was the fact that I had just acquired my family at a borax refinery. But why split hairs?

Like any proper road trip, ours involved a protracted game of I Spy—except that the boys, who were both first-timers, quickly tired of the rules and opted for a more direct approach. They'd simply point to a spectacle, of which there were plenty, and bestow a lavish name upon it. Some loosely translated samples from our drive-by dubbing spree: "the flamingo-ful red lagoon," "the big, brown, cactus-smothered mountains," and "the spitting image of the Irish countryside...if Ireland ever decided to promote the peaceful coexistence of llamas and flamingoes." Actually, that last one never got used—wrong crowd, perhaps—but nonetheless held true in at least a couple of spots along the way.

Yes, the scenery was amazing...and ever changing. One minute, a field of quinoa would pop up. The next, a cluster of red-rock spires—seeming defectors from Sedona. Soon to follow would be a series of rolling hills, first in deep red, then sulfuric yellow, then jade green. But however varied the landscape, there were two constants: extreme beauty and no trace of humanity. Well...almost no trace.

There *is* Julaca, a town with one train station, several adobe-and-corrugated-tin homes, and at least two dogs that don't particularly like each other. There's also Villamar. More an outpost than a town, it boasts a distinctly hotel-ish establishment that's got to be one of the foremost examples of the Concrete Cell Block school of architecture. Bonus: If you ask whether there's a light in your bathroom, you're told, "Of course!"—and a woman promptly shows up with the very candle that illuminated Scrooge's last days.

No matter where Paulino, Sra. Lidia, the kids, and I found ourselves, we made our own fun—from peek-a-boo among the junior set (the boys were really good at entertaining their sister) to career talk among us ancients (Sra. Lidia, for the record, is a municipal functionary somewhere in the greater Uyuni metropolitan area). Quickly feeling at ease with the group, I popped the big question during a rest stop: Would anyone be willing to show me how to work one of those stripy Andean carry-all cloths? I had always wanted to know, but had been too embarrassed to ask. No sooner had I broached the subject than Gabriel—my self-appointed go-to guy from the moment we met—was drawing me detailed diagrams in the patch of dirt where we had pulled over. After reviewing his renderings of folds, creases, and knots, I was ready for the real thing. So poor little Nilda was summarily removed from her sling, then endlessly wrapped and rewrapped for my educational benefit. Though anyone else would have caught on in about two seconds—this was hardly post-doctoral origami, after all—I clearly belonged in remedial folding. On approximately the thousandth attempt, however, I got the configuration right, and took a few baby-toting victory laps around the car.

Something else I learned en route: the fine art of *abrigando*. Though the conventional meaning is "putting a coat on," the contextual version is "insulating your car with whatever happens to be growing on the side of the road before you cross a massive, corrosive salt flat." So, during our final approach to the Gran Salar, we stopped at a patch of bushes and systematically relieved them of their twigs. Periodically, we'd present handfuls of said greenery (what florists would call "filler") to Paulino, who in turn would use it to shroud every square nanometer of the jeep's innards. Eventually, Gabriel and Eloy got sick of their roles as glorified hedge trimmers, and left for a piece of the real action (under the hood, of course). But by then we were almost done.

The last thing I expected after we'd finished *abrigando* was sudden-onset sadness. Yet there it was. Though an hours-long drive across the salt flat still lay ahead of us, I realized that our time together was waning. And all of what

I had quickly grown accustomed to was about to disappear.

What I would miss most was the way that Sra. Lidia could console, discipline, and crack up her kids—all without raising her voice above a whisper. Granted, I had encountered the Andean whisper before, and had even been warned about it during my first trip to Peru: "Don't think the women are talking smack about you or intentionally leaving you out," said my guide, who'd apparently seen tourists respond in the manner of Elaine at the Korean nail salon. "This is just how they relate to each other—it's an indigenous thing." Still, all my previous experiences with *cholitas* had been fleeting, leaving me with absolutely no idea of the whisper's full scope and power.

Something else I would miss: Gabriel's unfailing chivalry. If I started a conversation in which nobody was remotely interested, he'd be the poor soul to keep it going, long past the glazing over of everyone else's eyes. Or if I was roundly butchering the few words of Quechua I had proudly claimed to know, he would do everything in his power to suppress the guffaws I so richly deserved.

But in the tradition of all good things, our family road trip came to an end. Having completed the long, surreal, mirage of a drive across the water-coated salt flat, we arrived at Isla Pescado. There, as we sat among the giant, fuzzy cacti, we heard some chilling news: The *volqueta* that Sra. Lidia et al. would have taken from the refinery was now missing—and presumed irretrievably stuck or overturned.

Needless to say, I didn't even want to think about what would've happened to them had they been on board (nor what *had* happened to anyone who was). But I did pause to think about fate…and its mysterious taste in partners. Really—what are the odds that a couple of worrywarts in Tucson should ultimately (and unknowingly) keep a

Bolivian family off a doomed truck? As I was explaining
my parents' accomplishment to them the next night from
my hotel room in Potosi, for once they nearly conceded:
perhaps their daughter's dispatches from nowhere might
actually be worth the agita.

                        ♫ ♫ ♫

*Fifteen years into a women's magazine career, many of them spent
as a* Cosmo *contributor, Abbie Kozolchyk dreams of a day when
she's known for something other than her ability to use the word*
foxify *in a sentence. To that end, she recently took on the role of
contributing travel editor at* Martha Stewart Living's Body +
Soul. *For examples of the resulting columns, along with her other
work, visit her at: www.abbiekozolchyk.com.*

❦ ❦ ❦

Sand Angel

In Mali, the rough travel she sought softened her heart.

I was just getting settled on the boat to Timbuktu, arranging my backpacks, oranges, and burlap-covered jerry cans of water around me, when a burly African man appeared above me, blocking the sun.

"All these people are savages!" he boomed. With a grand sweep of his arm he took in the other passengers on the boat. "They have never been to school. They live like animals. Me, I don't like savages."

"Hello?"

"*Bonjour*, I am Touré. *Comment ça va?* What is your name?"

"Tanya."

"Excellent! I'd like to sit here with you, Tanya, to profit from your company." He plunked his canvas satchel onto my grass mat.

"You are not sleeping here," I said, alarmed.

"I don't sleep," he said impatiently. "I go days without sleeping. Where are you from?" He glanced at my bag. "America?"

I nodded, and his eyes lit up with a familiar gleam.

"I want to go there with you, Tanya, to your country. Can you help me to get a visa?"

"I don't work for Immigration."

"You can sponsor me. Vouch for my character."

"I—"

"I would like to go there and open a store for women's shoes. They say that women in America will pay two hundred dollars for a pair of shoes. One can easily get rich with shoes."

"It's actually not—"

"Very rich."

"There are a lot of poor—"

"Ha!" He stretched out his legs, propped his head against his bag and said firmly, his tone brooking no argument, "The poor in your country would be rich here."

The floor of the boat was piled high with sacks of grain, creating a treacherous, uneven surface. We spread our grass mats across it to stake out territory.

The *pinasse* was an oversized, pregnant canoe—about thirty feet long and nine feet wide—with a roof over the middle and a motor in the back. Sitting in its covered center, I felt like Jonah in the belly of the whale, looking up at a sturdy rib cage of bamboo poles with woven raffia stretched across the top. About thirty adults and fourteen children fit tightly atop the sacks, with about a foot of space between us.

"You people are educated," Touré said to me. He was spreading out his things now, making himself ever more comfortable on my mat. "You know how to make things:

telephones, computers, cars...and you all read. Not like these animals here. Me, I like to read." He produced a dog-eared French novel from his bag.

"You know, not all whites read—"

"Well, I never met one who couldn't. You and me, we are alike, Tanya. *Toi et moi.*"

I couldn't shake Touré. Whenever I attempted to converse with someone else, he placed himself in the middle. When I misplaced things, which happened at least every half hour, Touré asked, "What are you looking for?" When I grudgingly named the item (water bottle, socks, sunscreen, etc.), he performed a vacuumlike search of the surrounding sacks. Within minutes he held the missing item aloft, proclaiming proudly, "It is here!"

He was a muscular man, with a sly, wise face that seemed to smirk in repose. He ranted incessantly about the ignorance and stupidity of the other passengers, but at the end of these tirades he always burst out laughing. His laugh was infectious. For all his abrasiveness, he could win a crowd.

"These people are all thieves," he announced.

"Stop that," I shushed.

"I know them," he insisted. "I have been in prison."

"Really?" I paused to digest this. "What for?"

"Commerce."

"Commerce?"

"You know, commerce," he shrugged impatiently, then made a series of illustrative gestures: touching one nostril and sniffing, sucking on an invisible joint, tapping out a vein in his arm.

"I get the picture," I said dryly.

"So you see," he continued, "I know what it is like. I will help you to keep an eye on your things."

Five times a day the call to prayer sounded, and the majority of passengers rose like a wave and faced Mecca. I envied them this ritual, at once private and shared. *It must be a great comfort,* I thought, *to know that wherever you are, whatever you're doing, five times a day you—and everyone around you—will drop everything and speak deeply with God...or even just with yourself.*

One man kept drawing my eye. He was tiny—maybe five foot two—with small bones and delicate features. When he performed the prayer, bliss seemed to radiate outward from his entire body. His eyes turned upward in an expression of devotion more complete than any I had ever seen. I was transfixed.

On the second afternoon of the trip, after finishing the morning prayer, he turned suddenly and came toward me, pointing emphatically. His face was animated, his eyes urgent. He pointed at me and then pointed up. Then he looked back at me, hands spread wide, eyebrows raised.

Confused, I looked around for help.

"He wants to know why you don't do the prayer," said Touré. He tapped the man on the shoulder, pointed at me, then made the sign of the cross. "I told him you are a Christian," he said.

"But I'm not a Christian," I protested. "I'm an agnostic-leaning-toward-atheist Jew."

"*What?*"

"Just tell him I'm not a believer."

Touré looked at the man. He pointed at me, crossed himself again, then shook his head sadly and moved his hands across each other in a negating gesture, like an umpire calling "safe." He mimed bowing down in the manner of the Moslem prayer and repeated the negating gesture. Then, in a final dramatic action, he pointed toward the sky, sweeping his arm as if to include anything that could possibly be up there. He shook his head vigorously, as if to say, "Not a thing."

The man looked at me in disbelief. He made a gesture as though gathering up a fistful of grain and throwing it over his head, then looked up again to heaven. His face wore the purest delight.

Touré shrugged. "He says you must believe. God is there."

The man nodded at me, beaming. It was the same conversation I'd had a hundred times since arriving in Africa, but this man's passion made it fresh.

I shook my head at him. "I'm sorry," I said gently. "I wish I could believe, but I don't." I shrugged helplessly. "I can't."

The man simply nodded again.

"He says you will," said Touré.

On the third morning, we were passing a village when the little man approached me again. Excited, he pointed to me, then to himself, then to the village.

"He wants you to visit him in his village," said Touré.

"Is that it?" I asked, confused, pointing to the passing hamlet.

"No, no. In the desert. He will bring you there from Timbuktu."

"That would be fantastic. What does he do there?" I asked.

The man moved his hands vigorously from side to side. I looked at Touré in bewilderment.

"Isn't it obvious? He makes charcoal!"

"Obviously," I said wryly, seeing nothing obvious about it.

"He wants to know what you are doing on this boat."

"Me? I'm just...traveling."

Now it was the little man's turn to look bewildered. He spread out his hands and cocked his head inquisitively.

"Why?" I looked at Touré, who nodded. "Why," I repeated. I looked at the man. It was impossible to gauge his age, though I guessed mid- to late forties. The skin was stretched tight across the bones of his face. Deep smile lines had carved themselves beside his mouth. I tried to imagine his life: sweltering days spent digging holes in the desert and pressing the charcoal, walking for miles in search of water, eating rice and sauce with his family, sleeping curled between siblings and cousins in a tent, then dragging his heavy sacks on a bumpy camel ride to Timbuktu, where he would catch a *pinasse* and travel along the river, hawking the hard black lumps to the people in the villages he passed—people who had known him all his life—always delivering a smile with his goods. How could I explain my strange life to him? How could I tell yet another person here that with everything that had been given to me, I was still restless and unsatisfied? That I felt driven to wander the earth in search of some elusive key that would unlock the chamber of my own happiness? How could I explain that I chose physical hardship: dysentery, heat rash, dizzying rides in crowded vehicles down bumpy, potholed roads—hardship he had no choice but to endure—that I *chose* all of this, because it was the only thing that made me feel truly alive?

"To see things…I guess," I offered lamely.

The man pointed to my red spiral notebook. He put his head down and hunched his shoulders, making a scribbling gesture. He looked up at me with an inquiring expression.

"How can I see when I'm always writing?" I shrugged. "Good question. Sometimes I feel that when I'm writing is the only time I can see."

He looked at me in perplexity.

"Why don't you write at home, in your own country?" asked Touré.

I shrugged, turning to him. "I guess I was just born rest-less. Wherever I am, I always want to be somewhere else."

The little man shook his head sadly.

"He says you are a very bad girl," said Touré. "Your mother and father are so worried about you—they want you home. His mother too, she will be glad to see you, for his sister has gone far away, to work in Bamako."

"Did he really say all that?"

"Of course!" said Touré, mock offended.

I laughed. "Well, tell him I can't wait to meet his mother. What's his name?"

The man gestured helplessly, spreading his hands wide, palms up. Straining his neck, he let out a high chirping sound.

"He cannot tell you," said Touré. "He does not have letters."

The man was deaf! All this time I'd thought he was gesturing because of the language barrier. I'd imagined he spoke a regional dialect so different from Touré's that even they had to talk to each other in sign.

Suddenly the man pointed at my feet. He stroked his pale soles with a doleful expression.

"He wants you to give him your shoes," said Touré.

What? Here I am thinking this guy is some kind of guru, and it turns out he's just after my shoes?

"I need them," I said, my lips tight.

He wagged a finger at me and pointed to my backpack. With infinite care, he built a boot in the air around his foot.

He knew the sandals were not my only shoes. He'd spotted a pair of boots in my backpack, practically new. He touched his heart, then repeated a gesture I'd seen him make before, flinging an invisible handful of grain into the air.

"He says when you give, you are in the heart of God," said Touré.

"Is he still trying to convert me, or does he just want the shoes?" I snapped.

"I will ask him."

"No…. Don't."

What the hell was wrong with me? The man's feet were dry and cracked. When had I become so hard?

But what good would it do anyway, one pair of shoes to one person, in a year they'd wear out and—

Stop it. Look at this man.

I looked. The woolen skullcap, the slight body swathed in its cotton robe, the crinkled face and glowing eyes, the hopeful smile. I stood there for a long moment, suspended in indecision.

Just take the sandals off and give them to him.

I didn't.

Afternoon found me on the roof of the *pinasse*, basking in the sunshine, the wind tousling my hair. It was a perfect day, the sun warm but not oppressive, the breeze delicious on my skin. The Niger spread brown and languid before me. The sky was a pure, deep blue, the marsh grass to the left a vibrant green. To the right, spectacular red rock formations rose above the equally red earth.

The air was filled with birdsong, harsh and lyrical. Earlier in the day we'd seen three hippos, bathing serenely in the middle of the river, their backs rising from the water like the mountains of a sunken land.

Whenever we passed a village, children materialized out of nowhere and tore down the shore, pointing and shouting, waving wildly at the strange white creature perched on the boat. I waved back at them, feeling like the homecoming queen on her float.

Suddenly the captain of the ship, who'd been standing

a few feet in front of me, nose to the wind like a mascot, jumped off the roof to the deck below. The boat was heading straight for the swampy shore. He grabbed a pole and threw his weight against it, trying to deflect the nose from collision, but we were moving too fast—the pole jumped back at him. He sprang out of the boat as though someone had pushed an ejector button, and crashed into the water below.

I stared at the water, paralyzed. Where had he gone? Was he hurt? Just as I was about to scream for help, he hopped out of the water onto the bank, shouting and waving his arms.

At that moment, the nose hit the shore with a resounding crack. Wood splintered. Water poured in. A few scattered shouts from the deck below built quickly to a cacophony.

Wow, I thought, with a kind of dull incredulity. *This is really an accident.*

People started running off the boat. I suddenly realized my notebooks were still in the back of the boat, under the roof. The red one was loose; two others were in my daypack. There was over a month of writing there, precious detail I didn't want to lose.

When the flow of traffic stopped, I leaped lightly to the deck. The water was coming in slowly—only ankle-deep so far. Plenty of time to get my notebooks.

When I got to my mat, I found Touré dragging my packs and his own satchel toward the shore end of the boat.

"Here, put these on your back," he said, dropping them. I knelt to detach the daypack from the larger one.

"What are you doing?" he yelled.

"Detaching the daypack."

"There's no time for that! Put them on your back!" He headed off, toting his bag.

I tried to follow his instructions, but in my haste I got tangled in the straps. Out of the corner of my eye I saw the red spiral notebook sitting on my grass mat. I reached for it.

Until that moment, I'd never really understood the way a boat sinks. I figured that with the water coming in so slowly, it would be a good half hour before the boat was really under. What I didn't realize is that when the weight of the water hits critical mass, the boat just goes down.

Suddenly water—at my chest and rising. I tossed the bags and dove. But did I dive? Or was I just suddenly in the water? *My hat!* The leather braid yanked my head back, choking me. Ripped it off, paddling wild, roof coming down, dark. *Dark.* Underwater—how long?—turning, flailing in slow-motion darkness. *Which way is up?* Thrashing, heartbeat, loud—*Did I clear the roof?* Then light, murky and green, and I popped up into it, gasping.

The water was eerily calm. I looked around, confused.

Any children in the water? Fuck it—get to shore. What a selfish asshole you are.

I swam for the muddy bank, where children and adults were running down the shore, chasing after floating luggage.

"La blanche! La blanche!" A man extended a scratchy hand. I almost pulled him in, trying to gain my balance in the slippery mud.

Touré came running up the bank toward me.

"Look what happened to me trying to find *your* luggage," he shouted, showing me a gash on his arm.

Just then I heard a high-pitched sound, somewhere between a chirp and a scream. It came again and again, sharp and staccato, repeating at regular intervals like an alarm. I looked around, agitated, trying to locate its source. The brown surface of the water was smooth, undisturbed except for the end of the boat sticking up like a shark's fin and the baggage drifting lazily downstream.

"What's that sound?" I asked Touré, but he was gone. I scanned the floating debris for my things, wondering if the notebooks could possibly survive.

"Madame, your bag?" The captain's adolescent daughter appeared beside me, panting with exertion. Her chubby hand gripped my forearm too tightly. She parted the high grass and pointed to a soggy duffel.

"No, that's not mine," I said distractedly, watching the river. "Have you seen a small gray daypack? Or a red notebook?"

She shook her head, dragging me along the shore to where more items lay drying.

"This?" she asked, pointing. "This?"

"No."

People were darting among the luggage in a panic. A fight seemed to have broken out over a cloth-tied bundle.

"What is that sound?" I asked again. The shrill cries were coming at shorter intervals now, one after another.

The girl shrugged. "A bird, maybe."

Just then I saw my red notebook floating downstream. I ran down the bank, stripped off my skirt, and dove for it. When I got back to shore, holding my sopping notebook, the air seemed unnaturally still. The high-pitched sound, I realized, had stopped.

I turned inland to survey the landscape in which we were stranded. Sandy dunes surrounded by low shrubs capped the horizon, with spiky grass at the tip. The scenery I'd found so beautiful a half-hour before now appeared bleak: shadeless and unforgiving.

When the flow of luggage abated, the captain's daughter returned, still in a tizzy.

"I am so sorry we have not found your bag," she said despairingly, shaking her head.

"It's O.K." I clutched my notebook and laid a hand on her shoulder. My passport and travelers' checks were in a money belt around my waist, soggy but intact. "At least no one was hurt," I added.

She shook her head, eyes wide. "They say there was a man who died."

"Really?" A knot of anxiety formed in my chest. "Who was it?"

"I don't know," she said. "Only, an old woman, she saw him, trying to swim."

I searched for Touré, fear hardening and moving up into my throat. I found him arguing with another man, on the brink of blows. I grabbed his arm and pulled him aside.

"They say someone drowned."

"Yes, yes," he said distractedly. "Your friend. He is dead."

"What?"

He turned to face me. "The deaf mute. He was caught in the boat. He did not know how to swim."

"The...that man?" I imitated the hand gestures, and Touré nodded.

"Are you sure?" My mind doubled back frantically. Hadn't I seen him?

He shrugged. "I did not see it, but that is what they say."

"But—" I stopped suddenly. *Oh God. That sound.*

But how? I thought. *Those were not the cries of a person in the water. A person in the water couldn't have kept up such a steady stream of sound! He'd have been splashing, gulping, gasping, wouldn't he? How could the sound go on so long?*

Unless he was in the boat. The back of the boat was sticking up; his head could've been just above—But I was staring right at the boat, how could I not—if he'd been in there I would have seen—But I wasn't looking, was I? I was thinking of my notebooks. My notebooks—

Oh no. No.

"Why didn't someone save him?" I whispered.

"They did not see him in time."

Most people's things were recovered. The men cracked open the bamboo ribs of the roof, and things trapped within floated up, including my two packs. As they dove to dislodge stuck items, I held my breath, afraid I'd see a waterlogged body emerge, pale and softening. It never came. The current, swifter than it appeared, had long since carried him away.

Night fell. The darkness was alive with humming and whirring insects, punctuated by the occasional birdcall. Soggy and pathetic, we huddled around small fires at the foot of the dunes, holding clothing and blankets toward the flames to dry. I turned my bulky sleeping bag over and over, trying to dry it inside and out without burning a hole.

I gradually became aware of a thin man standing beside me, watching my manipulations with amusement.

"Are you feeling better?" he asked in flawless French. I shrugged, turning my face toward the flames.

"You know," he said, "when you cry, it brings everyone else down."

I looked at him in disbelief. "Well, they should be down. A man died."

"Men die every day."

"But it shouldn't have happened. The river's not wide; it's not even very deep. We could have done something, if

we hadn't all been chasing our luggage. Including me with
my notebook, God help me."

"That's right!" he said, with sudden energy. "God
helped you! It was our brother's time."

"I don't believe that," I said, wishing that he could convince me, that anyone could.

"If you'd seen him," he said, "would you have done
something?"

"Yes! I think so. I mean, God, I hope so. I mean—"

"*Did* you see him?"

"No, but I heard—"

"But did you *see* him?"

I shook my head.

"Neither did I. And I promise you, if I had seen him, I
would have gone in after him, even if I had died myself. But
why do you think, with all these people, the only one who
saw him was an old woman who could not swim?"

I started to say that I'd like to believe him, but that I'd
never seen any evidence that the universe was not completely, absurdly random—but my throat closed up. He
looked in my eyes for a long time, searchingly, as though
he might transfer some faith this way. I felt a sudden urge
to grab his narrow shoulders and kiss him, so hard that our
teeth knocked, to bite, to squeeze until we both lost breath.
My throat ached as though a stone were lodged there. My
face went hot.

"So you should not cry," he said.

"But we should remember," I croaked, eyes welling, "so
we learn from it." I turned my head from the fire. Cool air
bathed my face.

He sighed. "People have lost shoes, identity papers,
everything. Cakes and cloth they were going to sell are
ruined. They have nothing to bring home to their families,
not even money to get back to their villages. They must

keep cheerful. No one has forgotten. Each person, alone, will think of it. And around these fires tonight, people will talk of it. They are talking of it already."

His name was Yaya, and he was studying to be a minister, a Christian convert from a prosperous Moslem trading family. He'd been a student activist and lived in exile in France for two years when the political climate got too hot, hence his impeccable French.

"Do you know how you can tell that it is not yet your time to die?" he asked.

"How?" I asked skeptically.

"Because you are sitting here alive."

I woke to activity. All around me people were untying bundles and unpacking bags, draping clothing and papers across the tall grass to dry in the early morning sun. I went to get my backpacks, which I'd dropped behind a low bush. I found Touré next to them, standing guard.

"You've got to be more careful of your things," he berated. "You should have kept them next to you when you slept."

"Oh come on, Touré. Who wants my soggy backpacks? No one's gonna steal after this kind of tragedy."

"Oh, *please!*"

A few dunes away, a hubbub arose. The sound of shouting and slaps broke the morning calm. Touré and I hurried over to see what was happening. When we arrived, the whole population of the boat was there. Yaya stood at the edge of the group, shouting for order.

"What happened?" I asked him.

"They say that man stole clothing from people's luggage. They want to beat him."

At the center of the group stood a skinny old man in a threadbare *bou-bou*. Some middle-aged women were shoving him roughly back and forth. They shouted in piercing tones, shaking his shoulders with their stringy, muscular arms.

"I told them they must let me speak to the man," Yaya continued, "to find out why he did it."

"What makes them think it was him?" I shouted.

"The women noticed things were missing. They started opening bags to search. They found the missing items in his bag."

"Then they are right!" yelled Touré. "He is a thief. We must beat him and throw him in the water." He shoved his way into the middle, shouting and waving his arms.

"No!" Yaya pushed through the crowd. Standing at the center, he gained the group's attention with a piercing whistle, then dropped his voice and began to speak.

Touré interjected angrily. Some people cheered him, but others shouted them down. When the noise subsided, Yaya continued, his dignified demeanor commanding respect.

The old man stood off to one side, his blue-gray turban half-unraveled, staring at the ground. His face showed neither hope nor dread, but a kind of dull resignation, as though he were waiting in a soundproof chamber while a jury decided his fate.

Eventually Yaya prevailed. Holding the crowd at bay with sharp words and an outstretched hand, he led the old man over the crest of the dune and out of sight.

They were gone over an hour. At first people waited angrily, shouting and gesticulating, but after a while, they began to drift away. By the time Yaya and the old man reappeared at the tufty crown of the dune, Touré and I were all who remained.

"Well?" said Touré, leaping to his feet.

"It will not happen again," said Yaya. Touré moved to object, but Yaya continued rapidly, raising his hand as

though fending off a blow. "The women have their clothing back," he hissed. "Isn't that enough? Or will you beat
him now, by yourself?"

They stared at each other for a moment, locked in a
standoff. Then Touré turned abruptly toward the old man,
who took a step backward in fear. Touré turned back to
Yaya with disgust.

"I will be watching him closely. And you, too," he said,
poking a finger in Yaya's face. He stomped off across the
dunes, giving the other passengers a wide berth. The old man
slunk away, too, throwing Yaya a small, grateful smile.

"Would they really have beaten him?" I asked Yaya, as
we watched Touré's retreating back.

"People get very carried away when someone has been
stealing," he said slowly. "Often if a thief is caught in the
market, he will be beaten to death before the police can
even arrive. People work so hard for these things, for nothing. And they will give them to you. But for you to come
and take them...no."

"So why did he do it?" I asked.

"He said he could not help it. God made him do it. I told
him God would never do such a thing; it must have been
the devil. But he said no—it was God. God whispered in
his ear and told him so."

The midday sun was so relentless that even the marsh
grass seemed to wilt beneath its gaze. In the late afternoon,
three pirogues arrived from a nearby fisher camp, offering
to transport us to their camp for the night, then onward
tomorrow to the village of Aka, where we could catch a
new *pinasse*. Word had been sent back to Mopti to send us a
replacement boat, but no one knew how long it would take
to arrive. The men argued strenuously over what to do. As
usual, Yaya and Touré were on opposing sides.

"These men would divide the group," Yaya explained when I approached. "They say that those who can afford passage on a new *pinasse* should go forward in the pirogues, while the rest stay behind and wait for the replacement. I say it is not right that some of us should go forward leaving others here alone to suffer. A small group, alone in this place, will be vulnerable to bandits."

"And I tell him," blustered Touré, "that it is not right that you, Tanya, must get sick from the river water and burn your skin waiting many long days in the sun!"

"Oh no, please don't make this about me," I said quickly.

"Be quiet!" snapped Touré.

Touré's group won out. As the sun set, I sheepishly loaded my bags into one of two long, narrow pirogues, along with sixteen of the boat's more prosperous passengers. The river glowed rosy orange in the failing light. Several young men from the Bozo fisher camp waited on the shore, jousting amiably with the long poles they used to propel the pirogues.

I was surprised to see the old man who'd been accused of stealing among our privileged group. No one commented on his presence, but I noticed that he made sure not to ride in the same boat as Touré.

Touré climbed into the front of one of the canoes, and I squeezed in behind him. Yaya and I had shared an emotional goodbye, with prolonged hugs and promises to write. I was therefore startled to see him dragging his duffel toward the water, just as we were about to push off.

"What's this?" shouted Touré. "You will leave the very poor to suffer alone?"

"I will go forward to Aka and send word to their villages, so that their families will not worry," said Yaya primly.

"Oh, *please,*" groaned Touré.

Although the villagers in Aka offered shelter, Yaya and I decided to spread our grass mats on the beach. The night was mild, and I couldn't bear to trade its breezy freshness for the close warmth of a hut.

As we set up our camp, Yaya told me about Stacy, the American missionary waiting to meet him in Timbuktu.

"We pray every day that we will marry," he said.

"Why pray to marry? It's not like it's out of your control."

"We pray that conditions will be right for it to take place."

"Do you *want* it to take place?"

"Yes...I think so." He paused. "I am not sure," he blurted. "I love her, but...the attraction. I am not sure. That is why we pray."

I looked at him in surprise. Most West Africans I'd encountered considered a match good if the potential spouse came from a decent family and was neither abusive, dishonest, nor excessively ugly. Marriage to an American, with its implicit visa to the land of plenty, would be the answer to their prayers. Perhaps living in Europe had changed Yaya's perspective.

"I have similar issues with my boyfriend," I admitted.

"Yes?" He looked at me eagerly.

I told him about Michael: my profound love and equally profound confusion.

"I feel the same confusion about Stacy," said Yaya, when I had finished. "But I will marry her anyway," he added, after a moment's pause. "The satisfaction I seek can never be found in human love. I get my deepest fulfillment from the love of God."

We lay side by side on our grass mats. The sky arced above us like a speckled ceramic bowl, so thick with stars that every inch of space seemed crammed with pinpricks of light. Since Yaya had only a light blanket, I opened up my sleeping bag and put it over both of us. I rolled onto my side, facing away from him. He turned toward me and began massaging the tight tendons of my neck with brutal precision, working his way downward.

Something familiar was happening. I recognized it immediately and marveled at its universality, even as my heart began to cavort like a crazyball against my ribs. While his hands worked on me, I lay absolutely still, scarcely breathing. Suddenly he was pressed hard against my back, and his hands were around the front, squeezing my breasts with a muscular intensity that caught me by surprise. At once I was wildly, acutely awake, my head pounding, my body pulsing subtly against his. But I couldn't bring myself to make a definitive move, to turn around and kiss him, to commit.

My mind raced dizzily, trying to arrange the thoughts. What was wrong? He had a girlfriend, no, he was engaged! On the other hand, I wanted him. A *lot*. My body was responding to his touch with a yearning I suddenly realized had been growing since our first conversation, on the night of the accident. I remembered the deaf man, then, and sorrow shot through me. Suddenly everything felt false: Yaya's platitudes about destiny, his confession about Stacy, my own shallow grief and facile, oft-repeated words. I pushed him away with a throaty sound and rolled to the other side of the mat.

"I want to sleep," I said.

Silence.

"I'm sorry," he said stiffly.

I lay there, motionless, for a long time, listening to the sound of Yaya's breath. Eventually it slowed, grew regular, and quieted. Then I stuffed my face into the fetid t-shirt I'd balled up for a pillow, and cried.

Two days later, a new *pinasse* arrived. On the boat, Touré, Yaya, and I tiptoed through a dense garden of bodies, finally finding a small clearing in front of some soldiers. We wedged ourselves in, sliding down into the crevices between the sacks of grain. One of the soldiers' long guns, laid carelessly across his knapsack, pointed straight at me. I gingerly pushed its muzzle aside.

Out on the water, it became a running gag between the three of us that every time the boat slowed down, or brushed against a sandbar or a piece of floating wood, I faced the water, put my arms over my head in a diving pose, and said, "I'm ready to swim." Touré and Yaya were even joking with each other. Touré said they were cousins, Kulubaly and Tangara, but Tangara was the slave of Kulubaly, so Yaya ought to treat him with respect. Yaya said he couldn't respect a Kulubaly: they ate too many beans. We grew giddy with laughter.

Touré was looking through his bag for a photograph he wanted to show me, when suddenly he let out a shout.

"Hey! Where are the shoes?"

"What?" I asked stupidly.

"The ladies' shoes! I was bringing them to Diré to sell. I had three pairs; now there are only two."

"I think you sold a pair," Yaya said. Then, to me, "I thought he sold a pair."

Suddenly Touré was on his feet, picking his way through the mass of bodies with extraordinary speed. When he got to his destination, he reached down and grabbed someone's *bou-bou* at the throat. It took me a moment to recognize the old man who'd gotten himself into trouble on the first boat.

"This man is a thief!" shouted Touré. "He stole on the last boat and because of this...posing imbecile..." indicating Yaya, "we let him go free to steal again. And now he has stolen my shoes!" He yanked the old man to his feet. "I should have beaten you last time. This time you are going to pay. This time I'm going to open your bag, and if I find those shoes, I'm going to throw you off the boat."

"No!" shouted Yaya. He stumbled through the crowd, drawing shouts and curses as he stepped on people's limbs. "You cannot do this!"

Touré spun around. "You stay out of this!" he snarled. "I am tired of you telling me what to do, you who have left the faith and taken another."

"You see?" Yaya shouted, looking around frantically for support. "He oppresses me because of my faith! He oppresses me because I work for justice, like Jesus Christ himself was oppressed."

"You stand up for criminals because you do not know them," yelled Touré. Yaya had reached him now, and Touré let go of the old man and grabbed the top of Yaya's *bou-bou* instead. "You are a weak, soft man. You have never had to pay your own way. Stand back, weak man! Life is for the strong." Touré shoved Yaya, who stumbled and fell backward onto the legs of a child. The child screamed.

"And you," cried Yaya, lurching to his feet, "you feel you are fit to judge. You who are a criminal yourself, who have not been to school past the second form. Who can scarcely read!"

"I can read! I can read!" roared Touré.

"Then read for us. Read for us if you are so smart." Yaya reached into his robe and extracted a small black-bound volume. "Here is a book of Mali law. Read for us where it says that you may throw an old man in the river." He tossed the book at Touré's feet.

Touré looked down at the book, then slowly back up at Yaya.

"I do not have to read for you." His voice was low and fero-
cious, simmering with fury. "I do not have to prove anything
to you. You traitor! I will throw you off the boat!"

Touré advanced on Yaya. Yaya raised his arms to defend
himself, and their hands locked in the air like the antlers
of two stags. Touré had easily fifty pounds on Yaya, and in
no time he was propelling him backward toward the edge
of the boat, while the other passengers shuffled desperately
out of the way.

"Stop it!" I screamed, moving toward them.

"You stay out of this, *tubabu!*" Touré flung the words in
my direction. "This is not your place." It was the first time
Touré had called me a white lady.

From the center of the boat, an enormous woman
dressed in bright red cloth rose slowly to her feet.

"Stooooooop iiiiiiiiiiit!" she bellowed, her voice deep
and penetrating as a foghorn. "*Stop it! Stop it! Stop it!* You
are behaving like two small boys in the village who run
around with no pants on." Scattered laughter and cheers
came from the crowd. "You, sir," she shouted, pointing a
thick, authoritative finger at Touré. "You leave that old
man alone. You are talking that way to him because you
do not respect your father!" A rumble of assent from the
population of the boat.

"You go right ahead," she continued. "You go right
ahead and open his bag, but if you do not find your shoes,
it is you we will beat and throw in the water."

For an astonishing moment, there was complete silence.
Then Touré smacked the bamboo pole beside him, hard,
with the flat of his hand.

"Savages, all of you!" He turned his back on the boat
and faced the water. "Me, I don't like savages."

Touré moved his satchel to the roof and stayed there all
day. I peeked my head up and called to him a couple of

times, but he ignored me. Yaya and I sat in silence as well. The countryside around us was flat and sandy, with patchy grass, thorny shrubs, and flat-topped, spiky acacia trees. We were well into the Sahel now, where savanna and desert meet. Just a short hop to the Sahara itself.

In the late afternoon, the boat pulled up to the shore of a fishing village with a lively riverside market.

"This is Diré," Yaya told me. "Touré will descend here."

I accosted Touré on the rocky shore, pushing my way through a crush of young girls who plied me with bags of cakes and sticks of charred meat. I was determined to have a proper goodbye.

"Savages, all of them, idiots!" he spat, when I asked him how he was feeling.

"Oh Touré," I sighed, suppressing a smile. I put a hand on his arm. "Thank you for taking such good care of me. I'm sorry things had to end so—"

"You and me," he interrupted, leaning forward conspiratorially, "we are alike, Tanya. *Toi et moi.*" He grinned, then, and it was as though a spell had broken and he was once again his blustery self. He continued, "Some day I will come to America and find you."

"And then?" I said cautiously.

"And then? And then, Tanya, you will come to my house, and we will laugh, and say, 'Oh, you remember that boat ride, in Mali? It was so crazy, my friend, but it was *sweet.*'"

We arrived at Kabara, the port of Timbuktu, as dusk was falling. We were still about an hour's truck ride from the city itself. The port was unremarkable, with its long wooden dock and familiar assortment of colorful, dilapidated boats.

As we made our way off the *pinasse*, I found myself directly behind the old man. He seemed weak on his feet, so I took his arm. Stepping off the ramp, he stumbled and fell to his knees in the shallow water, spilling some of his belongings.

"Oh no!" I cried, "Are you all right?"

He nodded, fumbling around in the water for his things. I tossed my bags onto the shore and crouched down to help. Some ceramic beads had come unstrung; they floated on the greenish brown surface of the water like tiny inner tubes. I fished them out and then spotted a dark lumpy object, partially submerged. It was a woman's leather shoe.

Timbuktu was founded in the eleventh century by the nomadic Tuareg tribe, who used it as a seasonal camp. A hundred years later, the king of the vast Mali empire laid claim to it. By the fourteenth century, it had become the Port of Africa—the center of trade between northern and sub-Saharan Africa. It was also a center of Islamic education, with more than a hundred Koranic schools and a major university.

Ten days after my journey up the Niger began, I walked the streets of that mythical town. Having come with no real expectations, I wasn't disappointed to find that the once-glittering trade mecca was now a sleepy desert village which was gradually being buried in sand.

But those who told me there was nothing left in Timbuktu were wrong. The city's more than 30,000 inhabitants moved noiselessly through the streets in their full-length garments, their faces shielded from the sand and sun by layers of cloth. Their lives took place in those streets, and in the flat-roofed mud houses with their intricately carved, iron-studded wooden doors. These individuals didn't seem to know they were living in a ghost town. Contrary to modern mythology, they were definitely not ghosts.

There is a mosque—one of three in Timbuktu—which the locals told me was the oldest in West Africa. It was the third place I'd visited that claimed to be the oldest mosque in West Africa, but the others shriveled in comparison. Originally built in the late thirteenth century and rebuilt many times since, it is located on the western outskirts of Timbuktu, its hulking cone-shaped tower looming above the city's otherwise flat skyline. Since the mosque is no longer operational, I was permitted to enter. Walking among the pillars of its high-ceilinged chambers, I felt a growing sense of wonder. The silence itself felt old. Like everything else in Timbuktu, the mosque was made of mud, a product of the sand that surrounds it, the same sand which, in the not so distant future, will swallow it whole.

Stacy turned out to be a bible-thumping blond from Louisiana. The most endearing thing about her was the way she made the French language sound like a Tennessee Williams play. The least endearing was the condescending tone she took with Yaya. Her pet name for him was "Donkeyhead."

The last time I saw Yaya was on my third day in Timbuktu. He and Stacy came by my hotel room, and the three of us went together for a camel ride out into the Sahara to visit a Tuareg camp.

The desert landscape was less uniform than I'd imagined it. Instead of an unbroken expanse of sand, the rolling white dunes outside Timbuktu were dotted with thistles, patches of grass, and occasional scraggly trees. When we arrived at the camp, I sat on a small dune, writing in my notebook, while hard-shelled scarab beetles tottered over and around me. Below me, dome-shaped tents hunkered low to the earth. Golden-skinned Tuareg children with crew cuts and mohawks sat below me in the sand, watching me with avid curiosity. Their knees and elbows were knobby, their bony scalps covered with scabs.

I looked up. Yaya and Stacy were playing in the sand, unrolling his long turban and holding it like a sail in the wind.

I thought of him then, the deaf man. The light in his eyes, the questions he asked. He wanted to know why I traveled.

"To see things," I'd said at the time, but that wasn't right. I should have said, *To see what else is possible.*

I lay down and flapped my arms and legs against the earth. Grains got in my eyes and mouth. My teeth crunched. My eyes teared.

A few minutes later, Yaya came and sat down beside me.

"What are you doing?" he asked.

"Making a sand angel. Where's Stacy?"

"She's in the Tuareg tent, shopping for jewelry."

"I could tell her a thing or two about you," I said slyly.

He smiled. "But you won't."

We looked at each other. I smiled back.

"I miss Touré," I said, hugging my knees.

"You know," he said with some surprise, "I miss him, too."

On my last day in Timbuktu, I climbed onto the rooftop of West Africa's oldest mosque to watch a pale sun set over the Sahara. The rippling sand gleamed beneath it like an ocean of bones. The night air already held a chill.

Two weeks had passed since the day a devout man with cracked feet and glowing eyes had asked me for my shoes. I remembered the disappointment I'd felt when he asked. I'd taken him for an angel, and there he was behaving like a human being. I realized, suddenly, that I'd spent much of

my time in Africa befuddled by the notion that if a friend
asked me for something, it rendered our entire relationship
suspect. But what friendship isn't a balancing act, an ever-
shifting dance of altruism and self-interest? How naïve I'd
been, to imagine that *any* human exchange could take place
in a vacuum, let alone one between a person with shoes and
a person without.

It struck me, then, that the only changes we humans
are capable of are small ones. You can beat yourself up for
years, wishing you could be kinder, happier, more decisive
and secure. And then one day you realize you've made a
slight shift, moved your inner lens a fraction of an inch to
this side or that. Not a whole new self, a remade identity,
just a little change in perspective. A loosening, really, an
out-breath, a drop of acceptance in the salty ocean of the
soul. You haven't solved everything, maybe you haven't
solved anything, but if you're lucky, that small shift will
be the difference between holding your life in grace and
simply holding on.

I knelt and put my forehead to the dusty rooftop in
honor of the passenger on our *pinasse* who never reached
his earthly destination. I wanted him to know that he'd
made a difference on this earth, that he'd touched someone, even if it was only a wandering white girl of ques-
tionable faith. He hadn't gotten a proper send-off on his
new journey, so I did my best to give him one now.

"Goodbye, my friend," I whispered. "Go in peace."

*Tanya Shaffer has toured internationally with her original plays
and solo performances, including her solo show "Let My Enemy
Live Long!," which was based on this story. Her latest play,
"Baby Taj," based on her travels in India, was chosen by the* San

Francisco Chronicle, Oakland Tribune, *and* San Jose Mercury News *as one of the Top Ten Shows of 2005. Her stories and essays have appeared on Salon.com and in numerous anthologies. This story was adapted from a chapter of her book,* Somebody's Heart is Burning: A Woman Wanderer in Africa. *The book was selected as one of* the San Francisco Chronicle's *Best Books of 2003 and profiled in* USA Today *and* Vogue. *Visit her online at www.tanyashaffer.com.*

BARBARA KINGSOLVER

Changing the World: One Chicken at a Time

In Peru, a charitable donor sees first-hand
how her gift keeps giving.

$\mathcal{M}$y first sight of the Andes was exactly as I'd imagined them since I was a child: white, sharp points
laid row upon row, like the teeth of a shark yawning at the
sky. Crowned with permanent ice, the mountains stand
with their feet in green, humid tropics on the Amazonian
side while their western flanks include some of the driest
deserts in the world. Peru is a nation of surprises, where an
intrepid traveler with light baggage may encounter some 90
of the world's 125 classified ecosystems.

Our plane carried just this kind of traveler—a dozen
Heifer International devotees from the United States
who'd come to bear witness to the works we had supported
for years with our hearts and wallets. We would see places

as diverse as Peru, from the dizzying altitude of Cuzco (where we'd find out "dizzying" is not a metaphor), down to some of the world's most marginal inhabited lands in the coastal deserts. I had been told that just a few dollars' worth of assistance wisely spent, in these harsh places, can make the difference between famine and survival. This is what I came to see for myself.

When our plane touched down in a dust-covered coastal town, I shed my jacket in the heat and struggled to recall what month this was: November. Peru's Southern Hemisphere calendars would call it spring, but here in the state of Piura—just a few degrees south of the equator—the season is nearly always just called dry. We emerged from the plane into a town that felt profoundly reminiscent of the Arizona-Mexico border, where I lived for many years. In the skin-prickling aridity I felt strangely at home—doubly so as I chatted with Fidel Calle Calle, a staff member from Piura's Heifer office. As we passed through the city I was struck by another familiar sight—mesquite trees, old and enormous, shading the benches of the town square. Beyond the hopeful, spruced-up little park, Piura's crumbling adobe structures began to betray the truth—this is mostly a poor town with desperate outskirts unraveling in every direction.

We crossed the Rio Piura, a scant trickle over bone-white stones in a broad riverbed. The rainy season, technically, is January to March, but many years pass with no rain at all. Every few years El Niño revs up a good head of steam and drops some moisture. It's good for the land—the trees grow then, Fidel explained. This year the prediction was for medium rains.

At our hotel we changed into farm clothes, climbed into several pickup trucks and barreled out of the city. Fidel steered us skillfully around three-wheeled moto-taxis and crowds of people pursuing the business of their days, in endless districts of houses built as minimally as any I've ever seen. Connected one to the next like flimsy condominiums, running in long banks beside the road, the shops and residences were all made of crisp-looking, leafy dry bamboo cut from the riverbanks. The walls looked as substantial as a grass skirt, with roofs even more provisional. Of course, with no rain or cold to keep out, a structure that offers shade and privacy is presumably good enough.

The office's pickup was equipped with what we called in my childhood "4-60 air conditioning" (roll down all four windows and hit the gas). We inhaled the day in hot gulps. Between stretches of dry forest lay flat, white-crusted fields—former rice fields, Fidel explained, abandoned after years of being irrigated and fertilized until the land could bear no more insult. Flood irrigation evaporates quickly in this climate, leaving behind dissolved mineral salts that accumulate year upon year until the soil is ruined, too salty to support life.

We'd passed into a region of abandoned fields where the white, salt-crusted land looked strangely like tundra. Here and there a corn monoculture rattled crisply in the heat, evidence that some farmers were still trying. We drove up onto a long dike that had been built to hold the river away from houses and farms, in those unimaginable times when there might be too much rain. We bumped along for some dusty miles on the narrow road that topped the high dike, looking down on the desolate land, until we zoomed past a startling green oasis. Fidel stopped abruptly, executed a hair-raising turnaround atop the dike, and delivered us back to where a broad-shouldered farmer waved us down with a smile.

This was Julio Chero, farmer of six acres and leader of a community of twenty-five or so families who are living in an experiment. His family's home is simple, no more substantial structurally than any we'd seen earlier, but the sheltering micro-climate surrounding it offered relief from the desolation of this countryside. This small farm was the first thing we'd encountered that felt like shelter.

From inside a bamboo enclosure we heard the soft bleating of sheep. Heifer had given him five. Now he has twenty-five. He's sold a good many and, of course, he has passed on the gift. But more important to him than the gift of the sheep, he says, has been the gift of knowledge that Heifer also brought this community. Three agricultural workers from the Heifer office who'd come out with us greeted the family companionably.

"These men taught me everything about what you see here," Julio said with his arm around one of Heifer's staff agronomists. They come out daily to work with farmers, teaching them crop diversification, rotation, permaculture, composting. and organic pest management. Julio waved us into his fields to show us how he has incorporated these ideas. We walked among rows of thriving crops: five kinds of beans, which he rotates, always following corn with a legume to replenish the soil's nitrogen. Mango, avocado, banana, and guayanaba trees formed shady hedgerows between the fields.

"Diversifying our crops is not just better for the land, it's better for us," Julio explained. "Our family eats more different kinds of food than we did before, more protein especially: meat twice a week, and beans year-round." At the end of a row we stopped to gaze at the desolate field beyond Julio's: empty, salinized land, to all appearances the end of the world. But no, Julio insisted, not the end—even such damaged land can be recovered, with time and effort. His fields were like that, too, when the project began.

The new crop techniques are directed toward improving rather than further depleting the soil. Julio plows in sheep manure and fallen leaves before planting, using much less chemical fertilizer than before, to produce more corn. For pest control he grinds up a pungent weed. "This one here," he said, yanking it up by the roots and passing it around for us to examine—a sticky aster with a scent of marigolds. He ferments the macerated plant material and sprays it on his corn, effectively controlling earworms without killing the soil with more chemicals. Everything is recycled. Even the new, Heifer-built cement stove in the family's outdoor kitchen is part of the cycle; they cook their food with corn-cobs rather than using up the scant mesquite forest by cutting firewood.

The difference between Julio's soil and his neighbor's was astonishing. It was easy to see why Julio had become a community leader, putting to use the knowledge he receives from Heifer's Piura-based consultants and passing it on to other project participants. If I'd come here to be made a believer, I realized, I needn't travel farther. This diversified farm stood as an emerald island of life among the used-up monoculture fields surrounding it. We were witnessing something beyond sustainability—this was resurrection.

Julio deflected our praise. "I didn't invent anything here," he said. "Our fathers did these things. The land was all they had, and things like manure and biological controls. They saved seeds and had improvement plots to strengthen their seed lines. They knew farming. We came to do it another way, which we thought would be easier, relying on things we could buy, or chemicals supplied by the government—if we could get them. That's what hurt the land. Now we're learning to rely on ourselves again."

Compartir recursos—"passing on the gift"—is an event that draws people in from miles around. We were invited, too, to watch the ceremony scheduled that afternoon in a small village in Baja Piura. In the village's dusty center, a hand-lettered banner decorated a pavilion made of branches, and a white-shirted band of schoolboys with drums and trombones were tuning.

As I stepped out of the truck it crossed my mind that we'd happened onto the arrival of some local celebrity. Then I read the banner—Bienvenidos Familia Heifer— and realized the celebrity was us. A cheer went up from the crowd as the boys with drums escorted us to the pavilion. A row of first-graders gamely held up pink paper hearts, each one lettered with one of our names. Our group ranged in age from seventy-something down to my eight-year-old daughter Lily, each of us having come to learn in our own way what our support for Heifer International really means in a big, particolored world. Walking toward the sun-bronzed faces of a hundred or so expectant villagers, I had a shaky moment in which I wondered if I could possibly be what they expected me to be. I scanned the row of kids for the paper heart that said "Barbara," and my shy moment passed. I bent down to kiss the shrinking violet of a schoolboy who had the task of greeting me. They expected nothing of us, beyond a symbolic acceptance of gratitude. Heifer has changed this village. They wanted to show us how.

We took our seats on a long bench in the shade of an open shelter built out of sticks and branches. The festivities began: first, the *marinera*, a local dance interpreted by a teenage girl—barefoot and lithe in a long black skirt and yellow ruffled blouse—and a boy, dignified beyond his years in boots and hat, waving a white kerchief. To the recorded music from a battery-powered cassette player they moved sinuously and precisely, circling and raising their chins together like mating cranes. It was a breathtaking gift, a moment of beauty from this place to take home with us. Next came singing and a morality pageant about responsible behavior. The crowd laughed at the school kids' antics but also began to buzz with anticipation. We weren't the only ones who'd come a long way for this occasion. The crowd around us suddenly felt enormous as more and more people arrived from other villages to witness the event they've all heard about: *compartir recursos*!

A simple idea, put into practice, becomes magic. On this day, some twenty families that had received sheep or goats through the Heifer project were going to share the offspring of these animals with twenty other families. The village had agreed upon a list of people who were most in need—but there were not enough animals, so twenty recipients' names had been drawn by lottery. The selected beneficiaries now lined up against a wall at one side of a large corral. Out of sight, sheep and goats bleated behind a fence as their owners prepared them for the ceremony. As the crowd assembled I walked over to a tiny widow dressed in black who was soon to receive the gift.

"Will these be the first animals you've ever owned?" I asked her in Spanish, hoping my question would not insult her, if the answer was no. She leveled me with a flat gaze. "Of course," she said. "I've never owned anything. I'm poor."

I gulped, accepting an utterly indisputable definition of "poor." I studied her face, realizing that I'd received the impression "elderly" only from her clothes and demeanor. Her skin had endured a lot more sun than mine, and her hands, undoubtedly, more hard work, but she might have been about my age. I retreated to what every mother considers safe territory and asked, "Do you have children?"

"Six sons," she replied. Or sons and daughters, possibly in Spanish the noun for a mixed group is masculine. I looked around for some of these sons or daughters. For an occasion this important it seemed they ought to be here, but this woman stood alone.

"Are they here?" I asked.

"They're all dead," she answered, again without much emotion, and once again I adjusted my mental notion of small talk.

"I'm sorry," I said. She nodded curtly. Her emotions in this moment were surely too large to discuss with a stranger. What was about to take place was not, for this woman, any sort of sentimental pageant.

It was survival.

We stood together silently then, listening to the subdued bleating on the other side of the corral where animals were being shepherded by their handlers toward new ownership. I tried to imagine this woman's sense of who those shepherds were, over there, and what she must be feeling toward them: gratitude, of course, and perhaps some degree of awe. These neighbors were now benefactors, people who knew new things—animal husbandry, the luxury of household provision and perhaps most amazingly, the prosperity of having something to give away.

I wondered how this woman's life would change. Soon, perhaps already as I write these words, she'll have milk, manure for a garden, eventually meat to eat or sell. In a few years she will have something else. From one flat word, *poor*, her self-portrait will grow more complex as it comes to include the words *compartir recursos*, a ritual whose importance derives not just from the receiving, but also the giving. With luck and health, she will live to stand on the other side of a ceremony like this one.

Suddenly dust flew and the corral filled with the noise of hooves, shouts, and laughter. Eager animals pulled their handlers across the divide. Tether ropes wound up into knots as the skittish animals were handed across. A few men embraced, and several more wiped tears from their faces. Some members of our visiting group took pictures. For my own part, I could only watch and try to understand the depth of human transformation that lay behind the simple act of a tether rope changing hands.

Since the day I first saw a colorful Heifer brochure promising that my gift of a flock of chicks or a goat could change someone's life, I've believed that promise in an abstract way. Each time I wrote a check or volunteered, I pictured kids gathering eggs or a boy waving a branch at a water buffalo, driving it toward the plow. I imagined mothers milking goats and making cheese, preparing rich white protein to feed their children. Now that I've been on a Study Tour, I can verify that those happy images are true. High in the Peruvian Andes we saw women grinning from ear to ear as they received baby chicks into their aprons, round bowler hats and the bright folds of their skirts. We watched their daughters chase the pullets across a schoolyard, excitedly counting their eggs while the hens were barely hatched. In a remote desert in the lowlands, we watched a mother pat out goat cheese with her hands, dribble honey over it from her own hive, and bend down to give a nourishing bite to her toddler—after first sharing some with us, her guests. I was lucky enough to witness the pride and burgeoning health of families all over Peru who explained to us how they cared for their animals, how they used their new resources and skills to improve the health of the surrounding forests and soil, how they'd begun to count on a future they could not have imagined a few years ago.

What I never really understood before this trip, though, is what it means to pass a newly secured future on to a neighbor. The eradication of poverty involves more than satisfying physical needs. It means reaching, somehow, the soul of a woman who has lost husband and children and describes her entire life with the single word "poor." Her grief goes beyond hunger I imagine, into a sense of human irrelevance. To trust that our lives have meaning, everyone needs to effect some tangible change in the world. It's why I donate to Heifer. Why should I think I'm alone in that desire?

In Baja Piura, after the dust of the ceremony had settled, I ate dinner with Luis Gomez Abramonte, a staff member from Heifer's Piura office. An agricultural ecologist, he did research at the university before taking the job here. He greatly prefers working for Heifer, he said, because of the practical effectiveness of the work. Expansion is automatically built into the project through each recipient's contract to pass on the gift. Heifer has now reached more than two thousand families in the Piura area alone. I had a hundred questions, and sorted through them to try to get at the basic thing I wondered about: Does it always work this well? Does every recipient become a benefactor?

Luis answered me patiently: Sometimes animals get sick and fail to reproduce, though this is rare because the project provides veterinary training. This, too, is a gift passed on, since every technician trained in animal care agrees to train others.

I persisted, "But when there is an increase—a profit, you could say—it gets shared?" My doubts arose from a lifetime of having been scolded as a ridiculous optimist, I suppose—too many warnings that human nature is ultimately greedy. "Everyone always passes on the gift?"

Luis smiled. "For most participants, that passing-on is the best day of their lives. Why wouldn't they show up for it?"

Why, indeed.

Barbara Kingsolver is best known as the author of The Bean Trees, The Poisonwood Bible, *and* The Prodigal Summer. *She has been awarded the* Los Angeles Times Book Prize *for Fiction, the American Library Association Best Books of the Year award, and has been a finalist for the PEN/Faulkner Award. She has also been a contributing writer for a diverse range of publications including* The Progressive, The Nation, *and* Redbook.

ℬ ℬ ℬ

The Tree

Being able to say "thank you" can be one of life's
most rewarding journeys.

"I wish for you that when you grow up you will
return to Malta and visit the good Sisters at the
orphanage." Those were the words my father repeated to
me during his worst of times. I knew what he meant by
"the good Sisters" and how important it was for him that I
come face to face with them again, perhaps to thank them
for their kindness of so many years before.

Growing up, my father, Carmel Aquilina, would tell
me of my early history; that I was born in the small
Mediterranean country of Malta, sixty miles south of Sicily.
I knew that my mother died when I was twenty months
old. I knew of the struggles and heartache my father had
experienced as he waited to take us to America. His decision meant he could escape haunting memories of war, the
death of four of his children, and above all else, the death of

his beloved wife. As he made preparations for us to immi-
grate to America, he asked the Sisters at an orphanage if
they could find room in their hearts and home to care for
my five-year-old brother and me. My father needed time
to grieve, alone. The Sisters knew my parents because my
mother, I learned later, had visited the orphanage periodically with donations of clothing for the children. With open
arms the Sisters welcomed us, and in 1950 the orphanage
became our loving home.

My father would often tell me about the kindness of
the Sisters. He would speak of his visits and how I would
cry each time he would leave me—and how it broke his
heart. I had recently lost my mother, and each time he left
me, he knew I felt I was losing him as well. Sadly, he and
the Sisters decided that it would be best if I did not see
my father. Though he knew it was the right decision, my
father wanted to see me—even if I could not see him.

He and the Sisters came up with a plan: at a certain time
each day, I would be taken out to a small courtyard to play
with a ball. On the other side of the orphanage wall, there
was a tree whose branches directly overlooked the courtyard. Each day, knowing the time that the Sisters would
bring me out to the courtyard, my father would climb up
the tree and sit on the nearest branch, looking down at me,
watching.

A year later, our immigration papers were ready. We
crossed the Atlantic during one of the worst hurricane
seasons on record, but arrived safely in America. My father
could not have foreseen how difficult it would be for him
to build a new life. Unable to find work, with very little
money, barely able to speak English, and with two small
children, he knew he needed assistance once again. He
turned for help to a children's home just outside Detroit,

Michigan. There, he told himself, we would be well taken care of until we could be together again. My father continued to struggle. With few resources and fewer acquaintances, he was never able to provide the means for a life that included the three of us. Unfortunately, my brother and I would spend the rest of our childhood being passed from one foster home to another.

Yet I stayed connected to my father all those years. Like the tree that overlooked the orphanage wall, I felt his presence with me always. It was on our visits together that he would tell me of my mother and of his love for his homeland—and how he wished I could see Malta again and locate "the good Sisters."

My father had long been deceased by the time my husband and I planned our trip during a summer sabbatical. I would bring old photos with me, the most precious being a picture of my mother's gravesite. I had no idea where the orphanage was or if it still existed, but I was determined to try to find it. My journey began when our plane landed at the airport in Valetta, Malta's capital. As I slowly stepped off the plane and felt my feet touch the ground, a feeling of comfort and sadness enveloped me. A country that had been so far away from me physically and emotionally was now within my view. I was at long last home, though a stranger. And through me, it was as though I was bringing my father home.

I was born not in a hospital but at home with a midwife, as was the custom of many families at that time. The address I had repeated growing up was "9 Lampuka Street, Paola, Malta"—the place of my birth. So that would be my first destination.

Navigating the streets of Malta was easy—old green buses were everywhere. It was just a matter of getting on one of them, calling out your destination and somehow arriving where you had set out to go. As we entered Paola, we were surprised at how quickly we located Lampuka Street. We walked along the narrow sidewalk past a row of flat-topped houses, then a garage-type door, then front doors until we came to the end of the street. Between the addresses of 11 and 7 Lampuka Street was a garage door. There was no doorbell to ring and no answer to our knocking. I stood for a long moment on the small sidewalk, savoring the reality of where I was, and stared at the door. Whatever it had become, it was still my family home of so many years before—the place of my birth, and the place where my father believed he could no longer bear to be.

I remember my father telling me that we had lived next door to my mother's cousin, and I wondered briefly if any members of that family still lived there. At 7 Lampuka Street I knocked softly, nervous and unsure of what I would say if anyone answered. The door quickly opened and a middle-aged woman stood smiling, as if I was expected. Hoping she understood English, I quickly explained that we were visiting from America, and that I had been born in the house next door but had immigrated to America with my father and brother many years before.

I asked if she could tell me if anyone by the last name of Farrugia still lived in the home (I explained that Farrugia was my mother's maiden name and that my mother's cousin once lived at that address). In a burst of excitement, the woman exclaimed that she was Doris Farrugia and that she lived there with her husband Joey and his mother. We were invited into their home whereupon she hurriedly went to another room and began speaking to someone in Maltese. Within minutes an elderly woman appeared in the small living room, smiling at me as though she knew me. What she saw in me was my resemblance to my mother whom she had known until the day she had died.

Speaking Maltese and beckoning for Doris to translate for her, she explained to me that her husband, now deceased, was my mother's cousin and that she remembered my family well, especially my mother. I was told stories about my parents and our life at 9 Lampuka Street, that my mother had been a gifted seamstress who made elaborate costumes for church *festas* and Malta's Carnival, and that she was a good mother with a sense of humor but a worrisome nature.

It was a beautiful afternoon, one that connected me to my past more than any other time in my life. Knowing that I was sitting across from a woman who once sat in that very room talking with my mother filled me with awe. I would be blessed with that memory forever.

We eagerly accepted Doris and Joey's gracious offer to give us a tour of some of Malta's landmarks. They showed us rocky beaches and beautiful churches, such as St. Mary's in the small town of Mosta. It's known for its spectacular dome, which a bomb fell through in 1942, sliding across the floor without exploding. Many who were present at the time felt it was a miracle.

As the day was ending, I asked if Doris and Joey knew of an orphanage near Paola. I explained that my brother and I had lived with Sisters in an orphanage right after my mother had died, and I hoped I could see it again. To my astonishment they recalled that there was once an orphanage outside of Paola many years before, but were unsure of its exact location.

Joey drove us to the area. Suddenly I was aware of a feeling of familiarity as we passed by a large stone wall. Asking if he would stop the car, I rushed out and walked toward a large wooden door near the wall. I motioned to my husband to follow behind me. There was no sign or address marking the building; all I knew was that I wanted to go to it. I turned excitedly to my husband, "I think this is it...the orphanage."

"I'll videotape you knocking on the door," he said, "and then we better go."

As I knocked on the door, to my surprise, it swung open. It was unlocked. I looked back and proclaimed, "I'm going in."

"You better not," my husband said, but I ignored him. I wanted to know what this mysterious place was and why I was so inclined to be there.

The door opened onto a large marble floor entryway. I could see no one, so I walked in farther. Suddenly a woman with a mop in her hand appeared from around the corner, looking at me frantically and speaking loudly to me in Maltese, as if to scold me. All at once I realized I was tres-passing, and perhaps this was a private residence. Before I could gesture an apology for my intrusion, I could hear Joey and Doris walking quickly toward me on the marble floor. Together they began talking to the lady in Maltese, pointing to me, explaining something to her, hoping she would understand.

She raised her hand and said, "Wait." Joey and Doris explained to me that she was so startled to see me because it was her responsibility to make sure the door was always bolted. She could not understand how a person could be standing there looking around, for she never left the large door unlocked. They had told her that I was from America but had lived at an orphanage when I was a baby and that I was searching for that orphanage. Joey asked if this was an orphanage and she said that it was not. Disappointed, I began to wonder why I had been so drawn to that wooden door, and why it opened.

Within a few minutes the woman returned, bringing with her a small, frail, elderly nun. I wondered if I had walked into a convent or religious retirement home. The woman was busily talking to the Sister and pointing towards me. At last Joey began to speak, repeating his explanation as to why I was there, and apologizing for our intrusion. As he spoke, the elderly Sister studied my face, nodding slowly, not in agreement with Joey, but for a reason only she knew.

Then a look of joy came over her as she proceeded to put her hands on each side of my face. Her eyes telling me something, while her voice repeated, "One time I was your mother." Looking to Joey for help in understanding what she meant, it was apparent that it was unclear to him as well. Her broken English, trailing thoughts intertwined with Maltese made me feel that she was simply being kind to a visiting American who was searching for something she could not help me find.

Continuing to look up at me, wanting me to understand, yet recognizing that I did not, the elderly Sister took my arm and said, "Come." Together we walked as she led me out to a courtyard. When we came to a stop, she looked at me with tears in her eyes and pointed to a wall.

"Look," she said. On the other side of the wall was an old tree rising above it. "When you were here, I was your mother. I took good care of you," the good Sister said. "I put you in this courtyard every day so that your father could see you. He would climb up that tree and sit on that branch and watch you play. Your father loved you very much. Never forget how much your father loved you."

I was overwhelmed with joy and gratitude, for this was my beloved orphanage, a place that had once been my refuge, my home, a place where my father knew we would be loved. I could only look at her and at the tree whose branches allowed my father a haven to watch, and whisper the words he had wished for me to say to her: "Thank you." For the love and care you gave me so long ago, for the compassion you showed my father, and for the peace you have brought to my heart.

❧ ❧ ❧

Carmen J. Semler lives in Mountain View, California with her husband. This is the first essay she has written for publication.

ॐ ॐ ॐ

In Hot Water

What do you do when panic sets in?

T he day I visited Hot Water Beach, on the northeast-
ern tip of New Zealand, there wasn't a hint of cloud
overhead and the sky reflected a rich sapphire hue. I had
gotten a lift to the beach with two locals who see everything
through a surfer's lens: Graham, a long boarder, and Mark,
a boogie boarder, are people who look out at the ocean and
see snaps and tunnels, and talk about right-hand barrels and
rips, terms I only vaguely understood. That's why they were
swimming out to the big waves, whereas I planned to stick
closer to shore, to an area where the breakers seemed mild
and manageable, but still big enough to have fun.

Hot Water Beach is a crescent-shaped bay that's backed
by a natural trellis of limestone rock. This stretch of golden
sand extends for miles to the north, but quickly disappears
at its southern end under a pile of boulders that spills into
the sea. The beach is similar to others along the coast,

but it has one distinguishing feature: an underwater hot spring that bubbles up to the surface when the tide goes out. People come from all over to dig holes in the sand, and then when the hot water rises, they plop down in these natural tubs to soothe and soak themselves. If it gets too hot—temperatures can reach 150 degrees—they carve out canals down to the water's edge and let the ocean turn their bathwater temperate.

While Graham and Mark paddled out to the surf, I made my way over to the hot-tub crowd.

"How is it?" I asked a man who was submerged up to his navel in a homemade thermal pool.

"Sweet as apples," he said, a New Zealander's way of saying, "Faaantastic. Life is good."

Sitting next to the man, perched on the rim of her pool, was a woman in a pink bathing suit, fanning herself with her straw hat. Around them, people were digging and sculpting, using shovels, plastic beach toys, and their hands. A few had ringed their pools with wet sand, as if building walls around a fortress.

I decided to go for a swim first and then warm up in a thermal pool afterwards. No lifeguards patrolled Hot Water Beach, but I figured that was because people seemed to go there mainly to soak. I wasn't worried. I had learned to swim when I was three years old and spent a majority of my childhood underwater, diving for pennies and painted rocks in our neighborhood pool and searching for snapping turtles in local ponds. Later, I worked as a waterfront director at a camp and ran Red Cross programs, training people to be lifeguards.

After watching the man finish constructing his triangular tub, making a pillow out of sand, I waded into the water and strategically made my way toward the breakers. I studied the waves, like an artist contemplating her

subject, and then got into position. Body surfing requires
some intuition, the ability to read the water, and a lot of
luck. If you get too close to the breaking point, you may
miss the wave altogether; not close enough and you risk
getting tumbled by the frothy whitewater. I found what
seemed like the perfect spot and then waited patiently,
treading water. I was only slightly over my head and a
comfortable distance from shore. Farther out and off to
my right, I could see Graham, Mark, and several other
neoprene-clad surfers spread-eagled on their boards, just
waiting for their moment to jump up and dance across the
whitewash. Finally, a wave began to form in the distance,
swelling, gaining height, and then sweeping outward as
it expanded. I maneuvered around, waiting to see how it
would break and then eventually dove through it, deciding
it wasn't quite right.

I continued bobbing around—moving left, right, a few
feet toward shore and a few feet out again—and assessing
each wave, still searching for the perfect one. I could feel
my body shifting and swaying and rising with the water.
Better than a hot tub or a Jacuzzi, I thought, just a bit on
the cool side. I glanced back over my shoulder, toward the
beach-bound crowd to get my bearings, and was immediately overcome with fear: the bathers were now as small as
boats on the horizon and the limestone cliff behind them
resembled a thin pencil scratch across a giant canvas. My
body went numb and then started tingling, as adrenaline
shot through my veins. My breathing became short and
shallow.

I don't know how I hadn't realized that I'd been body
surfing in the wrong direction. While I had been studying
the water, and trying to read and anticipate the waves,
I had no idea that I was moving swiftly out to sea, out
over the coral reef, beyond the breakwater, and into the

deep blue waters—6,000 miles of ocean that stretched all the way to the coast of Chile, with hardly a bump of land along the way. The sandy shore was now far off to the right and I was in front of a rocky coastline with no surfers in sight because of the tall, rolling swells that I was supposed to be riding into shore. I was way over my head, the current was still tugging at me and a series of big waves—what seemed like an endless row of breakers—was heading straight at me.

And then I panicked. Despite a decade spent teaching people how to swim safely and handle fear, I totally panicked. I began fighting the water, wrestling with the current and trying to gain control.

I spun back around to face the waves head on and fought the pull of the water as it dragged me farther out. My legs were pumping hard, kicking and fighting, as I got ready to dive through the first wave. It crested and I lunged, tensing my neck muscles, clenching my fists and trying to keep my body pencil-straight. Cold water ripped through my hair and then rippled around me, and it was a long few seconds before I clawed my way back to the surface. I gasped for air, my arms flailing and slapping down on the water. *Keep your head up,* I told myself, *keep treading.* The waves came quickly, closer together now and another one loomed overhead. It was like looking up at a towering snow-capped mountain. Suddenly, it let loose an avalanche of saltwater as it began to crumble over me. I inhaled quickly and dove, my arms flapping at my sides, too tired to reach overhead. The force of the wave sucked more energy out of me and I kicked to the surface with little time for a quick breath before—Crash!—the next wave struck. My thighs burned and my lungs were gagging for air. I could feel the muscles in my throat convulsing, but I kept my lips tightly pressed. *You have to fight it*, I said to myself. *Keep going.* I swallowed a mouthful of water and started choking, saltwater shooting up and down my throat, confused which direction to go. I was gasping and coughing and trying to keep my head above water so I could breathe. My legs were on fire. My muscles were stinging. My feet flopped around, dangling at the end of my legs, useless, numb from exhaustion. *Don't go upside down,* I told myself, *don't get flipped.* The water spun me around and I went under, tumbling. *Get your head up. Where's the surface? Get up! Get up!*

Then, suddenly, there underwater, not knowing which way was up, I no longer cared. I wanted air, but I couldn't get to it. I couldn't fight anymore. I popped up from the last wave and felt a sense of profound peace wash over me, a moment of total calmness. I let go, no longer feeling the pain or the fear, and I remember thinking, *This is what it's like to drown.* My body melted beneath that thought, dissolved into the depths below me as I faced the next wave head-on, no longer afraid. The intense power of the ocean, I was no match for this force. I don't remember the next wave, whether it tumbled over me or slipped underneath me and lifted me up. I will never forget that moment of peace.

Seconds later, I realized the towering waves had passed, so I floated on my back to conserve energy. Soon the swells died down, too, and I realized that maybe I could swim again. I began kicking and paddling as hard as I could, angling myself away from the rocks so that I was heading diagonally toward shore. *Are the waves getting bigger again?* My stomach jumped, but I kept swimming. *Get away from the rocks*, I told myself. *Keep kicking.* The swells dropped down and I tried to remain calm, while desperately pushing myself forward. I kept an eye over my right shoulder, on the lookout for incoming waves. I couldn't tell if I was getting any closer. The beach looked like it was miles away, but I kept kicking and slowly, slowly I inched my way in. I thought I'd left all my strength in that last wave, but somehow it had nudged me along.

It took me about forty minutes to get back to shore, forty of the most draining and exhausting minutes I've ever experienced. I literally crawled onto the beach when I finally reached it. Then I stood up and walked twenty yards away from the water's edge, as if a wave would snatch me up and suck me back into the ocean, and out to sea. I stumbled and sat down, shaking uncontrollably from fear, from exhaustion, from disbelief, and from overwhelming relief. I was too shocked to cry. I was too stunned to throw up. I was too numb to think about what had just happened. I couldn't make sense of it yet. I sat on the beach for ages, hunched over with my arms balanced on my knees to hold me up, and stared out at the water and at the surfers who glided across the tunnels of death that had brought me to hell and back. They hadn't seen a thing. And for the first time in my life, I felt mortal.

I wanted to hug someone and cry. I looked over at the bathers, but they were busy chatting and digging and splashing water over their shoulders to cool down, or else leaning back with their heads propped on little sand pillows. No one had even realized I was in trouble out there. No one had seen me flailing and going under.

An hour later and still shaking, I walked up toward the car. I waded across a little saltwater stream that carved its way through the sand, and stopped to read a sign I hadn't noticed before: "BEWARE," it said in giant letters, "strong tidal rips can take you out to sea." I took a deep breath and walked away. *How amazing to be alive.* I thought. *Just as sweet as apples.*

❧ ❧ ❧

Kari J. Bodnarchuk is an adventure-travel writer who lives in Bellingham, Washington. She earned a Lowell Thomas Travel Journalism award for her story on Rwanda and is author Rwanda: Country Torn Apart *and* Kurdistan: Region Under Siege*, two children's books in an ethnic conflict series. She writes for* Outside Magazine, Backpacker, The Miami Herald, *and* The Boston Globe*, and has contributed to numerous travel anthologies, including* The Best Women's Travel Writing 2005 *and* 2006, *and* Her Fork in the Road: Women Celebrate Food and Travel.

ॐ ॐ ॐ

Living on Venetian Time

Once experienced, Venice never leaves your blood.

We ride outside, clinging to the sides of the racy wooden boat, pushed backwards by a humid wind. As we roar across black water, the boat's running lights flash past shadowed, hummocky islands, sometimes revealing a pile of crumbling ruins.

Only an hour ago, our plane swept into Venice's soaring, elegant Marco Polo Airport, poised like a beautiful bird on its jut of land. In our marriage, I do the Italian speaking, but in my exhaustion, I find my verbs have seeped away, leaving me stuttering a request for a water taxi in toddler Italian. Considering my mortification and the dispatcher's disdain, we lucked out in Filippo, our tall, bronzed, water-taxi driver, who ignores us completely now as he flouts the speed limits with abandon, a cigarette hanging from the corner of his mouth. Thrilled by our cinematic entrance, stunned by lack of sleep, my

husband and I stand, holding hands, for our entry into
Italy's Oz.

I wake in the half-light in the elegant, gray-shadowed
room with its beamed ceiling and two full-length, shut-
tered windows on a small canal, or *rio*, Rio dei Felzi. For a
moment I'm not sure where I am, then, at the same time I
hear the steady sound of my husband's breathing, I notice
the lapping sound of water. I feel warmth flow from the
center of my body into my hands and feet, and recognize it
as elation. After so many years, and so many trips, including a couple to other parts of Italy, we are finally here,
where we promised ourselves we would return twenty
years ago, after our first, honeymoon, visit to Venice.

The soft lisp of Venetian dialect brings me, padding
barefoot, to the window. I push open the heavy wooden
shutters. Only a few feet below, a boat glides slowly by,
low in the water from its cargo of drinking water, cases of
wine, and crates of vegetables—daily life, delivered on the
water as it has been for a millennia and a half. Tucked back
into our pillowy bed, I think about the bed in our pensione
twenty years before.

Two hard, lumpy mattresses connected in the middle to
form an old-fashioned *letto matrimoniale,* matrimonial bed.
The particular conformation of the lumps meant that, no
matter where you started, you always ended by meeting in
the middle. With its opulent decrepitude and simple furniture, the room, and even its hilly bed, were sufficient for us.
It's true we were a little surprised by the proprietor's definition of a room *con doccia,* with a shower. Strictly speaking,
there was a shower, not with the room but actually *in* the
room, a metal shower stall positioned against one wall. The
shower functioned well and was admittedly quite convenient
for tumbling into straight from bed. It would have been nice,

of course, if the shower had been part of the fully appointed
bathroom the *con doccia* had led us to expect, but we were
satisfied by the shared bathroom down the hall. The lack
of a sink or toilet was more than offset by the ancient fresco
that blanketed our entire ceiling with muted royal, rose, and
umber; in a patch above the shower it was mottled by mold
and peeling in flaky strips.

In those days, Dorsoduro was a fashionably funky artists'
section, though not nearly so expensive a place to live as it is
now. It was the ideal place to begin our days, one *vaporetto*
stop from the Accademia Museum, in a real neighborhood
where a ragged line of chattering children filed beneath
our windows each morning on their way to school. There
was no breakfast with the room, but powerful coffee was
just a minute away in the nearby Campo San Barnaba.
We sat at an outdoor table with a view of the elegant San
Barnaba church, which we would later recognize with glee
as the library visited by Sean Connery and Harrison Ford
in *Raiders of the Lost Ark*. A housewife leaned out the window of an upstairs apartment and called, *"Buon giorno,"*
down to a passing friend, who waved back; a man sat on a
straight-backed chair in the shade painting the scene. Life
in our *campo* offered an intimate counterpoint to exploring
the larger city around us.

At the Piazza San Marco, we, like all first-time visitors,
gazed in awe at the pink-and-white, piped-icing façade
of the Doge's Palace and wandered about the golden cave
that is the interior of the Basilica San Marco. One night we
shared a gondola ride with friends from San Francisco. None
of us could understand the gondolier, except for random
words that seemed to be Italian, English, Spanish, perhaps
German. Puzzled, we strained to decode the smooth patter.
Giggling, we finally realized the gondolier was speaking
a kind of Esperanto—snatches of several languages, the

whole entirely incomprehensible. The price was exorbitant, the singing off-key, but what made this extravagance worthwhile were the snatches of opulent rooms, brightly lit like stage settings, as we glided by in the quiet darkness.

For most of three dazzled days we two stumbled and floated, jet-lagged, sometimes lost, always drunk on beauty, shocked by the sheer impossibility of what we were seeing. We understood that we were in a place unlike any other: a place where the boundaries between air and water are porous, where the living Venice breathes, light on water; where dappled light plays on peeling walls; where your eyes are ravished by beauty everywhere you look, and you know you can never look enough to be sated.

Our visit was so brief, yet we knew something had happened that had altered us forever. Young and in love, with all of our lives together ahead of us, we had come to Venice. To come to Venice, in such a way, with an open heart and open senses, is to embark on an affair from which there is no recovering. Even then we knew that wherever we went after this, however marvelous or mundane, we would, as long as we breathed, be haunted by flickering images of upside-down, plaster-licked, Byzantine, Gothic, and Renaissance-windowed palaces no more improbable than their upright counterparts.

What we couldn't know was that this obsession would be like having a second, half-imagined life. With avid interest and heartbroken frustration, we would dissect the news of greedy and mismanaged efforts to save this floating mirage of a city, scrutinizing its progress toward annihilation from afar with the sort of tender grief felt toward a fatally ailing, still-beloved lover.

Twenty years later, the windows become our entry into life on the water. A couple of hours after the delivery boats,

I wake a second time to Carlo, my husband, bringing coffee. Eagerly, I carry the small, hot cup to the window. A casually-dressed man about forty emerges from a deep doorway in the crumbling three-story palazzo across the narrow canal. He turns his back and steps out into space, then finds a foothold on the wall. As I watch, the man moves along the wall like an insect, clinging to crevices in the brick and a few metal brackets. When he reaches a shabby, jaunty little motorboat, he casually drops into it and starts it up. The engine is ragged; then it roars and spits black smoke for a few minutes before he glides off. To our delight, this performance is repeated with aplomb every morning.

We often sit by the windows to read and watch the show. One late afternoon, I relax in the big chair by the window, book upside down on my lap, drowsy in the sun. For the first time during our stay, the shutters on the third floor of the house across the way begin to open. I look up, curious about who might live there. An old woman's face—beautifully, deeply lined—appears in the window. I smile shyly at her. She scowls magnificently down at me, grabs both shutters, and bangs them shut. Although I look for her to appear again, they remain shut for the rest of our stay.

All day the gondolas mingle with the neighborhood boats. The gondoliers call out, "*oiii,*" to let other boats know they are coming around the bend into our canal. After midnight, a teenage couple sometimes lingers in a little skiff nearby, murmuring and kissing, the boat affording them an opportunity for the Venetian equivalent to parking in cars. All day and into the night, we chat and make love and sleep to the sound of water slapping the wall beneath our windows.

Our hotel is in the Castello section, and "our" *campo* is the largest in Venice after San Marco, which is the only

square allowed to call itself Piazza. Named for the towering Gothic Church of Saints Giovanni and Paolo, the
campo is commodious enough to allow kids to ride their
bikes, officially forbidden, but, after all, this is Italy, where
breaking the rules is *normale*, as Italians say, and families
who choose to remain struggle for a normal life in this
impractical city. Our local bar pours the two-sip (or one
gulp) Venetian espresso that is the shortest in Italy. But the
crema on top is perfect and we sometimes stop for a pastry,
or a couple of *cichetti*—little snacks like bread with fish
paste or marinated anchovies—with the crowd of working
people from the 6 P.M. *vaporetto,* eavesdropping as the man
standing close by whispers softly into his cell phone, letting his wife know he'll be home soon for dinner. It seems
that Venetians often whisper, perhaps a natural outcome
of living where sound bounces and refracts back and forth
from buildings to water, and a conversation can often be
overheard. More Venetians live in our neighborhood, the
Castello, than in any other; when we walk back to our
room at night, we notice that other tourists drop off gradually until we find ourselves the only foreigners among the
Castellani. We speak very softly then, if at all, in an instinc-
tive effort not to intrude.

This time, we stay long enough to live in the rhythm of
the Venetian day: rising to eat enormous breakfasts—fresh
cornetti with jam, fruit juice, yogurt, cereal, and creamy
cappuccini—in the charming courtyard of our hotel, riding the *vaporetto* to the islands of San Michelle, Burano,
Murano, Torcello in the northern lagoon, resting at siesta
time. I find a *fruttivendola* close to home and, by the second
day, we greet each other familiarly. "*Buon giorno. Come sta,
Signora? Sto bene,*" we exchange each day as she carefully
examines her boxes of fruit and transfers from her hand to
mine, as carefully as though they were South Sea pearls,

two perfectly ripe peaches or a handful of tender plums.
Late at night, we visit the nearly empty Piazza San Marco,
when artificial light and the absence of crowds make its
vast space feel even more like a magnificent phantasm,
peopled by ghosts.

We are tethered to home on this trip in a way we
had not been twenty years before. On our way from San
Francisco, we dropped off our ten year-old son, Giancarlo,
with my family in New Jersey. The respite from vigilance
is invigorating as a whiff of pure oxygen, but I miss him,
especially when, riding the *vaporetto* out in the lagoon one
afternoon, I spot a group of boys, ten or twelve years old,
their laughing voices carrying across the water as they
race each other in their tiny boats. They are princes of
the lagoon, their expansive empire scattered with unin-
habited atolls and abandoned islands. They play their
games among the stones of forts and dwellings, some of
them shattered testament to legendary settlements long
ago lost to earthquakes, storms, or high water. I know
that hurricane, high tide, and an earthquake swept away
almost all of (the original) island of Malamacco, home of
the Venetian government before 809. And that another
earthquake, on Christmas Day, 1233, submerged forever
the lagoon islands of Ammiana and Costanziaca.

Everywhere we go—out on the water, in piazzas,
in cafes, even when lost in narrow nameless streets—I
find myself scrutinizing the Venetian women. I want to
understand what makes them seem so arresting. They
dress more conservatively than the tourists or even Italian
women from other cities. On high summer days when
visitors cower in ribbons of shade, they wear black or
brown fitted linen or cotton dresses; even in sundresses,
their display of flesh is modest. They tend to be deeply
tanned—not surprising given that sunblock at the *farmacia*

ranges from only SPF2 to SPF8. Without being obvious, they are at times startlingly beautiful. Almost without exception, they move in a way that is all fluid grace and ladylike provocation. I remember reading a novel once in which the Italian characters commented on a young English bride: they said she didn't know how to move. Now I think I see what the author meant. What is most mysterious is this: young Venetian women are often fresh and lovely; middle-aged Venetian women often alluring and elegant; and then, as though a bewitchment had been snatched away, old Venetian women seem to transform into bent and furrowed crones, sometimes assisted through cobblestone streets and up and down bridges by a solicitous daughter. I wonder when, precisely, the spell ends.

Several nights, we eat dinner at the same restaurant, Il Mascaron, near Santa Maria Formosa. It's a cozy, crowded place, popular with the locals, with a small bar, a half-dozen small tables, and several long, family-style tables. We seem to have the same waiter—large, indolent, amiable—every time. He always presents a piece of waxy paper with tonight's dishes scribbled in pen. We eat wonderful antipasti of roasted vegetables and bits of seafood and pasta with clams and the food and the price are both good, but it's always obvious that there are two levels of service: one for tourists and one for Venetians.

On our last night, when the waiter tells us what's available, I order the *branzino*, a fish from the Venetian lagoon, in season for only a couple of months each year. The waiter tells me it is very large. I say I have a very large hunger. As we sip our glasses of Prosecco, I notice the whole fish being delivered to a couple of other tables, where the recipient watches patiently as the waiter carefully bones it at the table. Finally, he brings me a whole, flat, sizzling fish that fills the plate, and walks quickly away. I am obviously meant to

manage, and probably expected to mangle, the big fish on
my own. But the waiter cannot know that I am an Italian-
American. My blood is as Italian (though Neapolitan, not
Venetian) as his. I grew up in a family where the worship
of food was taken as seriously as Catholicism. Years ago,
my father taught me to cut up a chicken and to bone a fish.
So I take the sharp knife the waiter has left, and carefully
slice off the top layer of flesh. Then with my fork, I remove
the bone in one unbroken piece, like a gleaming fossil
pulled unharmed from its bed, and set it aside. Except for
one bite for my husband, I eat every bit of the sweet, "too
big" fish, including the cheeks, which Daddy taught me
were the tenderest parts of all. Having seen this boning
performance before, Carlo grins at me, amused. When the
waiter comes to collect our plates, I smile my most satisfied
and delighted smile at him and he looks at my plate and,
only a bit unwilling, smiles back.

Awake in our bed that last night, I wish I could sleep,
and dream about Venice. Instead I leave open the shutters
and listen—listen to the rhythmic heartbeat of the canals,
smell the briny green water, and watch shadows silvering
the pale green walls. In the twenty years that I have been
reading and thinking about and hoping for Venice, her fate
seems more certain. Many scientists think she won't last
past the end of the century. Still, she is very likely to outlast
me. It's true I can no more bear the thought of her end than
I can of my own, but since it is unlikely that I can forestall
either, I lie there curled against my sleeping husband, and
close my eyes so that the sound of the lapping water makes
me feel as though my bed is rocking. And then I promise
myself, once again, that I will return.

The water taxi comes for us in the dark. This driver
is no Filippo: our progress is ponderous, tranquil. The

lagoon swirls with curls of vapor. Out of the vapor, bits of other boats reveal themselves like body parts. The mist tints pale yellow and rose with the rising sun. We join a sedate parade of boats, funneling between channel markers on what must be the "official" route to the airport. The water is a silver sheet; the mossy brine canal smell transformed here in the open lagoon into freshness, a sly metallic saltiness.

We look back, like all lovers, with regret. In the creamy morning light, Venice pierces the air with her red brick minarets, displays her pastel palaces, flashes her ornate windows, shows off her impossible surreal gorgeousness, shrinks into a chimera on the horizon.

❧ ❧ ❧

Francesca De Stefano lives in San Francisco with her husband and their son and is writing a book on traveling and eating in Italy. She credits her love of travel to one of her first childhood memories: standing at the dock in New York, holding one end of some streamers, her grandparents holding the other, as their boat left the dock for a visit home to Italy.

✂ ✂ ✂

Savorings

Sometimes getting in tune with yourself
requires the touch of another.

"Iarranged for our strongest man, Tunla, to come,"
the hostess smiled demurely while observing my
athletic build. "I hope he will please you." I had arrived at
the Tjampuhan Hotel an hour earlier, tense after a stifling
ride from Bali's international airport to the mountain town
of Ubud. After dropping my bags in my room, I wound my
way down the hillside dense with lush greenery on thick
stone stairs. The overgrown path was difficult to follow
and I had to retrace my steps when it would suddenly dead-
end at a fishpond or an unfenced lookout. I could not see
where I was going in the dense foliage and suddenly found
myself in a small clearing that led to a door illuminated by
a warm welcome light. I stepped inside. Mahaja stood up as
I entered, letting loose her flowing black hair that fell to her
slender waist. Her wrists, no wider than my two thumbs

pressed together side by side, were adorned with pink-, blue-, and gold-colored glass bracelets that complemented her sarong. Her skin was the color of smooth honeyed oak. I would have felt self-conscious by her subtle reference to my bulk, but her cheery greeting blunted the disquiet that had built up as I followed the convoluted twists and turns of the path I'd been on. Instead, I laughed.

Mahaja led the way to a room with one wall open to the jungle and river below. With the fresh ears of a small child, I listened to animal life prepare for nightfall. Reptiles tucked themselves into pockets of warm earth while bats flared their radar scales and stretched out their wings, readying themselves for night flight. Crickets' angelic humming replaced jungle birds' God songs. Whiffs of fragrant incense kept mosquitoes at bay and burning candles buffered the mysterious sounds of the jungle intruding into the world of human activity. Mahaja showed me where to hang my dress and as she was leaving said, "Tunla will knock on the door in a just a few minutes. Please make yourself ready to receive him."

I looked around the room for a place to set my glasses. Undressing had always been an awkward affair when I was anywhere other than at home, particularly so with my glasses off for I was never truly naked while wearing them and yet, without them I never really knew what I looked like. Deciding that the wooden hutch by the door would be a good place for them, I undressed and hung my clothes on a peg, the beige linen shift hiding my underthings, and set my plain leather sandals on the floor beneath my dress. I climbed up on the massage table, and slipped under the white top sheet. As I lay there, I noticed a spider spinning its web in one corner of the ceiling and realized I wasn't naked after all. I got up off the table to lay my glasses down on the hutch but they were too close to the edge and fell to the floor. I picked them up, set them on the hutch again. Now naked and several steps from the table, I felt like someone acutely aware that they were wearing clothes turned inside out, ragged seams, loose threads and pockets all exposed. I dreaded the possibility Tunla would walk in before I was securely under the sheet again.

Tunla knocked then waited a long moment before entering, his right hand covering his heart as he bowed in respectful greeting. His smile was warm but hesitant, conveying a deep shyness that didn't permit him to look directly into my eyes. The stark whiteness of his uniform accentuated his blocky build; his dark skin glowed like nebula in a moonless night sky. Swallowing my own nervousness, I returned his smile and asked about his family. He answered after apologizing for his halting English and I learned he was thirty-two and married with two young children. I was startled to meet what I did not expect, a body worker more self-conscious than me.

He asked my permission to begin and when I assented, I discovered his hands, despite his timid demeanor, take firm command massaging first the sole of my right foot and then the left with all the care of someone handling a living heart. He wrapped his fingers around each toe as if he were a baby reaching for his mother's breast. He worked his way up my shins, calves, and hamstrings, using his knuckles to cut hard muscle into thin curling ribbons. As he worked, I slowly drifted into deeper space, forgetting absolutely everything, even my name.

Tunla was a master musician of the body. My bones, ligaments, muscles, and skin became mere strings resonating with rich sound as he played my familiar body and also another one, one very different. His touch converted each and every cell to sonic sound waves that excavated dark, moist, secret places. My lungs filled with oxygen and released carbon dioxide in shared rhythm with earth's vibrations.

Time passed, time that was this day and yesterday, time when I was a child and when I was a sister, time when I was another mother and many mothers, time when I was a grandmother and other great, great grandmothers. I was in the Gobi desert, I stood overlooking the source of the Ganges River and I was with the bison freely roaming the Great Plains. I wandered this earth for a very long time.

I wanted to stay but I was called forward. Tunla's hands were taking new license in the cupping and squeezing of buttocks and the gentle pulling apart of thighs. A soft awareness of the room I was in replaced the wide-angle lens of my mind's eye as he loosened my arms from my sides and with his fingers and palms traced every curve along breasts, waist, and hips. His hands ran up my legs, back, neck, and down again to my toes caressing me into ripeness fuller than I'd ever known before, even when happily pregnant, and left me feeling the grace of a seal that leaves only the smallest ripple when she lowers herself into the depths. We were deliciously attuned and he didn't break the spell when he lifted the sheet for me to turn onto my back.

He savored the tops of my feet from ankle to toenail tips and then the bones of my lower legs. He rode bony knee caps and kneaded powerful quadriceps. The muscles in his face softened and his touch became more personal. The tips of my breasts stood up like an adolescent girl's, lushly pink, and my thighs relaxed into acceptance. He pulled on my skin from my clavicles down to my navel and then from my navel down to the cellar of my sexuality. As the remaining bit of sheet slid to the floor, his hands intimately worked to elongate inner groin; his fingers kissed outer lips. I was singing inside.

His hands traced pelvic bones, ribs and stomach, teaching me how each separate part belonged to the whole of me. He worshipped each breast encircling his hands clockwise and then counterclockwise until I too was enchanted by them. In the tradition of Bali where only women, not men, have the power to communicate with the gods, he had me offer up the nectar stored deep in the recesses of my milk ducts and the nectar was gladly taken. His hands taught me the ways of receptivity, of a world entirely eroticized. Body opened to heart whose only purpose on this day was to lead me to soul. His touch grew softer and lighter until his hands gradually withdrew; satisfied his message had been properly received.

Tunla floated the sheet above me reminding me to pay attention to the dim outlines of the room. Sounds coming from the hall slowly intruded as I tugged on my senses. Satiated, I barely noticed Tunla leaving. He returned carrying a clay bowl filled with a mixture of sweet oil and ginger-pepper scrub. He scooped out thick handfuls and spread it over my skin and scalp. He next cocooned me in a heated sheet and stroked my back before giving me his now radiant smile. He turned out the lights and I was left alone, enshrouded in white cotton and thrown into what felt like a searing fire. All I could manage was the sleep of the dead until the different pieces of me, body, mind, and soul, merged as hardened glaze adheres to an earth-fired pot. I was me, but a me I hadn't known before.

I woke to the sound of water filling the bathtub that was tucked into one corner of the room. Tunla was gently pulling on the sheet to loosen it so I could stand up. He very, very slowly unwound the covering to reveal all of who I had become and then, taking my hand he guided me to the bath. The inverted bowl shape of my chest that I had always depended on to guard my heart had been dissolved.

I stood upright and proud for him as he washed me with a fat soft sea sponge filling his powerful hands. I turned for him, lifted my arms for him and spread my legs for him. I was mesmerized by the cascading fragrant soapy water. Body and mind stretched outward, without boundaries. Again I traveled, this time to a long forgotten childhood when love still ran around loosely and generously, teaching me that no matter how I behaved there was a silent forgiving self who accepted all I have ever been and all whom I ever will be.

Tunla toweled me dry and then draped another towel around my shoulders while he retrieved my dress. He gently dropped it over my head and steered the armholes through outstretched arms. He slipped my feet into the sandals, handed me my glasses and stood back a moment to inspect his handiwork. With a satisfied smile, he withdrew. I stood awhile, pulling myself back into human form, no longer caring about the underclothes that had fallen to the floor. The light in the hall hurt my eyes so I leaned against the door jamb, pausing to get my bearings before exiting the room. A young woman passing by took my hand and led me to a table where the staff congregated between sessions. I was aware of their warm greeting—not the words yet certain they knew I had climbed onto an altar naked to myself. Invited to sit and take tea, I attempted conversation but my words came out as mush. The well-wishers giggled behind their hands, assuring me I would recover and urging me to drink the thick, sweet ginger tea. When I finished, I waited to see if my tongue would loosen up and when it didn't I said my goodbyes, offering my prayers first to Tunla and then to the rest. He walked me to the door, congratulating me on my return.

I ascended the same slippery wet steps one at a time, no longer confused by the path I was on. I savored the velvet feel of dark humidity, heard the fat molecules of water slide off iridescent green leaves and plunk against the hard backs of big black beetles. I tasted mold spores that leapt up from the decaying forest floor and searched for cosmic light through thick jungle tree tops. The walk back to my room seemed to take forever but I was in no hurry. The internal wisdom Tunla had stoked tethered me to earth's deep pulsating energies making me aware that this gift was an act of grace. I flung open the door to my room and was greeted by a four-foot-high blackened teak god swinging from the rafters of the balcony. Laughing foolishly, he danced in the wind while holding his two-foot-long, forever-erect phallus—impregnating everything around him.

❧ ❧ ❧

Victoria Q. Legg resides in San Francisco, staying close to her two, not quite adult, children while writing short fictional and non-fictional pieces. She is the editor of a tri-annual newsletter pertaining to parent education. When not writing she paints, largely as an abstract expressionist. She can be contacted via the web at www.victorialegg.com.

❧ ❧ ❧

Spirit Quest

In a monastery in the
Arizona desert, the author finds that
seeking the holy entails risk.

*I*t may have been the grayness that drove me to the desert. Through months of Boston winter there was no color—not in the ashen heaps of plowed snow or the papers to grade or the sullen faces of my grad-school professors.

Now, on an endless stretch of I-10 in Arizona, I squinted into the sun like some Northern-dwelling troglodyte unaccustomed to the light. The landscape, flanked in reddish-brown dirt, looked like the pictures sent back by the Martian rover: only this was Mars with billboards, tractor trailers, a Rooster Cockburn ostrich farm. Soon the land began to prickle with cactus—not the anemic, over-watered and under-sunned windowsill variety, but massive, man-eating things, their spiny arms bent at the elbows, reaching for the open sky.

Past Tucson I entered the high desert, its low-slung hills blue in the late light. In nearby Tombstone, player pianos romped inside Big Nose Kate's saloon and honest-to-goodness tumble weeds rolled past the jangling spurs of men dressed like Wyatt Earp. The town's namesake grave markers ("Margarita, Stabbed by Gold Dollar"; "George Johnson, Hanged by Mistake") stood shoulder to shoulder on a wind-swept bluff as foreboding as the town's violent history. But my destination was as far from the spirit of the Wild West as I could imagine: Holy Trinity, a Benedictine monastery in the tiny town of St. David.

I had thought it was the forced frugality of student life that led me to such an unconventional spot: at thirty bucks a night for room and meals, I could afford the winter escape I had dreamed about—sunshine and mariachis and festive bordertown buildings the colors of popsicles. But on first sight of the Celtic cross looming over the landscape, I felt the muscles in my chest pull taut as rubber bands. Around my neck hung my own crucifix. I never took it off, not to shower or to sleep, but through the years of graduate school it had lain under my sweaters like a dead weight.

It wasn't that I had lost my faith entirely. But I hadn't found a safe place to house it in the vaulted rooms of academe, where we were all busy intellectualizing and analyzing and deconstructing. My mind alone seemed a welcomed guest in that world; my faith felt like something I should have outgrown, like braces or turnkey skates.

Yet somehow I now found myself rumbling down a dirt drive, past the long rows of gnarled, squat trees I would later learn formed a pecan orchard, finding my way to a monastic guest house. A stoic brother appeared, led me past rusted farm equipment and barrel cactus to my sparse guestroom. He told me meals were to be taken in silence, gave me a list of Mass and prayer times, and vanished.

I wandered back out onto the grounds, surveying the mish-mash of Spanish architecture, a trailer park, a small thrift store that sold well-used items and the native pecans to poor Mexican families. I saw an adobe chapel the color of wet sand and what seemed to be a Japanese garden, its red bridge bleeding into the land. Peacocks wandered the grounds, their glossy blue-green chests reflecting like silver dollars in the afternoon sun.

As daylight faded, I watched the sun lowering over the Celtic cross. Outside the chapel, dark shapes were amassing in the trees. The peacocks were roosting there, massy shadows with tails pulled in like closed table umbrellas. There was something strange and unsettling about the silence and utter darkness descending, about the silhouettes brooding in the boughs, about the dry, warm air that breathed over the mountains on a February night.

Soon tiny beams of light began to flicker, swinging this way and that at odd angles over the desert. The residents of the Benedictine community emerged from their solitary cells and joined a silent, twinkling parade to the dining hall. I was to join in a hushed meal with all of these strangers, who followed one another through the cafeteria line with shuffling feet and downturned faces. But then the meal wasn't exactly taken in silence: one of the brothers pushed a button on a portable cassette player, and we slurped our soup to a Baroque trumpet voluntary.

It was over breakfast, the only speaking meal of the day, that I met Susan, a ruddy-faced woman with a Dutch boy thatch of silvery hair, and Peter, a bearded college dropout in a stiff-brimmed cowboy hat I had seen working in the orchards. They leaned in to the table and invited me in little more than a whisper to go with them on a nighttime desert hike. I liked the vaguely conspiratorial flavor of their tone and was enticed, too, by the possibility of spotting javelina, strange pig-like creatures that travel in packs by moonlight, munching on the spiny leaves of the prickly pear cactus.

So off we went into the high desert that very night. I was armed with only a meager flashlight, which illuminated the tips of my boots and little else. My head bobbed from the ground (this was rattlesnake territory, it suddenly occurred to me) back up to sky, where, even given the glow of the gibbous moon, more stars festooned the heavens than I had ever before seen.

I walked as quickly as I could manage, far more nervous that I thought I'd be, swinging my flashlight accusatorily at every desert weed that crossed my path. But my new friends were loose and unbothered, batting monastery gossip back and forth like ping pong balls. *Monastery gossip*. I hadn't realized there was any such thing. Weren't monks, well, monkish? Quiet, pious types, with no sin in their hearts? But apparently Brother somebody-or-other was depressed again. Another brother was showing signs of Alzheimer's, continually forgetting the words to the "Glory Be." Yet another brother was such a motor-mouth no one could get his work done, and there were whispers of petitioning the Pope himself for a transfer.

I learned of other desert intrigue that night, of the illegal aliens running across that precise strip of land, of the occasional altercations, sometimes violent, there with the authorities under the placid stars. I came to realize why I had found empty gallon water jugs along the dried-up San Pedro river basin on the Holy Trinity property. Peter said the water was so heavy, the families couldn't carry any other belongings, not even food. They had shed only their empty bottles on their flight.

Soaking in that story, I doubted more deeply the wisdom of trekking into the high desert when it was so late and so dark, so far from any help. And then I heard it: the first cry of coyotes breaking the brittle spine of the night. I stopped short, and for several long moments I could not move. There it was again—that insistent cry of longing or pain, nearer this time, impossible to know how near in the blinding darkness. There was a purity and urgency to the sound that seemed to shake something loose in me, something that had frozen over in Boston. It at once terrified and thrilled me.

Sometimes, I was beginning to learn, the sacred felt scary. Sometimes finding the holy was a risk.

There was a quotidian rhythm to life at the monastery. The mornings were cool and clear. My first sight each day was the sun beaming over one of the outstretched arms of the cross. Peter and a few other men cleared brush and planted in the garden; a tiny bell was rung from the adobe chapel; the peacocks and hens stretched and walked dotingly across the land. There was time to mediate in the Japanese garden; to sit in full February sun, baring my pale arms to the light; to follow the bird sanctuary trail around the pond, which rustled and flashed with feathered color.

I began to notice the subtleties of nature: the first green, pale and tremulous, pushing its way to the tops of the cottonwood trees; the three-inch thorns of the acacia, where the so-called butcher birds impaled their prey; the huge, succulent spines of the blue agave, taller than I, filled with the clear sap to make tequila; the curling, rust-colored manes of horned steers in the blond fields.

Never before had I attended Mass daily. There was a rhythm to that, too, to the daily Eucharist, to feelings of constant prayer, washing over me in steady waves.

But when I wasn't in the chapel, with its beamed ceiling and tree trunk-hewn altar, I wanted to be outside every moment, day and night. I wanted to sleep outside and to eat outside and to pray outside and to take every night the desert hikes under the stars.

It was during another of our moonlit walks that Susan and Peter confided that they were members of a clandestine group of poets who held secret meetings deep into the night. "Wow," I said, "how many people here are involved in that?" They looked at each other and replied in unison, "Two."

I followed them one night into the dark monastic library, down long musty rows to a little corner lit only with a rubber-necked lamp. Truth be told, I was curious but not expectant: I was, after all, a Ph.D. candidate in literature, jaded from overexposure to wannabe poets. I vowed to myself I would be polite, supportive; keep my theorizing and deconstructing to myself.

But I didn't have to.

The poems, about God, and to God, and for God, were sometimes angry, sometimes beseeching, sometimes peni-tent, but were made so purposefully, humbly—the words placed atop one another in a careful climb, like a pilgrim ascending stone stairs on his knees. Hearing them, I was witness to something intimate and deep, something that mattered: sincere and naked struggles with faith.

Susan, I discovered, had been a noted San Francisco psy-choanalyst who was following her own spiritual call all the way to the novitiate. She traveled the country, staying as a guest in monasteries and convents, trying to find the right fit, the order to which she would belong. And Peter turned out to be a wayward millionaire who had renounced his tycoon father's worldly lifestyle. He left it all behind, *all* of it, to labor in any corner of the world he was needed.

As I walked through the warm darkness that night,

poetry was in my mouth, my gut. Passing under the shadowy peacocks in the trees, I thought of Wallace Stevens's "Domination of Black": "the colors of their tails / Were like the leaves themselves / turning in the wind, / in the twilight wind." I remembered, too, the words of Pat Dawn, the old Yaqui woman and curator of the small museum on the monastery grounds. "The desert is mystical," she had told me. "The desert *changes* people."

I saw her daily, sitting outside her little museum, silent and grave, her jet black hair pulled tightly against her skull in a thick bun. Her eyes, deep-set and sunken over high cheekbones, stared out to the desert. One day I followed her to the dim back rooms of the museum, which were crammed with bizarre trinkets. The place was like the rich repository of a grandmother's attic and she showed me around with the same matriarchal care. We moved slowly through the Victorian room and the room of Arizona history and another room displaying liturgical objects; we scanned over sheet music, uniforms, Native American baskets. There was an entire room dedicated to nativity scenes from all over the world, Bolivia to Madagascar, some 168 sets in all. Overwhelmed by the display, I took my time, examining each one with respect, aware that Pat Dawn was also examining me.

"I could teach you the medicine wheel," she finally said, in a tone full of import and quiet pride.

I followed her again to one last, small room and seated myself on a low stool. Pat Dawn sat with her eyes closed. Then she took a breath, let it out, and began to speak. From somewhere within her skirts she withdrew a hand-drawn diagram, a circle pierced with four arrows, one for each direction of the compass. Mind, Spirit, Emotion, and Flesh were all given a compass point; each section of the circle was also designated with a color, season, and an element—earth, wind, fire, water. I saw that they also encompassed the seasons of life, from infancy through adolescence, aging, and what was called "dormancy," the wintertime, death. Below the wheel hung three feathers, representing freedom, strength, and power.

I didn't quite understand in that moment, sitting on the stool beneath the medicine woman, afraid to ask or interrupt, what precisely the wheel was for, or why she had chosen me to share it with. Her stories about it were like the Lenten prayers recited in Latin that I'd heard at Mass as a child: I didn't grasp their literal meaning, and yet there *was* meaning and mystery in what was happening, meaning *in* the mystery.

Looking more closely at the drawing I realized that the feathers were also designated with Christian names: Father, Son, and Holy Spirit. And suddenly I began to understand this Holy Trinity—and the monastery of the same name— in a way I had not understood it before. It was no wonder Pat Dawn was so proud of her museum: it was a tangible manifestation of her very self, part Native American, part Christian. The whole monastery was like that—an ecumenical paean to God. A Celtic cross loomed over earth alternately called Yaqui, Apache, and Spanish names. A young Greek-American volunteer read Joseph Campbell after a French service held in an adobe chapel. A Japanese garden offered a sacred space where one could pray the rosary.

I would become part of that rich and paradoxical fabric, too, as the northerner in southwest territory, as the academic who had discovered in the depths of the desert that she could still feel the existence and transcendence of God.

Pat Dawn told me I was to be given a new name. A Yaqui name. But not yet. Not until she received the seven confirmations from the desert spirits, the seven signs of grace from her Christian God.

And in that moment a door was unhinged. I spoke, at last, about my own faith: confessing that the academic life had too often felt to me like the long Boston winter; that I felt such isolation; that I had kept God out of my writing, like a shameful secret. It was as though I was supposed to choose between my own depths, I told her, intellect and soul. But here, the strong skeletal frame of the wheel was charted with mind and spirit, flesh and feeling—all equal, equivalent, necessary.

Sitting with a medicine woman at a Benedictine monastery, I did not have to choose. I could round my back like a circle, stretching to embrace the line of spirit that had fallen away, but was not lost.

On my last night at the monastery everyone was hushed and expectant for Taize, a mysterious service with French origins. The chapel was lit only with oil lamps and votive candles in gold and green holders, assembled to form the shape of a cross. Entering the chapel that night was like entering a canvas. The light was too dim to make out more than the faint brushstrokes indicating eyes and mouths, but the aggregate presence of the supplicants created something, a virtual hum in the small, palpably sacred space. I found myself holding my breath, just so I could hear it.

Then one by one, from different corners of the chapel, people began to speak. At first I didn't know what they were saying. I could tell only, from the strength and reverence of the voices, that they were uttering prayers—prayers for people no one else knew, for troubles kept too long in the solitary confines of their minds. Every name was a toll: speaking them aloud was like ringing a bell. I wanted to cry, and I didn't even know why. Up at the tree altar the priest was crying, too. Over his shoulder, through the open apron of windows, I could see the panoply of desert stars.

Afterward I was like a rung bell myself, my skin resonating to some spiritual frequency I had not felt since I was a child. I yearned for one last desert walk, perhaps to find at last the elusive javelina, or the owls whose low calls I sometimes heard in my dreams. Peter agreed to go with me and we walked along the riverbed, through fragrant thickets of mesquite and cottonwood. There I was, in a short-sleeved shirt in February, looking for owls, saying poetry and prayers in whispered breath, holding my crucifix between thumb and forefinger and feeling, at last, like it meant something.

Faith, I knew, feeling my way through the dark fragrant night, is a risk, and I wasn't the only one who had to navigate its streams. Everyone, even the residents of a Benedictine monastery, struggled in his or her own way with a private faith—each of those faceless people in the hushed chapel, offering prayers to nothing but darkness and stars.

In the morning, I stopped by the museum one last time. Pat Dawn invited me to return to the mystical high desert, to embark on a spirit quest. I thanked her warmly and promised I would return. But before leaving I had to ask—what was my Yaqui name? The medicine woman smiled. That would have to wait, she said—until the spirit world confirmed the signs; until faith finished its unfolding.

෴ ෴ ෴

Jennifer Carol Cook finally finished graduate school and received her Ph.D., her faith still intact. She currently lives in the Boston area, where she teaches writing and American literature at Bentley College. She continues to embark on solo travel adventures (and misadventures) every chance she gets, and her spirit quest continues.

⁊ ⁊ ⁊

Getting Clean in Chiang Mai

A teacher says goodbye to the life she
lived in Thailand.

*T*he day's steamy heat has nearly crested, and as I walk
home up our lane after teaching my last class for the
day, my body wants the rain. It will come, I know. Trudging
along with my book bag, my faded umbrella shielding me a
bit from the sun, I stare at my sandal-covered feet, taking on
more dust with every step. Bua Jin will have filled the clay
jar at the foot of our stairs, and I crave this simple foot wash
as I grow closer to our house.

I'm nearly there, passing the hourly-rate hotel, where I have
sometimes gone to use the phone. As I round the corner, and
Wat Chang Kien, our neighborhood temple, comes into view,
a few of the boys in golden monk robes call to me, rousing a
cat that's been dozing in the sun, atop the plaster wall.

"*Ajaan! Ajaan!*" they call, laughing at one another, and the bravado of shouting at me, the American woman who lives in their neighborhood. I shout back a greeting, playing at this small transgression in their young monks' vows.

"*Sawat dii, kha! Sabaay dii, leeu, kha?*" Hi, how are you? I answer, tossing them a big grin. All three settle back to their rhythms, one sweeping the temple yard, the other two bent over a bit of grass, watching a bug of some sort.

Our house comes into view, the coconut tree in the front of the yard visible over the gate, a few water-starved fronds drooping over the fence. As I open the gate, Bua Jin comes out from behind the shower house, where she has been watering some of the hibiscus. She sees me as she approaches the well to refill the empty bucket she uses every morning to water the yard, and fill our water jars. Today, with the humid air seething, she will water the yard twice, a trail of bucket-spill dampening the dusty soil in her wake.

"*Pay nay maa?*" Where are you coming from? she asks me, as she does whenever I return home. "Finished teaching already?" she adds.

"*Kha,*" I reply. "Yes, it's so hot today. I can't wait to take a shower," I add.

At the bottom of the steps leading into the house, I stop to slip off my shoes, dip water out of the jar, and rinse my feet. I savor this small domestic habit, knowing that soon it will be just a memory. My departure from Chiang Mai, where I have been teaching at the university, is coming all too quickly. The fellowship that has financed my time here will end, and I will head back to the States. The season of goodbyes has begun, goodbye to all these people I have come to love, whose habits and smiles I have come to share, whose language and jokes have become familiar.

Bua Jin, too, has been thinking about the departure. The other night, as Roberta and I sat on the cool teak steps inside our house, correcting the semester's final exam papers, Bua Jin lifted her head from the sewing machine, where she stitches clothing and sarong skirts for the neighborhood women every night, earning a bit of extra money. That evening, she was clearly thinking of our coming departures, mine the first, just weeks away.

"*Ajaan*," she asked, as I parsed the best way to gently correct the paper of one of my shyest students.

"*Ajaan*, once you're back in the United States, will you remember how to come back here, to this house, and to all of us in Chang Kien? " she asked. "Will you remember the way?"

I smiled at her simple understanding of the distance. And then I reassured her.

"Of course," I said. "Of course I'll come back to visit. I'll never forget the way to Chang Kien and all of you. This will always be my home."

Indeed, two years into my stay in Thailand, I had managed to cross to the other side, living within a culture that had once been utterly alien to me. Although I was sometimes confronted by my own foreignness, most days I no longer experienced any real sense of being different. Yes, there were moments when I realized I was the *farang*, or foreigner, like that afternoon in a doctor's waiting room, when I found myself sitting amid his other patients, who were all Thai and Hmong people from the mountains. Clearly, what they saw was a white American woman wearing strange shoes.

But in my own head, the traveling, the pleasantries of being a tourist, had ended a long time ago. I was no longer a visitor; my life with Bua Jin, with my students, my fellow teachers, was lived much of the day in Thai, moving in and out of the routines that had become my life there, and were now so intimately normal.

If I was foreign, it was in the back of my head, because Thailand had become home. Only the sudden sight of my own pale skin, blue eyes, and curly, light brown hair in a shop window or mirror would sometimes, unexpectedly, thrust me back into my American identity and life in the United States. Chiang Mai was home, and life was now a series of treks to the university to teach, trips into town to do errands, visits and jaunts with friends to nearby villages on the weekends, and the everyday details of life in our small, teak house in Chang Kien.

Such a perfect fit, it seemed that Bua Jin would often insist that I must have been Thai in a previous life.

"*Ajaan,*" she'd say, "Your soul is so Thai. I know you were Thai in one of your earlier lives." Most often it seemed a gentle joke, but sometimes it set me to wondering about whether transmigration was the reason I'd been gravitating to the East since my childhood.

I had always been drawn to the foreign. As a child, I could spend hours fingering the pages in the encyclopedia where all the traditional garb of the world was laid out, like paper dolls with costumes already permanently affixed. I lingered over the Asian figures, and the East European, savoring on my tongue the whispered names of places I could barely imagine. I became addicted to the geographic series called Lands and Peoples, which illustrated a different country every time, where an abundance of time-blurred black and white images could be counted on to help purge the boredom of living among Levittown houses, strip malls, and blacktop parking lots naked to the sun.

I had always hated the suburban sameness of the place where we lived, where all the houses were identical, and all the trees had been bulldozed away. But I see now that suburban sterility was the prod to my imagination; I saw futures elsewhere, of shimmering bronze bells, of densely textured monks' robes, of women in brightly colored sarongs leading water buffalo amid rice fields.

Twenty years later, in 1976, I would traipse across the globe to escape the too-narrow confines of the life my parents had in mind for me. I needed to break through to the other side of the world, and prove to myself, at least, that the world was benevolent, could be trusted, and that—a year after the Vietnam War had finally ended—all that was foreign and Asian was not necessarily your enemy.

Now, as I mount the steps to the Chang Kien home that I soon must leave, I smile thinking of the way Bua Jin spoke of the distance that will soon separate me from this place. A gust of wind sweeps the house, and suddenly the wooden shutters are banging against the house, and I hear Bua Jin shout to me, as I slip into one of my sarongs.

"*Ajaan, Ajaan*! The rain is here! It's a storm—close the shutters, it's coming down strong!"

In an instant, the garden is awash in a downpour, the dust-covered leaves drinking in the water that has broken from the sky, the smell of the wet earth rising like a potion, intoxicating. The slow, lazy early evening has suddenly become a fast cacophony of shutters slamming shut, water slapping the banana tree leaves and hitting the tin roofs of the shower house and water closet. Bua Jin calls to me, "Look, *Ajaan*, look!"

She stands by a corner of the roof, where the water is rushing off, wild and thick.

"Come here, *Ajaan*! Take your shower here," she yells, throwing me a broad smile.

As I head outside, Roberta peeks out of her room.

"What's going on?" she yells.

"Come on outside," I call to her. "The water's just pouring off the roof!"

Within minutes, we three stand under the rain, laughing as we become soaked together, each of us wrapped in a flowered sarong. Bua Jin has run into the house to get soap, and now we're sudsing up, turning to do one another's backs, yelping in glee as we play at this game of rainwater showering.

This moment will soon be a memory, I think. Let me remember how it felt, I implore whatever gods there are. Let me feel this water, this lush garden of fruits and jasmine, this woman who's become part sister, part mother, in a language that is not my own. Let me remember that this is how I lived, in an Asian place that once was foreign but became my home.

That shower in the rain now seems lives ago. Indeed it is. Exactly thirty years ago—before my first marriage and my divorce; before falling in love with the South American musician who would chase Thai from my head, replacing it with the Argentine Spanish that even our daughter now tells jokes in. Many lives ago, that shower was.

When I returned to the United States in 1978, my personal landscape had been utterly transformed. Home was no longer a thirty-block radius in one of Boston's neighborhoods, or even my parents' place in Connecticut where I had spent adolescence. Home was much larger, and much farther away.

"I'm a citizen of the world now," I told people when I came back. And indeed, there was a lot of truth to that. Foreign news datelines were no longer faceless.

Immigrants, once I had moved to the city, no longer seemed "foreign." Homesick for Chiang Mai, I soon took work teaching refugees from Vietnam and Laos, feeling an almost immediate familiarity that revived something dying in me. I craved this connection; sometimes I stumbled on it by surprise, in the face of a stranger on a train, looking like one of my Chiang Mai teachers, or in the quick patter of a Thai waitress, whose accent sounded just like Bua Jin's. Each contact left me dislocated on a tide of longing.

Over the years, there have been many such unexpected "encounters" with people I left behind in Chiang Mai, even if only in my mind's eye. Whether because of uncanny resemblance or the simple memories that come through reverie, these friends live in me still. We are told the world today is a global village, and yet, in the desperation of headlines and competing national destinies, of armies and weapon systems locked on the radar of human heat, it sometimes feels far simpler, and even necessary, to retreat, to surrender to the years, and the distance. To yield up the past, and to let it be just that, to let it be over, ended.

But that would be a terrible deprivation. When I think back to that moment in the rain, outside our small teak house in Chang Kien, I am washed anew, cleansed of the daily preoccupations that keep us isolated in our current lives. The traveler in me lives again. The world, and its far horizons, is mine, and I embrace it.

♫ ♫ ♫

Laurie Covens writes for a hospital in Boston. In previous lives, she authored speeches for two Boston mayors; penned editorials almost faster-than-a-speeding-bullet for local TV; and was a daily news reporter. This is her first published travel story.

K. GREGG ELLIOTT

❧ ❧ ❧

What Can't Be Spoken

A "guest journal" reveals the inner life
of friends made along the road.

T was being swept along by the other passengers
debarking the Gibraltar ferry to Tangiers. They
were mostly tall thin men wearing flowing djallabas and
burdened with all sorts of packages. Immediately upon my
arrival, a tout ignored my steadfast refusal and escorted me
into the cool den of a Moroccan shop, where I sat drinking
mint tea and admiring each richly-colored carpet rolled
out for my inspection. "*Mais, je n'ai pas beaucoup d'argent!
Je n'ai pas l'espace!*" I said, mainly to convince myself, as my
hosts exchanged knowing glances and refilled my glass to
the brim.

The next day, clad in a beautiful new kilim-weave coat,
I set out for the Rif Mountains, famous for both their
remoteness and their thriving trade in hashish. I was in
search of the former. For days I wandered through nar-

112

row cobblestoned streets, past whitewashed adobe houses trimmed in violet and lemon. Each morning, as the sun rose higher in the sky, the immaculate dwellings suffused the air with blue-white light, mirroring the surrounding snow-capped peaks. Barefoot children pushed wheelbarrows of fragrant loaves of bread—still warm—through the cool streets, jostling foot traffic, goats, and bicycles. Steep twisting alleys beckoned with the promise of new surprises at every turn. In the tiny village of Chouan I met an American woman who introduced me to the Turkish baths, where we joined the village women in pouring extravagant buckets of hot water over one another's lathered heads and bodies. Back outside the baths, these same women turned anonymous, hidden behind the folds of their veils.

People do it all the time, but what is the reason for traveling, for backpacking alone to a remote and foreign place? I suppose I wanted to escape the heavily touristed Iberian coast and have my own personal experience of the exotic. I wanted the conversations I had with strangers to yield shards of meaning. I wanted to apply my travel journal to the road, like a pickax to a vein of gold, sifting the dust of my journey for a wider comprehension of the world.

In Rabat, where many of the Muslim women simply wore headscarves rather than a face covering, I finally met a young Moroccan woman eager to speak with me. She was a university student. Saida had a round intelligent face, a ready smile, and spectacles. She was filled with ambition, pursuing a career in teaching. But her future included no plans for a family.

"I will not get married," she told me, gazing into the distance. This seemed to explain everything. I had begun soliciting guest entries in my journal. I proffered a blank page to Saida:

"*J'observe partout...*" she wrote, "I observe everywhere in Morocco that wealth plays a very important role, provoking a comparison between rich and poor. Our society has little means of constructing factories for improving life or eliminating unemployment. Unemployment is the state of young Moroccans, and jealousy reigns everywhere." That same day, after lunch at a sidewalk café, I watched as a frayed man in a filthy djallaba slipped onto the patio where I sat alone in the late afternoon sun. He hurried up to an uncleared table, snatched up a half-full glass, and drank rapidly and a little unsteadily. A bread crust disappeared into the folds of his garment. Once he paused and glared straight into my eyes. I could not hold his gaze. He continued until he had consumed the remains in every glass and on each plate, then disappeared as quickly and quietly as he had entered. I sat in stillness afterward for a long time.

One morning in Rabat I visited the medina, the old market quarter that sits at the center of every Moroccan city. I purchased a round of freshly-baked bread and began eating, tearing off huge chunks as I inched my way through the bazaar. A piece slipped from my fingers. Instantly a tall Moroccan youth with a mustache and penetrating eyes was at my shoulder offering me the bread. "*Tu l'as perdu.*" You've lost this, he said.

"*Non, merci*, I dropped it."

"Take it," he said.

"I don't want it, thank you."

"Are you English?" he asked.

"No, American." His eyes narrowed and immediately I became the subject of a piercing inquisition during which my interrogator loudly announced his antipathy for the American government. I managed to blunt his hostility somewhat by agreeing with many of his criticisms then asking him to explain his politics.

He paused in mild astonishment, then answered, "That will take some time."

"Time," I said, "is precisely what I've got."

We spent the day walking through the city, discussing politics and philosophy, consulting my French-English dictionary to look up the big words. By mid-afternoon, having made short shrift of Moroccan history, we had begun tackling Western versus Muslim attitudes toward women. Abdelkhalik spoke with conviction, but when I asked if he would marry he became silent.

At some point I must have passed an indefinable test, because Abdelkhalik looked at me with new eyes and invited me for supper, saying I'd have to spend the night because it would be too dangerous to make my way to the pension after dark. I was young and struggling to know the world. This was pre-9/11. He was not after the usual prize, of that I was certain. My intuition gave a nod, so I accepted.

Abdelkhalik was from Salé, the slum across the river from Rabat, home to the majority of Moroccans who work in the capital city. The narrow, grimy streets overflowed with garbage and people hurrying home from work. Abdelkhalik stopped and bought two tomatoes and an onion from a sidewalk vendor. I offered to pay, in return for his offer of hospitality for the night, but he refused.

Most dwellings in Salé were of corrugated sheet metal with dirt floors. Abdelkhalik led me to a small room at the end of a decaying building. The room had cement walls, a concrete slab floor, and one barred window high on the wall. One cot and a sleeping mat on the floor, a tiny gas cookstove, a few kitchen implements, and two scarred wooden chairs were its total contents. Pictures of beautiful women from *Elle* magazine were taped over cracks in the wall. A latrine consisting of a hole dug into the bare ground in a dank closet leaked the smell of urine and human waste.

We ate our meal of sauteéd tomatoes and onions over rice, and I invited Abdelkhalik to make an entry in my journal. He took the pen, paused, set the tip to paper, paused again. When the words finally came, he wrote quickly. He handed back my journal with the intricately scrolled serifs of Arabic flowing across the page.

"What does it say?"

"You will find out," he answered.

After supper, Abdelkhalik offered me his sleeping mat. He would sleep on the floor.

"Who is the other bed for?" I asked.

"I can't afford to live here without a roommate."

"Where is he?"

"I don't know. He usually returns late." Sensing my unease, he added, "Do not worry."

Too exhausted to ask more questions, I mastered my distaste, used the latrine, and we fell asleep as the murmurs of the city beyond the concrete walls faded. I awoke to the sound of a man bellowing in anguish. With wide-open eyes I strained to see through the cavelike darkness. I smelled alcohol and heard an unfamiliar voice spew an incomprehensible stream of angry Arabic. I froze in fear. I lay awake the rest of the night as Abdelkhalik's roommate snored in his cot, occasionally shouting or moaning his alcoholic rage. I thought of Abdelkhalik's lively intellect, hobbled by lack of opportunity in the hard, narrow track of his life. I recalled his reluctance in speaking of a future with family, and his reticence no longer seemed such a riddle. When dawn outlined the window bars against the purple sky I arose, gave Abdelkhalik a hug of thanks, and taking care not to rouse the swarthy middle-aged man sprawled on the cot, I left—simply because I could.

Memories of Salé faded in the sultry desert air of Marrakesh. For several days I explored the labyrinthine medina and gorged on succulent dates after being taught how to first pull them open to check for the worm that sometimes lives inside. From the taxi drivers, I gathered travel tips and decided to head next to Essaouira, a small town on the coast south of Marrakesh.

After three years of drought, February rains had resuscitated the withered landscape, which overflowed gratefully with buttercups and tiny flowers the color of blue and white porcelain. I found an *auberge* located four kilometers from town amid budding acacias and succumbed to the beguiling rhythm of desert life. Each morning began with the sensual aroma of *café au lait* served in an outsized ceramic bowl with a handle on either side. The soft susurration of the windmill blades above the well pump accompanied morning bird song. Next I would meander toward the ocean, lost in the beauty of the resurrected desert. Once I stumbled upon a shepherd boy helping to birth a lamb. I watched until he was vigorously rubbing down the newborn, a wide grin on his face. The lamb's tottering first steps toward its mother's teats and the shepherd's careful ministrations imparted a biblical quality to the scene. There was no need to speak.

The beach was the widest sweep of sunburnt sand I had ever seen, and utterly deserted. One afternoon, I was invited to tea by some local fishermen. These men were Berber, the original natives of Morocco prior to Arab colonization. They had brown, deeply lined, handsome faces and arresting sky-blue eyes. They explained to me the significance of the mint tea imbibed so regularly throughout Morocco. The tea is prepared in three rounds using the same tea leaves, but adding fresh mint and sugar with each draught.

"The first draught," said the old man preparing the tea, "is bitter, like life. The second draught is sweet, like love." He continued stirring the tea as he impaled me with his impossible eyes, "and the third is gentle," he said, "like death." I realized, with something akin to shame, that for me life had never seemed bitter, and I wondered whether death would ever seem a thing of mercy.

I slept fitfully on the night bus returning to the departure port of Tangier, awaking at each stop. Once, very late, we arrived at a cantina in a tiny village. The yellow light of gas lamps illuminated four men with traditional flowing headdress playing cards, and a dog lying half-hidden and motionless behind the men's feet. People began exiting the bus and with dawning horror I saw the dog was not a dog at all, but an emaciated man without legs. He used his arms and hands to drag himself with surprising dexterity through the mud to beg for a few dinhas. The tableau through the window was silent, but I could see him speaking rapidly, one arm outstretched toward his fellow men. Passengers walked by, absorbed in conversation. The gentlemen at the table dealt another round of cards.

In the ferry queue I made my last random Moroccan acquaintance. I don't remember how we met, perhaps Hassan was watching me observe the surreal stream of people laden with Western goods disembarking from the ferry. Somehow this particular place revealed the nonsensical nature of international borders: A person like every other, born into the struggle for survival, steps over an imaginary line on the earth. Suddenly he has to worry that customs will disallow his meager load, purchased for resale to help support a hungry family.

Hassan was a sophisticate who had lived and worked in Paris for years. His long thin face was always arranged in an attitude of merriment and his laugh was very attractive. Hassan's journal entry reads: "Traveling, for me, is discovering what is important in life. Thanks to travel, you know that life is short. Try to make it happy by seeing through to the truth of things."

I requested a translation of the Arabic script that Abdelkhalik left in my journal. Hassan read to me one and a half pages of geopolitical rant that ended with these words: "I do not know the political secrets of war. I can explain to you the rich and the poor. Me, I am poor. And truthfully, I do not want to tell you my feelings after all."

Hassan and I traveled together for several more weeks until we reached Paris. Years later, we are still friends. We correspond and even talk on the phone occasionally, in a mixture of French and English. But it is Abdelkhalik who speaks to me, across a gulf of hardship and unfathomable poverty, wordlessly.

♨ ♨ ♨

K. Gregg Elliott currently lives, teaches, writes, and raises her daughter in the Midsouth—land of fireflies, chiggers, bald cypress, barbecue, indigo buntings, and Southern belles.

꿈 꿈 꿈

The View from Below

In Ecuador, a surprising revelation awaited this climber.

M y former racing buddies thought I was crazy when I emailed them about the most magnificent day of my life... the day I *failed* to reach the summit of Cotopaxi, one of the highest active volcanoes in the world located along the eastern cordillera of the famous glaciers of Ecuador.

It was a plethora of firsts for me—first attempt at something that grand, first ice climb, first outdoor adventure since arriving in South America. I had spent the previous three months in Venezuela attempting to hone my Spanish skills with a native family. At that point, I was ready to get back to something familiar, something I was somewhat good at, something that invigorated my soul and connected my spirit with nature.

I felt prepared by the handful of fourteeners in Colorado as well as the circuit of sixteeners I had already completed in Ecuador. The chance to climb Cotopaxi had always been a dream of mine. Having done a few expedition adventure races, I always felt the hand of the Universe at my back. As far as I was concerned, there was no "Plan B": it was summit or bust.

Clad in layers upon layers, drowning in all of my superlight, wind-buster, bomb-proof, ain't-nothin'-gonna-give-me-the-shivers apparel and my bright yellow fluorescent jacket, I was deemed "La Banana de la Montaña." I was a Sherpa's yak weighted by jingling metal, carrying a silver steel "T" in one hand and my life in the other.

Cargo and all, I felt confident. I was a twenty-seven-year-old, traveling solo through South America, one of only two females on the mountain, and the only North American. How many people in the world had the chance to do what I was doing?

I would entrust my life on the glacier to Rafael, our guide, and my co-climber, Alexi, a twenty-six-year-old Peruvian medical student who was equally enticed by the magic and the challenge of the volcanoes.

We'd spent most of the previous day in deep conversation about our uniquely different cultures. Ecuador was the first country he had ever visited. He was from a family of seven who lived together in Lima. He spoke of his daily ritual which entailed waking up at 6 A.M. to eat breakfast with his entire family. Then he would ride the bus to school, return home to eat *almuerzo*, go back for afternoon classes, and be home by dusk to help his grandfather fix any electrical or plumbing problems. He would spend his weekends tending to the vineyard and fig groves on the family farm.

And here I was. Unlike Alexei, I had already traveled to five other countries in the world and would be spending the next year exploring this entire continent. All I had to do was buy a one-way ticket using my credit card and within the click of a mouse, I was on my way to Latin America. I quit my job, sold my car, and was about to climb a volcano in the Andes. How did I become so fortunate?

Rafael was a former mountaineering champion, who had crowned Cotopaxi more than 500 times and was one of the fastest to summit Aconcagua, the highest peak in South America. His encouraging and compassionate smile reconfirmed the privilege I felt to have him lead me to my first glacier summit.

"*¿Han visto mis guantes?*" I muffled through my face mask.

"*¿Que dices*, Estefi?" asked Rafael. No one yet in South America had been able to pronounce my name without placing an "es" in front.

Giggling, I poked my mouth out the bottom, "Have you seen my gloves?" I whispered again in Spanish.

It was pitch black as we crept about the *refugio* with our blinding headlamps. The other mountaineers were still snuggling in their bunks as we attempted to move stealthily across the hollow wood floor in our boots as if we were trying to quietly use a jackhammer in a library.

I had just returned from a chilly outdoor bladder relief session to release the two-liter water jug I had pounded to stay hydrated. It was one of those rare moments in life when I wished I were a guy. I must admit, it is an impressive skill that we women must possess to be able to squat and aim in a hole the size of a saucer, swathed in eight layers of clothing, literally freezing our buns off, do "the do," stand up, tuck in the thermals, pull the suspenders up, regroup, all without knowing if we've wiped ourselves with the actual toilet paper or our gloves!

"*Aqui estan*," said Alexei as he sweetly offered to put them on my already numb, dysfunctional, circulation-challenged hands.

We sat down at the breakfast table with three wobbly legs to await our midnight *desayuno* prepared by Rafael. He pranced out of the kitchen like a vicuna, carrying a loaf of fresh baked *pan de Guayava* and strawberry yogurt topped with Frosted Flakes. *Frosted Flakes!?* Suddenly, any preconceived uncertainty or nervousness dissipated as I was immediately back to childhood Saturday mornings in my PJs with Tony the Tiger. We ate abundantly before loading ourselves into our thirty-pound packs.

The old door of the *refugio* squeaked out a loud, haunted closure behind us, demanding that we not return until we had accomplished our mission. The wish-wash rhythm of our rainproof pant legs was the only sign of human presence. We were among the first few teams to tiptoe into the darkness, anticipating a perfect eight-hour, 8 A.M. arrival at the summit. No one said a word. Instinctively, we retreated into our own humility, silently praying to Mother Earth, our ultimate guide, that she graciously allow us to tread on her sensitive flesh to the heights of her beauty. A stadium of twinkling spectators waited to cheer us on as the spectacular creation lay ahead: Cotopaxi, or in the Quechuan translation, *Smooth Neck of the Moon.*

We set off into the night, three florescent headlights in space, like the belt of Orion, steadily ascending up the glacier. It would only be an hour before we reached ice and attached our crampons (or as Alexei called them, *"dientes de los tigres,"* tiger's teeth) to our comfy neon-green plastic boots with dental floss shoestrings. Rafael, Alexei, and I, respectively bound by rope, began plodding our way to the top. Little by little, *poco a poco*. Step by step, *paso por paso.*

Coming from someone who, let's just say, has an affinity for being in the front of the pack, I must confess that bringin' up the rear really does have its benefits. Not only did I have a set of footprints to follow, but there wasn't any pressure to set a pace or worry about those who were behind. With the anticipation of multiple consecutive hours of hiking ahead, I found myself drifting into my own little world of tranquility.

I relished the heightened awareness of my senses as I crept farther away from the tangible world and time slipped into infinity. The *hisssssss* of the long, dry, weather-stricken blades of grass dancing at every sigh of nature's breath revitalized me with a long-awaited sense of peace. Existence soon became nothing but the biting mountain wind whistling over the top of my hood and the shock of the icy oxygen molecules that snuck through my face mask and onto the rims of my cracking lips. I was finding my pace along the steadfast volcanic rock, my place in time-lessness.

Right…inhale. Left . . . exhale. Righti . . . inhale. Left . . . exhale. By now it had been almost two hours since we had left the inert nests of snoring climbers in the *refugio*. Although I considered our progress good, Rafael informed us that we were getting passed by other teams who had left much later than us.

"Tenemos que caminar mas rapido. Mantengamos nuestro ritmo." We have to walk faster. Let's maintain our rhythm, he commanded.

Our physical energy had not synchronized with the emotional and spiritual energy we shared at the beginning of the climb. Rafael set the initial cadence. Meanwhile, Alexei and I scuttled behind like little ants on a search for pastry crumbs. Alexei had been having difficulty setting a steady pace and appeared to be favoring one leg…one, two, three, four, five, six steps…stop and rest. One, two steps…stop and rest. Eight steps…stop and rest. This could have partly been due to the crappy gear he had rented back in Quito. Who in their right mind would give an inexperienced climber plastic tinker-toy, blister-causing boots with torn shoestrings, cotton thermals and pants with holes, cracked goggles that fogged up every four minutes, and no face mask? I cast blame as I lingered in and out of my *own* internal zone. I wasn't necessarily contributing to any rhythmic procession either. With our *dientes de los tigres* strapped to our boots, we vowed to pick up the pace, *paso por paso*.

As we got higher, the air got thinner. Right...inhale, exhale. Left...inhale, exhale. Two more hours had passed during our attempt to *"caminar mas rapido"* up the steepest section of the trek. Alexei's hip flexor began to bother him and he was limping. Meanwhile, the salsa in my own steps went from *caliente* to mild as I savored every chance to take my backpack off and close my frozen eyelids.

Momentary fuel stops allowed for muscular and pulmonary relief, but now we were higher and the wind was pelting our faces like a thousand tiny razor blades. My teeth performed a Riverdance tap duet as the accumulated sweat formed little, microscopic icicles on my body hairs.

All blissful thoughts of the summit were being kidnapped by the intent little dust bunnies inside my head. With every huff and puff, I began to wonder, *Why the hell am I doing this?* The more I pushed and fought my way along the smooth neck of the moon, the more I questioned. *Did it really matter how fast I was going? What was the true purpose of this experience? Just to get to the top? To say "I did it?" Why did I have to be on the top to appreciate the moment? Why couldn't I enjoy the feeling of knowing I "was doing it?" What was I trying to prove?* I was going my fastest and my fastest wasn't fast enough. So what? I realized in that moment that my entire life had been a race. I was in a hurry and I didn't know how to stop. I had thankfully been raised a goal-oriented and time-efficient woman, but I had consistently taken on too many challenges at once and had ended up climbing, pedaling, paddling, scrambling, battling through everything just to find the treasure. But where was the *real* treasure?

My wandering feet searched for Alexei's fresh tracks as if they were warm cozy slippers. *I don't have to do everything perfectly,* I thought. I never had to. The only pressure I ever felt was that which I put on myself. I never *had* to work thirty hours a week in high school. I never *had* to score the highest on every exam in Organic Chemistry. I never *had* to work out seven hours a day training for sports. At what point in my life did quantity surpass quality? I was tired of running.

For the first time since we had begun the climb, I heard it. My own breath. I heard its completeness and listened to its affirmation. Inhaaaaale, exhaaaaaale. It was in that sweet breath where the moment awaited me: the timeless moment in which all life becomes One, when I was the Universe and the Universe was me. We are consistently given opportunities to seek the beauty, truth, and goodness in everything that surrounds us. I looked to the west to see the moon rising from behind a distant peak. The mountaintops and valleys celebrated her arrival and within moments, as if the spotlight of the universe had been turned on, our entire path to the summit was visible.

Before I began this excursion, everything had revolved around the "summit." I had written to all my friends and family back home boasting about the fact that by Saturday morning I would be on top of Cotopaxi and would be sending warm wishes to them across the vast lands.

But we were dragging. We slogged for what seemed like infinity, fuel stops became more frequent, and we weren't adhering to the scheduled plan. By this time, the moon had slithered to the other side of night and the pale purple dawn was crawling out of her slumber. As I struggled with my own internal battles, I could now clearly see Alexei struggling to lift his right leg to complete each step. It was 6 A.M. and we were breathing in the freshness of morning 18,000 feet above the sea, just 1,000 feet away from our grand goal.

Then Rafael's words singed my tender ears...

"*No podemos seguir,*" said Rafael. We had to go back.

In that instant, as if the planet had stopped turning, my heart sank.

"*Es demasiado tarde y no nos queda tiempo de subir y bajar sin peligro.*" It was too late and we didn't have enough time to gain the summit and get back down safely.

With the waking sun, the snow would become too soft and the potential for an avalanche would increase ten-fold. At that moment, the little girl inside of me began to pout. I plopped down in the snow next to my ice axe, pulled a frozen Snickers out of my pocket and pondered the dreadful return back down to the *refugio*. Tears threatened the corners of my eyes as I looked down at our long trail of footprints. I started to blame everything and anything. *Why didn't we get up earlier? Why couldn't we have started off faster? Why didn't I prepare better? Why didn't Alexei prepare better? Why didn't he say anything about his leg before? Why did the rental company give him such crappy gear? Why didn't Rafael mention our lack of speed sooner? All of this for* nothing, I thought. *All of this preparation, time, effort and money. For nothing.*

I looked at Alexei who was massaging the top of his thigh. His expression of anguish and pain dissolved into one of relief upon hearing that we were *not* continuing. I realized that even with all of the disastrous equipment and clothing he was given, never once did he utter a squeak of discomfort. ¡*Que impresionante*!

I looked up at Rafael, who still wore his contagious smile and whose eyes glistened even underneath his Top Gun sunglasses. Then I looked out toward the horizon of the world in which I was etched. As if someone had reset the alarm clock of my life, everything began to make sense. *All for* nothing *Tiffany? How could you think this is* nothing? *Look where you are.*

Never in all of my adventure races had I seen or felt anything remotely close to what I was experiencing in that instant. This was a different kind of adventure race with no cut-off or finish line. The sun had risen to a point just behind the peak of the glacier, allowing the shadow of Cotopaxi to be cast clear across the valley on the opposite horizon, above which, the full moon hovered like a loyal companion.

Down below, a sea of clouds carpeted the valleys as the snowcapped cones of every surrounding volcano popped out into the silk sheet of morning light like lotus flowers, reassuring me of the balance between foundation and creation. For a moment, all human limitations became an afterthought and I contemplated running off the glacier into the playground of goose feathers. The golden papaya sunrays gracefully kissed the life-size icicles and jagged crevasses. Splashes of a new day peered through the windows of crystal and magnified like a prism into our presence, confirming that in every creation of nature, there existed an infinitely glowing spirit. From here, I not only saw every beautiful and essential detail of the mountain, but also the majesty of the summit.

Does it matter that you are not up there? From here, you can see everything and more! On top you wouldn't experience the same sensation. You wouldn't be able to see the teams of little black ants following their trail up the white peak. You wouldn't be able to see the snow being swept off the top of the volcano as if God were blowing chalk off a pool cue. You wouldn't be able to look up and soak in the magnanimity of the mountain, appreciating the significance of her wondrous presence on earth. On top, it's just a view and one can only look down upon everything. But here, here you are in it. You are a part of it. You are enveloped in this cradle of nature. You are standing between the sun and the moon, each in its full strength and glory, forming perfect harmony, like yin and yang, a complete balance of nature's rhythm.

An intense and profound breath awakened me to the uniqueness of each passing second and the fact that I would *never* experience that moment again in my lifetime. A moment of honor, humility, love, and connection with the entire Universe, I was a part of timelessness. My heart pounded as I whispered to myself, "I *am* this mountain. I *am* the glacier. I *am* the moon and the sun. I *am* the myriad of stars and the blanket of clouds. I *am* that shadow and that reflection. I *am* the summit. I *am* the journey. Along the smooth neck of the moon I wander...step by step, *paso por paso.*"

⚘ ⚘ ⚘

Tiffany Grimm is an aspiring yoga instructor, therapeutic personal trainer, and marketing coordinator for an environmentally conscious clothing company. She has published work in Ocean Magazine *and is writing travel articles for* Backpacker Essentials *in Australia. She recently returned from a fourteen-month trip traveling solo through South America.*

❧ ❧ ❧

The Silent and the Loud

A traveler discovers the power of Italian ex-votos.

*J*had no destination that afternoon beyond a break from speaking Italian, the intoxicating sound of which made me happier than any other language. Producing it on demand for my relatives, though, was doing me in. I knew just enough to think that I grasped the gist of almost every conversation they eagerly volleyed at me, like tennis balls from an automatic serving machine. If I could grab a second to flip through my dictionary for an unfamiliar verb, do a quick conjugation in my mind, and get back to them . . . but who can take time out every single sentence?

I stood on the outside of Italian, not the inside: an exile—an underfluent—a word I'd just made up, which is what I was doing more and more frequently in this isolated state. I, who craved communication, made gaffe after gaffe, reduced myself to stammering, unable to remember tense and agreement and, most elemental of all: what was masculine and what feminine. *Il dramma, la mano!* So I mumbled an excuse to my cousins that I needed to take care of an errand and escaped into the crowded downtown streets of Palermo, seeking silence in the midst of noisy humanity.

By late afternoon the city was choking on itself. My ears—already warm from listening so hard—were hot and pounding. I trotted along the loud boulevards breathing their strange formula of three parts oxygen, one part diesel, one part carbon monoxide. There was no way to counter the mad exhalation: even the plants were suffocating on their stems. Wisteria hung limply from the sides of buildings. The banana trees' sensitive leaves which normally picked up the simplest breeze didn't rustle a single finger in the leaden air. I dashed past hundreds of cars, past a young bicyclist with a basketful of schoolbooks; a policeman on a podium directing traffic, and a lot of good he was doing, too; a bent, white-haired man pushing his mink-coated wife in a wheelchair; a small truck painted like a Sicilian cart hauling a heap of pearl onions; an African man draped in jewelry and beads for sale who beamed a wide grin at me—one thousand kilowatts—maybe because he recognized a fellow foreigner. I waved to him as I rushed forward. A shop owner tracked my movement as if he were a lion and I were a wildebeest. My great-grandmother probably endured a leer from his great-grandfather a hundred years ago. Would she have looked away or stared him down? It was tricky either way. I avoided his pricking glance, but how I would have loved to tell him off in good Sicilian style, my hands speaking for me!

I'd made it to the crossroads of Palermo's two major streets, known as I Quattro Canti. Autumn's fountain splashed steadily, unconcerned with the creepy byproducts of internal combustion, uninterested in the black stripes of

soot and grime upon it. I ran my hand through the water
to cool the back of my neck. Which way now? I drifted to
the front of the convent of Santa Caterina. Maybe today
the silent sisters had baked. I took the grand steps two at
a time up to the big green door with a half door cut into it
and knocked. It cracked open. An antique nun enrobed in
black and white peered out.

"*Suora*, are you selling pastries now?"

She nodded solemnly, her eyes downcast.

"Uhh . . . " I made a ring of my two hands, "something
about this size?"

She shut the door. The hallway echoed. Should I have
shown her my money? Was there a password I didn't—
couldn't possibly—know? Had I blown my one chance
at confectionery heaven? Minutes passed. A milk-white
hand appeared in the opening, sliding towards me a square
of waxed paper bearing a light-brown cake, a perfect
rounded pouf with a rosy-pink dab on top. Four fingers
flashed the price. I placed the bill in her pale palm and
pranced down the stairs holding my delicacy before me.
This fragrant creation looked like, but couldn't possibly
be a . . . breast with a meringue nipple pointing straight to
heaven. What on earth?

I bit through the smooth marzipan icing which gave way
to a layer of pistachio filling, sublimely suspended above a
tier of sponge. Oh sinful sweet, devoured in church. Whose
breast? Something about a pious virgin who refused a suit-
or's advances and was thrown into a brothel, whose breasts
were cut off and placed on a plate—Santa Agata. I stopped
at this marble step to taste hazelnut filling, that one to
savor chocolate, the next to chew for a while, another to
swallow. Glorious. I paused at the street portal, looking
around, licking the paper and feeling the sugar surge into
my bloodstream.

I decided to return to I Quattro Canti and, using it as a compass, spin around until the next direction revealed itself. I searched the baroque statuary above at each corner, wondering which contained the likeness of Santa Agata whose breast I'd just eaten, but from street level I could not tell who was who. The saints were higher than the four kings who were higher than the four seasons. I chose south-west, and crossed the intersection, smug that I had used a mere handful of words so far.

Inside the church of San Giuseppe dei Teatini, I dipped my fingertips into the broad brown seashell of holy water held by a white marble angel. She hadn't landed yet, her wings were still extended, her feet still above her. She gazed discreetly left. That was the direction I took. One of the chapels, illuminated by a bank of tranquil candles, drew me in. I dug at the bottom of my bag for coins, dropped them in the metal donation box, and selected a taper from a stack, white and pure. The wick caught easily, the flame throbbed, then calmed itself. An all-purpose candle for burdened souls never allowed to lighten their loads. I sat nearby watching it pulsate until a third of it disappeared into spirit. My mind eased. No questions, no answers, no talking.

I wasn't yet through with remaining mum. I couldn't face getting back on a bus, walking in the door and resuming conversation. Out the church and back through I Quattro Canti, wandering to the other side of San Domenico Cathedral, I found myself in an alley called the Via Dei Bambinai. I whipped out my mini-dictionary—The Street of the Nursemaids. A tiny woman about my age wearing platform shoes leaned against the stoop of her store, as if she were expecting me.

"Wax dolls, *ex-votos*, come in and look, *signorina*," she lisped.

I nodded. I was having an I've-been-here-before-and-know-what-to-do-next sensation. She unlocked the door with a large key at her belt. I'd heard that creaking raspy turn already, in a dream, through gauze and veils.

"A lady like yourself would do well to own a wax baby."

I looked at her confused. "Me? A baby? What about the *ex-votos*? What have you got?"

"We have every body part, *signorina*, for healing maladies and human distresses."

She pulled out boxes of pressed silver hearts and livers, kidneys, gall bladders, brains, stomachs, legs, arms. They glowed in the gloom, these three-inch pieces of human form, and I sat intrigued, but nothing yet called out to one of my body parts. From tissue paper she unwrapped noses, mouths, ears, hair, knees, fingers, feet both single and by the pair. She kept her eyes on me during this anatomical procession.

"Do you have left hands?"

She regarded me for a long moment. "Absolutely." From a shelf, she located a box and unwrapped more tissues, right hand after silvered right hand saluting as each emerged. I doubted she had any left hands. I knew that they signified something evil, evidence of the devil or the dreaded *mal'occhio*.

"May I?" I touched a packet. She blinked, which I took as an agreement, though she never broke her serious frown, her hands never stopping. We unwrapped together in silence.

"We lefties make up 10 to 15 percent of the population," I commented, prompting no response. Finally a slender hand of tapered fingers with carefully neat nails and crimped edges appeared. It could do the beseeching of a southpaw like myself.

"I'll take it, and do you have good eyes?"

"We have excellent eyes." She searched through a box labeled "*OCCHI*" and held each crimp-edged mask up for inspection. "They always come in pairs, the right and the left."

"Uh-huh," I nodded, "yes."

"They're all identical, *signorina*," she said, humoring me.

"I'm looking for an exact pair," I insisted. I found them at last, slightly crossed, with etched brows, cousins to the eyes of the mosaic Gesù Cristo of Monreale and to Santa Lucia's beautiful eyes, so gorgeous that she plucked them out and put them on a plate for her admiring suitor. "Here they are."

"Anything else?"

"*Tst.*" Listen to me, saying no just like a native.

"A baby?" Evidently she had recurring visions of my future motherhood.

"Not this time. Maybe the next."

I asked if she had a boxful of high-quality boyfriends somewhere.

"I have many men."

"Guaranteed good quality men?"

"All our *ex-votos* are of the highest quality."

"For the man, I need a guarantee."

"*Tst*. A heart?"

"*Tst*. I already have a heart, I hope." I paused, waiting for her to react to my joke. She did not. Heartache I've had, but I didn't want to get into it with her. Tongues lay nestled on the table. I needed to be able to speak with fluidity.

"And one of these."

We bargained over the price. Of course she knew I was a tourist and tried to charge me an arm and a leg, ha-ha. Second only to pushing, haggling was the other Italian custom I hated pretending I knew how to do. I set my face in a grimace mirroring hers. We agreed awkwardly, tensely, on a sum. I wouldn't dare tell my cousin how much I'd put on the table. She would have lamented my being cheated and why hadn't I waited til she came along with me in order to get a fair price? I had purchased a sure hand with which to write and eyes with which to clearly see. I bought the language I needed to speak. The lady's practiced hands wrapped my three items in brown paper and string. Thank you for being exactly the person you are, for awaiting me as I turned the corner. Thank you for understanding my tarnished Italian. Thank you for trying to rip me off—I thoroughly enjoyed it! Thank you for selling me these talismans. Thank you from the bottom of my crimp-edged heart.

I returned through the Vucciria market, stepping on sawdust and fish scale sequins. Smells of overripe greens and dear departed fish hung in the air. I took refuge near a stall of warm hazelnut nougat. Big, smoothed, swirled slabs of pink and white candy stood stacked like pieces of quarried marble. I moved on through the vegetables, distracted by a mound of skinny, violet asparagus. "Try one." the vendor stretched his arms the width of his stall. "Go ahead. Taste for yourself the superior flavor of wild asparagus."

The tender stalk snapped between my teeth. "So delicate," I marvelled. "I'll take a half kilo, please." My cousin would love them.

Another haggling over price, another package tied with string. "*Mancino.*"

"Yes, I am left-handed," I smiled, reaching for the packet, "and proud to be so."

"So am I," he cooed, squeezing my baby finger for a moment before sliding off.

My eyebrows flew up in surprise as I looked slightly cross-eyed at him, but no words came. I stood staring longer than I wanted to. Some *ex-votos*, I gathered, worked more quickly than others. On the way home, I slipped the tongue out of the package and rubbed it. A faint tarnish appeared on my fingertips.

₰ ₰ ₰

Natalie Galli's articles have appeared in the San Francisco Chronicle *and* The Berkeley Monthly. *Her work of creative non-fiction,* Three-Cornered Island, *details her search for Franca Viola, the first woman in Sicilian history to publicly refuse the tradition of coercive marriage.* Ciao Meow, *her children's book about a free-wheeling cat, boasts illustrations by her sister. Look for her contributions in* Travelers' Tales Italy *and* Italy: a Love Story. *She lives in San Rafael, California.*

※ ※ ※

Border Crossing

A sister negotiates the politics of grief
in the Middle East.

*T*here is a tank in my living room. It stands about three
feet long and one foot tall and its turret holds a soldier
who carefully aims his gun at my piano. Coming to deposit
or pick up their kids, Cambridge parents stop short. In the
capital of East Coast political correctness, a huge remote
control tank forms a separation fence between us. Some
parents go quiet, beginning to wonder, I'm sure, about
our politics. Others laugh uncomfortably as if we have just
planted the greatest joke. In a city where it would not be
strange for a parent to call prior to a play date to verify that
we don't keep guns in the house—and they would usually
mean toy guns—a tank is an embarrassment. Still in its
packaging, it doesn't know what to do here. The cat chews
at it, unafraid.

Most Americans, no matter what their politics, have

never seen a real tank. This is the luxury of living in a country that always fights its wars on someone else's borders. Even post-9/11, and despite the Iraqi war footage, tanks do not belong in the American psyche.

This replica was a gift to my son from his seven cousins in Elon Moreh, Israel. They had arrived in New York for a Sabbath in which my father was being honored by his synagogue, and they had simply brought the biggest and best present they could find for their cousin whom they had met only once, briefly, two years before. Their father, my baby brother, had been killed in the first week of the second Intifada in October 2000.

We all arrive in Brooklyn at the same time. My father, aged beyond his years by the double scourges of illness and bereavement, is being fêted in true Aleppan tradition by the Syrian Jews he has led and mentored for half a century.

And so my sister-in-law has managed this long trip to the land where her husband grew up—to the house in Brooklyn where he presides in large photographs over the living room, first as a bespectacled eight-year-old, then on a hilltop with an Uzi. She has arrived with seven children, five suitcases, myriad gifts, and this tank which—it turns out—was made in America.

My nieces and nephews take me in shyly: the aunt who has been a mystery. They have only seen me once or twice. Very little compared to my parents who visit them three to four times a year and have a vacation home in their settlement, and compared to my sister who visits them two to three times a year. She has had no trouble riding through that dangerous territory in a bus, an army jeep escorting it on either side, or in bulletproof cars. She believes, as do my parents, my sister-in-law, and their seven children, that they are agents in God's plan to reconquer this land, to hasten the coming of the Messiah.

A bit of history: I was born and raised to be a settler. I think I know how it is done. The ideas and allegiances are shaped early. In the land of Hollywood and malls, it is easy to capture an adolescent's need for meaning and bravado. Add to that Biblical studies taught with the immediacy of current events, a few personal encounters with anti-Semitism, a couple of fiery seminars led by homegrown right-wing thinkers.

From grades one through twelve, I attended a Jewish Day School whose stated mission was to combine a modern Orthodox education with a superb secular education, but the religion in the school was really a fervent, jealous, unquestioning Zionism. Casting doubt on anything Israel did was tantamount to treason and would earn you the title "self-hating Jew," putting you in the company of other such vile creatures, who ranged from Woody Allen to Spinoza. The school was made up of second generation Americans, as well as the children of Holocaust survivors, and the contrast between the two groups was startling. My "children-of-survivors" friends had older parents and small apartments compared to the rest of us. There were whispered rumors of first families that had been entirely lost, of a parent who may have been a Kapo. Many of my friends with American-born parents enjoyed the fruits of their parents' youth and their fathers' prosperous careers. It seemed no one knew what to do with so much money. A husband and wife in my neighborhood would drive down the streets in their matching white Bentleys and the bar mitzvahs competed to outdo one another until they seemed out of some Jewish version of a Fellini film, the *pièce de résistance* being one bar mitzvah boy lowered into his party on a crane. Everyone would sigh in admiration at whoever was moving to Israel. Many people claimed to be on the verge of doing so, but remained in the U.S. another year and another and another.

My own love affair with Israel began in 1968. My parents had only been once—on their honeymoon in 1955. Now, just after the six-day war, it was impossible for my father, who had participated in the clandestine loading of guns onto boats in New York harbor in 1947, to wait any longer. And so from 1968 on, we began what would become an annual pilgrimage to Israel for the entire summer. I was twelve that first summer, and dissolved next to the handsome soldiers we picked up hitchhiking along the road. If asked to summon my first brazen, unbridled crushes, the images that rise to the surface will always include uniforms and guns. We drove back and forth through the newly captured West Bank, my father pointing out what was now "ours." He told us the biblical history of the hills and described the large cities he imagined would emerge and flourish, all the while saying, "Kids, if you hear any shooting, drop to the bottom of the car."

In 1975, with the excuse of a college year abroad, I made my way to Jerusalem on my own, and over my parents' protests, decided to stay. I had done what I'd been raised to do—I'd fallen in love with all of it: the silent, spectacular glow of the sun receding from the ancient walls, the pink haze of the Judean hills stretching from the final villages that cling to Jerusalem, the colorful trails of Bedouin women walking by the side of the road that wove through the stark desert hills downward to the Dead Sea. I was in love with Jerusalem—the old city with its alleys and spices and the Babel of all its tongues.

But my parents thought I was staying for my boyfriend, whom they disliked, given his long hair and his motor-

cycle. They were also quite frightened by my now undeni-
ably secular lifestyle. After some debate, I had accepted an
invitation to spend a couple of days at their hotel to talk
about it.

When I arrived, my mother looked at her watch and,
avoiding my eyes, told me to meet them downstairs by the
pool at 2:00. I didn't know what they were up to and took
a long, luxurious shower, slipped into a bathing suit, and
took the elevator down to meet them. By the time I came
out of the double glass doors onto the large stone-ringed
pool, the heat was at its peak and not too many people were
sitting in the sun. But there were my parents. My father
in his three-piece suit with a stack of Talmuds at his side.
My mother, who usually loves to swim, in a long-sleeved
blouse and skirt, with her legs tucked demurely beneath
the chair. Next to them sat a man who looked like he'd
been dropped by the pool directly from the Hasidic section of Brooklyn—black suit, white shirt, pants too short
for his height, pale skin, a beard, and a black hat which he
pushed back every few moments to wipe the sweat from
his forehead. This, I realized, had been the purpose of their
invitation. To introduce me to this man. This was to be the
antidote to my boyfriend, to Jerusalem, to the Sinai, to the
life I was falling in love with.

I approached them half amused, half frightened. My
mother caught sight of me and her eyes widened as she
took in my tropical print bikini. She made a movement as
if to swat away a fly. I came up behind them. They did not
turn around. The man had seen me approach and whether
or not he'd figured out that I was his "intended," he was
blushing profusely, his eyes riveted to the ground.

"Hello," I said, and my mother turned around and
motioned me away with a very unambiguous swing of her
arm. My father turned to the young man and asked him

something about the seminary in which he was studying. I stood there a few moments, stunned that they would actually ignore me.

"Mother," I said, but my mother took advantage of their conversation to turn around and hiss at me, "Go away!"

Later over kosher filet mignon and silence, I turned to them and said, "Well, my brilliant parents, if you wanted me covered from head to foot, why the pool?"

They clearly lost that battle, and I stayed on with no intention of leaving.

Four years later, an illness that was not getting properly diagnosed in Israel sent me reluctantly back to New York. But even the few years in the States seemed temporary. I never imagined that I wouldn't return. But after graduate school and an Israeli boyfriend, the man I would marry turned out to be a Chilean living in Boston. He already had a young child, which rooted us to Boston for a long time. I began to travel to Chile with the frequency with which I had once traveled to Israel. Perhaps, I remember thinking, my connection to Israel was not so deep. Perhaps it was all that was exotic there that I had loved, and I could trade one "exotica" for another. But Chile, with its gorgeous vistas, its deeply entrenched machismo, its parched and elongated desert ambling down to the sea, only stirred the other memories and longings.

Home became Boston—Cambridge specifically, and a permanent longing for the Israel I had known became another bit of baggage that I dragged with me. The prospect of traveling to Israel became freighted with complexities. Not only would I need to travel to a very dangerous area to visit my brother, but there was the added fact that my brother had still not revealed my marriage to his kids. Afraid to contradict all that he was teaching his children, whom he sheltered from even secular television, he never told them that they had a cousin in Boston. I wouldn't go pretending I didn't have a family and so there we were—each landlocked in our own land.

And so, unbelievably, and terribly painfully in retrospect, ten years went by without our seeing one another. Still, the love between us persisted. It was deep and profound. Eight years older than Hillel, I had been something of a second mother to him, and then a friend when he was struggling with the confusions and pressures of being the Rabbi's son. Ironically, when I told my family about my marriage, he was the only one who still offered his love unconditionally. My sister stopped speaking to me after my son was born, and my parents, after years of threats, did not in fact disown me, but the connection we maintained in those years was careful and tenuous.

After those ten years apart, I was to see my brother three times before he died. At the events surrounding my sister's wedding, and then twice more a year later, as our father suffered a stroke, and later, infection and septic shock, and Hillel made two emergency visits.

And then, as it has for so many, that landscape that I missed and cherished, and that crept into my writing and daydreams, became stung through and through with personal tragedy. As anyone who has lost a loved one to violence will tell you, a lot of energy is expended trying not to imagine their death. As the details of my brother's death came in, one more painful than the next, I clung to the hope that it had been quick, but the evidence said otherwise, and so this is part of what I carry with me in private, what I wear in the lines on my face.

I had always feared it would come to this. Still, it was an impossible reality to absorb. A night after my brother was found, I sat up late into the night, still not believing. My brother dead; my baby brother with his beautiful spirit, his difficult views. Walking to Joseph's Tomb, had he been in a religious trance or was it a breakdown? Either way, a state beyond states—but couldn't one sole rational voice break through the blackness, the solid wall of fire in his mind and toward which he marched and say, "Turn back, turn back."

Over the months that followed, there were those eager to enlist me as a poster child for the left, and others eager to enlist me in the growing song of martyrdom. Instead, I insisted on my private, unfinished grief—the one in which I see my brother—at two years old on my lap, or leaning against my door to take in the rock and roll I was submerged in, or arriving at my first apartment in Boston, his hair to his shoulders, before he did an about face and found his new life on a hilltop.

We had been considered the two "sensitive souls" of the family, and were more alike than not in our willingness to trade material possessions for something more essential. We had taken our quest for transcendence in very different directions—mine into the joys and uncertainties that comprise a writing life; and his to the Judean soil clenched in his fist and God's voice in his ear.

When I think now of the time we missed out on, of the many years that passed before those few final meetings, it feels both tragic and strangely inevitable.

Come back, I want to say to him. Let's do this again. Let's do this differently.

But one always wants to say that to the dead.

In October 2001, a year after my brother's death, the second Intifada and my grief were in their twelfth month. The events of 9/11 were only one month old. A large envelope arrived from Elon Moreh. It was rare that I received mail from my sister-in-law so when I recognized her lovely Hebrew scrawl, I was more than curious. The day before my brother's funeral, her voice tinged with both hesitation and threat, she had said, "There are letters he left you. There are messages," and I wondered if she had finally sent them. In that conversation and others, I had sensed that it was weighing on her, the uncompleted work of my brother, the mandate to save my soul. But a year had passed and she had not yet thrust the letters and messages like a bomb into my life.

I slit open the envelope, took out two identical pamphlets—the covers of which stopped me cold. On both my brother loomed over the two low rising hills of Mount Grizim and Mount Eval. He was wearing his *tfillin*, holding a giant Torah, and he was smiling.

The proportions were almost funny, but the collage made its point boldly and preposterously—Nablus was a small scattering of toy houses. Between the mountains, a sketch of Joseph's Tomb hung like a prophecy, and my brother's torso emerged from Mt. Grizim with all the entitlement of one carrying out God's mission on earth. His eyes blazed with certainty. Whoever had put this together had made the Torah look like a flag he was about to plant on an Arab moon.

For twelve months now I'd been trying to see behind those images and interpretations aimed at portraying my brother as a highly spiritual being, a saint, a martyr whose death at thirty-six hinted at the profound meaning behind his earthly presence, whose death came to teach us the true nature of the Palestinians, of this ill-conceived illusion of peace.

For a year I'd been squeezing my eyes shut and summoning him to me, the little boy who had worshipped me. The boy who had come to me for refuge when he needed it. The teenager who had once driven me to a beautiful mountain outside New York as a surprise for my birthday. The young man who, before he moved to Israel, would pick me up at any airport, drive me miles to where I needed to go. The man who discovered true joy with his lovely wife and family, and who, when he grew certain of his set of truths, tried delicately, carefully to save my soul.

Saving souls is always tricky territory. Particularly when the object of those attempts doesn't consider him or herself in need of salvation. And so those who remain still tiptoe around me, wondering how they will accomplish this. And with the rich irony that life provides, I carry with me not guilt, but sometimes a profound sadness at my own inability to save Hillel from the zealotry that consumed him.

In March of 2001, I finally traveled to Israel for my brother's second eldest daughter's bat mitzvah. They were holding the party in Jerusalem so that I, and other family members who didn't relish travel to Elon Moreh, could come. Held back by my husband and friends who were worried for my safety, I had not traveled to my brother's funeral in Yitzhar but had ended up watching the funeral procession being shot at on the evening news.

At shabbat dinner in the cavernous dining room, the bat mitzvah girl suddenly crossed her arms in front of her chest and said, "I will not eat food served by Arabs." My nieces and nephews looked at each other, not sure whether to follow her lead. But everything escalated before they could decide. The waiters, having overheard her, began to tease in a tone laced with threat and mutual hatred. "Yes, I wouldn't eat it if I were you. We're going to put poison in it." The atmosphere felt tense and suddenly dangerous. The maitre d' was summoned and pulled his waiters aside. Five minutes later, dinner resumed as if nothing had happened, the masks were lowered once again, the roles re-assumed.

But at this table, the territory became treacherous again very quickly.

Two yeshiva boys who had studied with my brother had become inseparable from his family—making sure that my brother's sons had a "man" to take them to synagogue, to sit with them on the other side of the *mechitza*, to lift them on broad shoulders, to be an ear should they wish to talk about my brother. My brother's sons wouldn't talk. The oldest boy in particular had descended into a pained silence. Thinking he now needed to be the head of the house, he was barely sleeping, aware that he was only four-foot-seven and had no Uzi. The yeshiva boys were talking loudly, or rather one was talking, berating the other. Apparently, his friend had stopped on the road to assist a Palestinian family stoned by a group of settlers in retaliation for a stoning earlier in the week. "How could you help them?" he was saying. "You should have left them to die. They are not human."

At this point my allegiance and love for this family were stretched. I stood up and left the table. It was statements like this that stirred the silt of hopelessness. That made it so clear how deeply we were mired, how much hatred there was to overcome. The tensions of the visit and the conflicted love all swam up to the surface and I suddenly needed to be alone to cry. But one of my brother's daughters began to trail me like a sweet puppy. "Why are you crying?" she asked, never letting more than half a foot of distance grow between us.

Here's the paradox, the strange territory of my life: These are people I love. Whatever we may think of each other's views, there is something else there between us. The problem is that when I cross into their world, I am literate in it, bilingual. But it's a one-way border. It doesn't work in reverse. They are not literate, and do not want to be, in another point of view.

So it is with all this history that I have traveled to the event honoring my father. In New York, on these familiar streets, in this house where we all grew up, my brother's death is real. I see him everywhere in his children's faces—here, his eyes—there, his mouth. The grief returns, a knot in the stomach, a stab piercing through the sunlight that is dancing on the buildings, filtering through the lace of treetops that arch above the street. And for a moment, I see it, the road stretching out before my sister-in-law, long and winding and bare. I see the huge space that he has left, and the questions and the unending silence. I see his children, their longing lifting from them like wisps of smoke.

After the events at the synagogue, we have three days together; three days for my son to get to know his cousins as we move between the houses of relatives. I wonder how it will go, coming as they do from such different worlds. But their love for him seems immediate and boundless. Their English is rudimentary, as is my son's Hebrew. So they pick up guitars and flutes and they are off and running, making music, teaching each other chords, words. And it strikes me how for so many years, my brother had fretted about the contradictions of wanting to keep his children close and within his world, while at the same time, wanting them to know the sister he loved. And here the children were—falling in love with each other over music, all barriers, for the moment, invisible.

At one point, outside the Museum of Natural History, the cousins pose together for a picture—my son, with the sweet, awkward body of an eleven-year-old boy, and my nephew, side curls trailing behind his ears, a mischievous smile dancing on his face. It was my nephew's idea I think, their exchange of identities. My son's red baseball cap is perched jauntily on his head. On my son's head, the large rounded yarmulke of a settler. And for a moment, I see the future I most dread: idealism—no, zealotry—coming to claim him as it did my brother.

I corral everyone towards the Chinese restaurant my sister has recommended. Kosher, of course. The waiter is Chinese but speaks Hebrew from a few months of work in Tel Aviv. The manager is from a settlement my sister-in-law knows. At the end of the meal, they sing "Happy Birthday" to my son as the waiter brings out a glowing candle melting into vanilla ice cream. They lift him on a chair like a bar mitzvah boy. Toss him upward eleven times. I can see that he is scared and thrilled and honored to be the object of so much affection. An only child except for a much older half-brother, he is suddenly a member of a large and sprawling tribe that thrills in him, that wraps its arms around him and says without any words—you are one of us.

On our last day together, the children are all glued to the window watching the neurotic scampering of squirrels in the treetops. They have never seen a squirrel before, except in books. One of them asks my son, "Do you have a lot of squirrels in your neighborhood?"

"We do," my son says.

"And we have a lot of these in our neighborhood," my sister-in-law says, pointing to the tank that stands in the middle of the room, and we all dissolve in laughter.

When we have said our goodbyes and are in Penn Station waiting for our train, my son bursts into tears. "I'm so worried that something will happen to them," he says.

"I know," I say, taking him into my arms.

Then we are on the train, speeding home. The lights of New York recede and for a long time, we travel in a thick fog that clings to the coast. How tragic it all feels to me. I wonder again, as I have so many times, how we will find our way out of this morass. As a species, we have split atoms, peered into distant galaxies, cracked our own genetic code. We have discovered too that matter itself shies away from being absolute, that ours is a relative universe, where the perceiver can affect what is perceived. That alone should make us shudder at claiming one version of reality as truth over all others.

When we arrive home, maybe it's my own projection, but my son looks tired, older, as if he too has assumed the weight of worry I carry through my days. I go to my study and pull down a blue folder labeled "Hope" that I keep high on my bookcase where the cat can't get it, and where I am not tempted to toss it in the garbage with every bomb and with every new outpost that gets reassembled in the middle of the night. I bring it to my son's room. "Look," I say, and show him the clips I've saved about the Jewish-Arab school planned for Jerusalem, about the Jewish-Arab Musical Youth Orchestra in which Israeli and Palestinian teenagers play everything from violin to oud. He takes the orchestra clip from me and reads it carefully, examines the photo of the young oud player. "Can I keep this?" he asks. "Of course," I say, and as I say goodnight and am leaving his room, I see him perch it gently on the shelf where he keeps a few of his most treasured things.

❧ ❧ ❧

Tehila Lieberman's fiction and non-fiction have been published in Salon, Nimrod, *the* Colorado Review, Cutthroat, *and* Salamander, *among other places. Her stories and essays have won the Stanley Elkin Memorial Prize for Fiction and the Rick Dimarinis Prize for Fiction, and have been nominated for the Pushcart Prize, among other awards.*

Higher Ground

Traveling through China with her mother,
she learns how people can surprise you—
even people you've known all your life.

M y mother and I are inside the women's restroom
at San Francisco International Airport. Mom is
wearing one of her lightweight, color-coordinated, wrinkle-
free traveling outfits. I'm in jeans, and I'm watching her pour
cool bottled water into two plastic juice glasses brought from
home. When the glasses are full, she drops a round, white
Airborne tablet into each one. The water fizzes and turns
slightly orange. Mom explains that it's a potent combination
of vitamins that helps fend off germs on long flights.

"I never go anywhere without my Airborne," she says.

This is the third time she's said this in the last five minutes.

Mom and I are inoculating ourselves because in thirty

153

minutes we will embark on a fifteen-hour flight to Beijing for a three-week, no-spouses, no-siblings tour of China. Just my mother. And me.

The trip was Mom's idea. She wants to cruise down the Yangtze River before the massive Three Gorges dam project completely swallows the river, its black rock canyons, and the historic cities along its banks. She's been to China before but wasn't able to see the river, and when she told my father she'd like to return, his response was straight out of the I'm-Over-Seventy-and-Don't-Have-To-Do-Anything-I-Don't-Want-To handbook.

"Have fun," he said.

Thinking the trip might be a way for Mom and me to connect on a tender and more intimate level, the level that self-help books say mothers and daughters are supposed to connect on, I told her I would go.

Looking back, I believe I may have made this offer after several glasses of Chardonnay.

Our first day in China finds us traveling in a small white bus: Mom, me, and twelve other tourists on the "Splendors of China" Tour. We're weaving through Beijing's crowded streets to Tiananmen Square, the first stop on a day-long tour of the city.

Our guide, Leslie, a tall and slim young man with crumbs at the corners of his lips, is reciting a litany of facts about Beijing. There are 11 million people here, he says, and roughly 8 million bicycles. There are 108 embassies. And since China opened its doors to world markets five years ago, fifty McDonald's restaurants have opened in the city, and there are plans to add fifty more in the next twelve months.

As he says this, our bus zooms past a shiny new McDonald's.

"Look!" Mom says, pointing at it with a glossy red fingernail. "Isn't that amazing!"

Her thin eyebrows are raised high above her glasses as if she is truly dazzled by this sight. As if seeing McDonald's in the middle of a busy city is as wondrous as a finding a rare mongoose in Madagascar.

We continue our tour and Mom finds many things to be amazed about. The price of postcards is amazing. The size of Tiananmen Square is amazing. The number of cars is amazing. It starts to rain and that, amazingly enough, is also amazing to my mother. Never before in the history of recorded travel has the commonplace been give so much credit.

Day four and we're at the Great Wall of China, which stretches some 4,000 miles over rolling green hills across the northern end of the country. Our tour group travels to a portion of the wall 40 miles outside of Beijing. Here, the wall climbs steeply, stair after stair, rising 1,000 feet before the steps end and the smooth concrete pathway begins.

Mom and I step off the bus and start to make our way toward the wall. She walks several steps behind because she's seventy-three and her pace has slowed, and because I'm forty and inconsiderate.

I walk up the first set of stairs and turn to wait for her. The sun is warm, and after the gray, noisy congestion of Beijing, the peaceful green countryside is a welcome relief. I look down at my mother, at her short, pale red hair. Her skin is smooth for her age, but whiter than it used to be. And as I watch her making her way toward me, I realize it's not just her pace that's slowed. Her overall demeanor is more cautious. When did this happen?

Mom starts up the steps. A small black video camera is slung around her neck and she cradles it close to her chest with one arm. She rises one step and starts to approach the second when the tip of her shoe catches the step's rough edge and she falls, swiftly and without warning, to the ground. Her camera hits the pavement with a hard metallic thud.

I rush down the stairs.

"Are you O.K.?"

"I can't believe I fell," she says. "One minute I'm standing, the next minute I'm on the ground." She chuckles, but I sense the laugh is for my benefit. I help her up and she wipes dust from the knees of her royal blue pants.

"Are you hurt?"

"Oh, no. I'm fine. Just clumsy. You go ahead, honey."

I glance sideways at the wall and feel myself stretched in painfully opposite directions like some crazy cartoon cat: an aging mother tugging one arm, a selfish little girl yanking the other. I want to climb the wall, but...

Another member of our group saw Mom fall and she comes over to tell me she will sit with her.

"*Neither* of you needs to sit with me," Mom says.

And so I begin to climb the hard stone steps. One by one, up and up and up, past bundles of German and Japanese and Spanish tourists. I feel tense, like I shouldn't be here, but the views of the jagged green hillside are so stupendous I begin to relax. I stop, look at the hazy horizon and thank God for the ability to travel to such awe-inspiring places. I climb some more and stop again, this time because I realize I've just spoken to God, something completely out of character. But I'm on the Great Wall and, well, if you can't talk to God here, where can you?

But between these entry-level prayers of thanks, I'm also begging God to keep my mother healthy, and promising that if he does I will be kinder and more forgiving when my mother repeats herself, makes inane comments, or otherwise dares to be herself as opposed to my unattainable Hollywood ideal of what a mother should be.

Ninety minutes later I rejoin my mother on the bus, where she begins telling everyone about her fall.

"Just call me Clumsy Betty," she says.

Someone chuckles at the Clumsy Betty comment and this encourages her. She repeats the story, dialing up the volume and adding little embellishments.

"And then Clumsy Betty fell on the second step…"

"So then Clumsy Betty waited at the bottom…"

"That's just me, Clumsy Betty."

I'm not sure, but I think God is testing me.

The next day we prepare for our flight south to Xian on our way toward the Yangtze River. Mom and I are in our dimly lit hotel room and she's repacking her suitcase. Unlike me, my mother is an organized traveler who believes if you've got a travel bag for your clean underwear, and a travel bag for your dirty underwear, why not allocate travel bags for everything in your suitcase, including socks, shoes, film, clothespins, make-up, shampoo, pens and pencils, books, medicine, slippers, sunglasses, passport, jewelry, and hair dryer.

Mom has been zipping and unzipping her travel bags for the last hour and it appears she's organized herself to the point of paralysis.

"Let's see now," she says. "Where did I put my make-up?" She reaches to the far end of her suitcase. "Nope. Not here." She steps back, drums her fingers on her lips, and makes that absent-minded clicking sound she's being doing ever since I can remember.

"Maybe it's under my nightgown." Click. "Nope." Click. She snaps her fingers. "I know! It's in the bathroom. Now. Where's my film?"

I screw in my earplugs, turn over in bed, and attempt to sleep.

We're standing in front of the Big Old Goose Pagoda, a Buddhist temple with seven stories signifying the seven steps to Nirvana. At the entrance to the temple, people are kneeling on yellow satin pillows and bowing with bouquets of smoky red incense. Watching them, I think about the Buddhist ideal of right mindfulness, of the need to let go of attachments whatever they might be—thoughts, embarrassments, annoyances. I think how much more content I would be if I could only embrace the Buddhist ideal of living in the present. But while I'm thinking about Buddhism, I'm also thinking about my mother and our trip and I'm thinking perhaps I've been a bit impatient with her. After all, she's never interfered in *my* life. Never made me feel guilty for not coming home at Easter. Never judged the choices I've made in clothing or relationships or jobs, and I've made hideous judgment-worthy choices in every category. I'm thinking about all of this as I step onto a smooth, slanted piece of concrete. My sandals, which have flat, well-worn soles, don't have enough traction to hold me upright and I fall, swiftly and without warning, to the ground. My camera, which is slung around my neck, hits the pavement with a hard metallic thud.

We've been cruising down the Yangtze for two days and I'm feeling more relaxed. The boat's gentle rocking and the long stretches of quiet have allowed me to settle into my role as traveler, my mother my constant companion.

At present, we're sitting together on the ship's windy back deck and Mom is telling me for the second time that there are 109 tourists on board.

"I know Mom. Leslie told us that yesterday."

"I just find it fascinating. Most of the ships I've been on are so much larger."

"I know Mom."

She's quiet for a moment. The briefest of moments.

"Did you know the captain has sixteen years of experience?" she asks.

My mother embraces details like this, collecting them like tiny shells on a beach, as if together they might create something grand or at least suitable for a bathroom decoration. She routinely reports the exact time, every morning, when our daily schedule arrives. She monitors the temperature fluctuation in our room. And she gleefully announces when our scheduled day trips actually depart as opposed to the time they were scheduled.

"Why do you care, Mom?"

"I just find it interesting."

I look at the misty riverbanks. Over the last two days, we've disembarked to visit villages and museums and temples, all of which will be submerged when the Three Gorges Dam is complete and the natural course of the green river abruptly ceases. Seven years from now, the jumble of houses and schools and factories that line the riverbanks will be nothing more than quiet underwater ghost cities. Altogether, 2 million people will be displaced by the rising water.

Perhaps my view is naïve, but I sense the Chinese people who live here are resigned to their fate; resigned to losing their pagoda-roofed homes, their goldfish ponds, and the craggy rocks where they've fished with grandchildren for generations. Here, time flows with the river, and people seem to understand that the only way to adapt to the distressing changes wrought by time is to move—willingly or not—to higher ground.

We're now halfway through the trip. Today, we'll be traveling by sampan up the Danang River, a narrow winding tributary of the Yangtze. To get there, we must leave the ship, hike a muddy hillside, and board a bus that will take us to the river.

We disembark and I link my right arm under Mom's left arm and together we start up the muddy path. Thin red strips of carpet have been laid to make walking easier, but it's raining lightly and the carpet is soaked through. The air smells like damp grass and rotting fish and diesel exhaust.

Slowly, Mom and I make our way up the hill, stopping to make sure each step lands on firm earth. Mom is gripping my hand so tightly her knuckles are white. Halfway to the top, it starts raining more heavily, and we stop to retrieve the umbrellas in my backpack. I open them and hand one to Mom. Her round pink face is shiny wet from the rain. She hugs the umbrella close, grabs my arm again, and we continue our slow, step-by-step ascent.

My stomach is knotting with acid worry. I'm worried about the rain. I'm worried about getting up the mountain. I'm worried about getting back down the mountain, and I'm about to suggest we return to the boat when my mother stops and looks up at me, her shoulders bunched up like a little girl's with secret news to share.

"Isn't this exciting!" she says.

Startled, I look over at her. Her bright open expression tells me she's not kidding. She really *does* believe this is exciting.

Her comment is so unexpected and so genuinely honest I almost begin to sob. The lenses of her glasses are fogging. Her white shoes are dirty. She has half a hillside still to climb—bad hip and all—and she's having a jolly good time of it. If she were not already my mother, at this moment, I would desperately want her to be. She's no longer the aging mother I have to worry about; she's the cool mom who makes the most perfect sandwiches on the block.

On day seventeen, we're in Guilin, a southern city surrounded by tall, emerald, up-and-down mountains. The scenery here—the winding Li River, the flat green rice paddies, the green peaks shrouded in mist—draws landscape painters from all over China.

We stop at an art school and visit its sales gallery. Every space on every wall is taken by paintings and scrolls and calligraphy. I immediately spot a painting I want, but the price—$4,000 U.S. dollars—is more than I can afford. The salesperson, a short man in a pink shirt, offers to negotiate. Within seconds, we go from $4,000 to $1,200. I tell him I can only afford $300. He walks away.

Thus schooled in the art of Chinese negotiation, I find another set of paintings. They are seasonal landscapes: one, an energetic green summerscape; the other, a peaceful rendition of the river in fall.

The man in the pink shirt returns. My mother joins us. He starts the negotiation at $500 each. I shake my head. My mother shakes her head. The price drops to $400.

"No thank you," I say and start to walk away. This isn't a tactic; I really don't want the paintings that badly.

"Offer him less," Mom whispers, while poking me gently in the side. And then I remember—Mom is a deal-driven shopper. She's been known to combine newspaper coupons, senior discounts, and credit-card rebates to create a trifecta of price discounts during a single department store transaction.

And so I resume negotiations. Soon, I'm wanting the paintings like a child wants presents.

"Four hundred," he says. I shake my head. "Three

hundred." I frown. "How about two hundred," I say. "For both."

The man scowls.

"He's mad," Mom whispers. "That's good. See if he'll go farther."

And so I ask him to throw in a book of the artist's work.

He leaves to go check with the manager.

Mom is *beaming*.

The man in the pink shirt returns and we agree on $265. But when he rings up the purchase, it's clear he thought I only wanted one painting.

"No," I tell him, "$265 for *both*."

He marches off to speak with the manager again. We wait by the counter. Mom is as excited as I've even seen her. Any moment now, I expect her to start barking and clapping her hands like some crazy carnival seal.

The man returns and silently wraps the second painting and the book and hands me all three for $265.

Mom and I return to the hotel where I'm immediately struck with buyer's remorse. I chide myself for getting seduced by the bargaining. I wonder where I'm going to hang two Chinese landscapes in my Rocky Mountain home. But when my mother starts telling our companions about my extraordinary negotiating prowess, I forgive myself for getting carried away.

Suddenly, $265 seems like a small price to pay for a mother's adoration.

Two days after our art negotiations, I call home and learn my father is desperately missing my mother. We've been gone more than two weeks, and it's the longest separation my parents have endured in fifty-three years of marriage.

I tell my mother Dad's missing her.

"Really?" she asks, her voice softening. "He *misses* me?"

"Yes," I tell her. "Debbie said he's really struggling without you."

"*Struggling?*" she says. "Wow."

All at once, she looks bewildered and pleased and uncertain, as if she's just been given the gift of magic for one day and is not quite sure what to do with it. And then she gets giddy.

"I think I'll give him a call!" she says.

I get into the shower to give her privacy. And as I wait for the water to heat, I think about how people can surprise you. Even people you've known forever.

After the brown and crumble and haze that is mainland China, Hong Kong's crisp glass-and-steel skyscrapers and penetrating blue sky inject us with a burst of renewed travel energy. Feeling celebratory and closer to home, Mom and I spend our last day of vacation doing what one does in Hong Kong: shopping.

We buy cashmere sweaters, jade bowls, knock-off watches, and opium pipes. We visit a jewelry store and allow a woman behind a long glass counter to talk us into two identical gold necklaces, one for "mama," as the sales clerk calls her, and one for me.

That night, we meet our group for a farewell dinner at a swanky hotel restaurant. Our meal is extraordinary: heavy silver, thick linen napkins, and a seemingly endless succession of shrimp, spring rolls, satay, halibut, lobster, and several gooey, perfect desserts. I buy my mother dinner, and in the elevator, she thanks me.

"Oh, honey," she says. "I felt so special dining in such an elegant place. I'm not used to that kind of treatment." The elevator opens and I step aside. That's too bad, I think. She deserves that kind of treatment.

We walk into our room and Mom spends the next hour packing for the flight home. She's just about through when she remembers her Airborne, and spends another fifteen minutes digging through her satchels for the fizzy vitamins.

Once found, she holds the tube of Airborne triumphantly in the air. "I never go anywhere without my Airborne," she says.

"I know, Mom," I say, smiling at her across the room. "I know."

ॐ ॐ ॐ

Shari Caudron is a Taurus, recovering business journalist, and San Francisco native who traded the California coast for the Rocky Mountains twenty years ago. Ordinary people impress her more than celebrities. She believes happy endings are worth the wait. And she's jealous of Barbie collectors for reasons that are tough to explain here, but you'll understand if you read her latest book, Who Are You People? *Caudron is also the author of* What Really Happened, *and her work has appeared in* The Thong Also Rises, Fourth Genre, The Christian Science Monitor, *and* Reader's Digest.

❧ ❧ ❧

Where Silence Is Never Golden

An American widow in Italy confronts her grief,
menopause, and a deep need for elbow room.

*E*xhausted after a long train ride in sweltering weather,
I climb aboard a nearly empty city bus parked outside
the train station in Livorno. There's one other passenger on
board, and he's asleep at the back, stretched out, dead to
the world. Dragging my luggage down the aisle, I grab a
seat near the middle of the bus and begin fanning my fifty-
five-year-old menopausal body with a magazine, hoping to
generate a much-needed breeze. It's early afternoon here
in my adopted hometown, and the locals have deserted
the area—the streets, the parks, the buses, and railroad
station. In their modest, well-scrubbed homes and small
cafes and restaurants, Livornese are enjoying *pranzo*, the
midday meal.

Moments before the bus is scheduled to pull away from the station, a gaunt, well-dressed young woman climbs aboard, saunters along the narrow aisle, and proceeds to do something that most of us Americans would consider very suspicious, dangerous even, something that might justify conducting an immediate threat-assessment. In a nearly empty public vehicle—a bus, that is, with plenty of available seats—this young woman elects to remain standing. Quite naturally, she attracts my attention.

People who prefer to remain on their feet while traveling on nearly-empty buses and trains and ferries, or even airplanes, for that matter, are welcome to do so. Though I may question their judgment, they have my blessings and can do as they please without any interference or cheeky comment on my part. What unnerves me, though, is *where* this young woman elects to stand. Incredibly, she plants herself next to one of *two* occupied passenger seats. Mine.

This makes me very nervous. Since I find this action hard to fathom, immediate panic sets in. Is this individual disturbed in some way? I wonder while furtively glancing around, seeking confirmation of my suspicions from the passenger asleep in the back; trying, at the same time, to assess the possibility of an escape route. Why is this young woman standing next to my seat? Why is she breathing down my neck? Why is she leaning over my shoulder and glancing out of my window? Is she not aware that this vehicle has plenty of windows with unobstructed views?

By the time our bus travels from the train station to the center of town, my emotions have escalated from alarm to barely suppressed outrage. Now that it's apparent no mishap or violence is likely to occur to my person, now that it appears the eccentric young woman blocking my way is probably harmless (although one can never be really certain about these matters), I am suddenly ready to blow.

"Perhaps you'd be more comfortable sitting in my lap!" I mumble in English, though I'm reasonably certain the woman can neither hear nor understand me. Too cowardly to ask her to move away, I nevertheless continue brooding about her presence. Then, quite unexpectedly, I begin to feel giddy, almost hysterical. I'm upset, of course. Yet I can barely control the urge to burst out laughing.

It's insanely hot and muggy inside the bus; I'm tired and sweaty; and my nemesis is undoubtedly contributing to the wave of hot flashes now irradiating my face, neck, and underarms, all of which are sweat-drenched. Moving to another row of seats would provide some relief, of this I am certain. Yet I'm grimly determined to remain where I am. After all, an important moral principle is involved: I was here first. Giving up my bus-space to a smartly dressed, yet blatantly clueless interloper is not an option.

Being left alone to stew in my menopausal juices, on the other hand, would suit me just fine. Actually, I am convinced that harmony would be restored to the Western world if this young lady would move just a few paces away from me—if she would go and stand guard next to any number of empty rows of seats. But of course this doesn't happen. You see, in Italy, unaccompanied standing or sitting is prohibited. There is, in fact, a cardinal rule here: Thou shall not be alone.

From time to time, my widowed friends Giuliana and Miranda, or another one of my geriatric running buddies here in Livorno, an industrial seaport southwest of Pisa, will grab my hands or gaze intently in my eyes and ask once again for an explanation. Still amazed, after all these months, by what I've done, they'll say, "*Dimmi*, Telma (pronouncing the "th" sound in my first name always challenges them), *perché ti sei trasferita nel nostro paese?*"—Why did you move to our country?—and I'll reply, without hesitation, and with the utmost sincerity, "So I can learn to be more like you Italians."

It's a simple answer to a weighty question. Not the back story my friends expect. But it's the best I can do, given my resolve to avoid dwelling on the past. Telling my friends here in my adopted hometown about my husband's death is difficult. I've tried a few times. And although almost six years have passed since the day I became a widow, the words I use to describe that moment always sound garbled: they swell in my throat and nearly strangle me. What I've found somewhat easier to share, however, is something about the type of person I was (and suspect I still may be) before moving to Italy nearly two years ago.

In the spring of 1993, I was a fifty-three-year-old widow battling depression and a tendency to withdraw from people (a legacy of growing up with a mother who was overly fond of milk laced with scotch). I was a lost soul still reeling from losing her husband in 1988 and her widowed father the year before. A stressed-out mom obsessively worrying about her grown daughters while working in a challenging technical editing job. A self-anointed martyr who, years earlier, had struggled to pay the mortgage and other bills while her husband was recovering from two heart attacks and open-heart surgery. A so-called "good girl" who, for two decades, had tried to balance caring for her husband and kids with helping a healthy but demanding grandmother and a younger sister undergoing near-yearly operations on her joints.

My life rivaled the messy, convoluted plots on a soap opera. And then, one spring morning, I collapsed at my job. Which turned out to be a good thing. Responding to my colleagues' frantic 911 call, rescue crews from two ambulances and a fire truck arrived at my workspace, stretched me out on the floor beneath my desk, tried to find my pulse and start an IV, and finally rushed me to Kaiser Hospital in San Francisco. Days later, learning more about all of this who-shot-John from my colleagues and my brother Raymond (who worked nearby and had been called to the scene), I came to a very important decision: enough was enough. What had caused my close call was a mystery to the doctors in the emergency department. But not to me.

And so, in keeping with the time-honored tradition of other not-so-merry widows seeking rebirth and adventure, I fled to Italy, where my mission—and I was more than willing to accept it—was to start over. To live abroad for a few years and learn to enjoy life. It was time to concentrate on me-myself-and-I, but in a healthier, less obsessive way. Furthermore, all of these positive changes would take place in a country that had been the object of my affection from the time I was a ten-year-old and had heard my piano teacher, Mrs. Justicia Scott, of Oakland, California, utter the lovely words *allegro* and *pianissimo* for the very first time.

Over the decades, the melodious, undulating musical terms in my John Thompson piano books had come to represent a vibrant culture, a place where people were passionate and creative, friendly and nurturing. Positive changes would take place in Bella Italia, I told myself. While living in the country of Puccini and Donizetti, of Michelangelo and DaVinci and Modigliani, of exuberant, life-affirming people, I would become more spontaneous and adventurous. In my safe haven, a country that I had visited a few years earlier with my daughters Pamela and Ashley, I would learn to live my life *alla italiana*.

In this country, friends and family members devote nearly each day to reaffirming their ties with one another.

Eating *pranzo* and *cena* with their husbands and wives and kids, with siblings and uncles and aunts, with parents and grandparents; congregating in piazzas with their buddies; strolling along the seafront with relatives and acquaintances they've lived near all their lives; gossiping with neighbors while sitting on rickety chairs dragged over to a mini-park in front of the apartment buildings where they live: these are the rituals that give form and substance and meaning to people's lives here. Not surprisingly, there's a phrase for this tradition: it's called "*stare in compagnia di amici*"—hanging out with friends.

Embracing such healthy Italian customs as *stare in compagnia* would be good for me, I reasoned, on moving here in October of 1993. But in spite of my desire to change— my eagerness to adopt new and healthier customs and values, to live my life with exuberance—my old, disengaged self insisted on coming to Italy right along with me. Which would explain why, one afternoon, some three months after settling in the city of Pordenone (near the U.S. air base in Aviano, where I hoped to find part-time work), I found myself staring in disbelief, cringing as five adults, each one munching on a *panino*, crowded onto the same bench in front of the city's downtown bus depot. Three men and two women squished together as compactly as the ingredients in their dripping, toasted sandwiches. Maybe they're family members, I remember thinking.

From an early age, Italians are trained to express themselves in front of groups. As young students, they must pass the usual battery of written exams. But they must also pass tough oral exams. No one is exempt from these orals or *interrogazioni*, not even kids in the lower grades. During oral exams in elementary school, for example, a student may be grilled by the classroom teacher or by a panel of teachers. Adding to the ordeal, the student may have to respond in front of a group of inquisitive classmates.

In a country in which silence is considered an aberrant, anti-social tendency, this school tradition produces the desired results. People here seem at ease when speaking in public, as well they should, since they often have to endure some eight to thirteen years of taking and passing oral exams in their elementary schools, middle schools, and high schools. Sitting around gabbing is a cinch for individuals raised in such an environment. Still, when I imagine a panel of teachers grilling an unfortunate fifth grader in front of other students, I break out in a sweat. Had I been required to pass an oral exam at Longfellow Elementary School in Oakland, California, I would still be there.

In a popular, nationwide television commercial, Italian singer-actor Adriano Celentano portrays a typical passenger traveling by train. Despite his trademark deadpan expression, Celentano generously extols the virtues of train travel. As he speaks, a skein of yarn unravels, inexplicably, from his outstretched hands. Then the camera pulls back to a wider shot and the television viewer sees not only Celentano but also another passenger. Seated across from him is an elderly lady. She is busy knitting. And chatting him up, naturally.

Featured in the railroad commercial's second scene is a spiked-haired teenaged boy wearing a headset. While he gyrates in his seat, the television viewer is treated to a little of the raucous acid rock that has so enthralled him. Suddenly, the young punk rocker yanks off his headset, hands it to the unsuspecting nun seated next to him, and urges her to listen. She does, of course, and then reels back in shock, assaulted by sounds that have traumatized her eardrums. On recovering, she smiles indulgently. Over

both of these slice of life scenes appears the following message: "*Sul treno, c'e la vita*!" There's life on the train! Too
much, if you ask me.

It's 7:45 in the morning on a commuter train bound
for Florence. I'm heading home to Livorno, following a
four-day visit with friends in a tiny alpine village northeast
of Venice. Though it's early on a Monday morning, the
tradesmen, bureaucrats, and students onboard are loud and
energetic, especially the group of teenagers from Treviso,
a few of whom are still streaming up and down the aisle,
trying to locate adjoining seats so they can sit together and
gossip in their booming, surround-sound voices.

Clusters of businessmen are talking animatedly, having long since cast aside their newspapers. Young men
in military uniforms are cheerily singing and chanting—something they do often, especially while waiting
on open platforms for their trains to arrive. College students are holding intense discussions. The joint is really
jumping. It's Club Med on wheels. Amused by all of the
activity and drama, I find myself thinking about the commuter trains operating between Silicon Valley and San
Francisco, wondering if the sleep-deprived passengers
onboard ever raise this much early-morning ruckus.

Here's what had happened some forty minutes earlier.
After fighting my way onboard at Pordenone, the largest
city near my friends' home, I make a very pleasant discovery: I am traveling on a train with "open" coaches. Riding
on trains with six-passenger compartments is something
I dread. In open coaches, on the other hand, I feel more
comfortable and far less confined. I also feel freed from
the tedium of sharing my commute experience with as
many as five other passengers, all of us squeezed into a
tiny, stuffy cabin, some of us struggling to disguise the

sounds of a churning stomach intent on digesting its meal, and at least one of us (that would be me) trying to avoid touching other people's knees.

The train heading towards Florence is packed, perhaps overbooked. Yet I'm confident I'll find a seat. While making my way from one crowded coach to another, I think about how much I'm going to enjoy sitting down, staring out the window, and slowly drifting off to sleep. But, alas, I soon make a second discovery, one far less pleasant than the first. To foster intimacy between strangers, state officials have arranged most of the rows on our train into conversational groupings, or love seat pairs. For all intents and purposes, each pair of love seats duplicates the seating arrangements inside a train compartment. Compartments without walls, is what they are.

I am crushed. Bitterly disappointed. Disgusted. Nevertheless, I continue my search, determined to keep looking until I find the type of seating I prefer. Gripping my purse and bulky overnight bag even tighter, I stubbornly push my way through several crowded, split-level coaches, searching upstairs and down, looking for rows of seats that face in the same direction. All I want to do is find a seat that will allow me to stare at the back of somebody's big head. My search proves futile, however. Giving up, I plop down in an aisle seat, directly across from my love seat partner. We smile politely.

Sharing a compartment with strangers is not always an ordeal, though. There are times when I actually manage to achieve a level of comfort with my cabin mates, despite the fact that we've barely shared more than three or four words and an after-dinner mint. On such occasions—usually at night—the compartment is a warm, quiet cocoon. As the train speeds along, I sleep fitfully. Drowsy, I awaken each time the train stops at yet another small town to relieve itself of seasoned passengers and welcome new ones.

At the door of our cabin, a newcomer inquires, "*E libero questo posto?*" Is this seat available? Hearing our sleepy replies—"*Si, Si*"—he gingerly steps around us, makes space for his luggage, and settles down in an available seat. Soon, I close my eyes and the cycle begins anew. Nighttime rides are often enjoyable—solemn, and strangely calming. Surrounded by sleeping companions, I feel very comfortable. I communicate better with Italians when all of us are half asleep and capable of expressing nothing more profound than "*Scusi*."

So, there it is. After moving all the way to Italy, I've come to discover that living my life like the Italians is going to be a bit of a struggle, one that I never anticipated. Because I'm menopausal, fifty-something, and cranky, I'm sometimes exhausted and exasperated by my encounters here. And, yet, living in this country is a rare blessing. I've had the good fortune to develop strong ties with many wonderful individuals, with women who are generous and warm and inspiring. Each day, they teach me, by example, to approach life with enthusiasm. When I'm faced with the most mundane of tasks, they'll shout "*Coraggio!*"—Come on! Courage! When I show signs of withdrawing—declining invitations to dine with them or to take day trips or vacations with them—they'll simply refuse to let me hide out. They'll call me incessantly. Or, since everything in this country is larger than life—which is to say, operatic and noisy—they'll drop by my apartment for a confrontation that will last until I finally yield to their demands. Naturally, I am learning from all of this: learning not only to indulge my unfulfilled penchant for theatrics, hysteria, and spontaneity, but also to trust others. So who knows? Perhaps the day will soon arrive when I, too, will find myself living large. Like my friends, the Italians.

≈ ≈ ≈

Thelma Louise Stiles worked for several decades with the private sector and the federal government before moving abroad in 1993. After living in Italy for four years and London for two years, she reluctantly returned to the States. Her short stories have appeared in Essence Magazine, *and her one-act play is included in* Center Stage: An Anthology of 21 Contemporary Black-American Plays. *A widow, mother, and granny-nanny, she now lives in Northern California.*

Friends Like These

A harrowing drive through civil-war-torn
El Salvador tests two public health workers'
friendship—and their mettle.

At the close of each day in the war zone I experienced a kind of euphoria. I was treading on the edge and I did not take my life or safety for granted. But it wasn't until a squad of government soldiers stopped me on a dirt road in Chalatenango, El Salvador, that I felt like I was falling over and I had no idea where I would land.

As René and I bumped through the town of Dulce Nombre de Maria in the *carrito azul*, the worn-out blue Toyota Land Cruiser that had come with the job, I was trying to feel positive about this round of village visits. I was grateful not to have to travel into the mountains alone, but René was my boss and we were not getting along. He was the same age as my older son, but that had nothing to do with it. I had been a full-time volunteer with CODIPSA, the Diocesan Health Commission of Chalatenango Province, since February 1991 when I had gotten my master's degree in Public Health, and here it was June and not once had I received a word of acknowledgment or encouragement from him. Although he was sitting next to me in the passenger seat it felt like we were miles apart.

Just before leaving Chalatenango City on that humid, overcast Sunday morning, we had thrown the medicine into the car in order to save the village health promoters the long hike down to the Diocesan office. If all went well, our own hikes between the four villages would take about eighteen hours.

I was still nursing hurt feelings from René's criticism the last time he had come with me. I couldn't remember what he said—it had been two months—but I did remember feeling as if he had slapped me. Maybe he thought I hadn't gotten an air bubble out of a syringe or that I hadn't checked a child's immunization record. Whatever it was, he scolded me in front of the people lined up for their shots. I felt like running away, but I didn't yet know my way on these mountain trails. I had to force myself to pretend it didn't matter. Later, we'd hiked to the next village, just the two of us, on narrow dirt paths for hours, hardly speaking.

It had taken me almost the whole two months to finally figure out that René was mourning a loss and taking it out on me. He was angry that I was not Marcos, the North American public health worker who preceded me. Mark and René were both gregarious, assertive, and the same age. For two years they had worked together in Chalatenango, sharing confidences and dangers, developing trust and becoming good buddies the way men do when they have taken risks together. But Mark left El Salvador at the end of 1989 after the Armed Forces assassinated six Jesuits, their housekeeper and her daughter. One year later René got me as a replacement, a quiet fifty-year-old woman who was unsure of herself and had two grown sons in the U.S. and nothing in common with him. Even if René and I worked together for ten years, we'd never end up as good buddies.

At five-foot-eight René was half a foot taller than I and one-and-a-half times my weight. Glancing at him, I realized he wasn't fat, just a little more fleshy than the skinny *campesinos* with whom I spent most of my time. His black curly hair was thick, and in the beginning when I had felt comfortable with him, I had imagined his wife taking pleasure in running her fingers through it. The new eye patch covering his good eye added panache. With adequate medical attention the other one, the "lazy" eye, could have been corrected in childhood. Now the chances were not great, but *seguridad social* provided health benefits, and surgery was scheduled. Even before the patch I had trouble looking René straight in the eye. It wasn't only because his gaze went in two directions at once. I guess you could say we didn't see eye to eye.

My grip on the steering wheel drained the blood from my knuckles as I tried to avoid the dogs, pigs, and people in the street. We passed a white stucco church, a bleak central park, two bakeries, and a *bodega* that sold baptismal baby clothes, bottled water, motor oil, yard goods, and everything in between. If we had been going up to vaccinate, I would have stopped there to buy a couple of bags of candy. Our immunization protocol called for sticking little Juanito in the arm, or if his arm was too skinny, his thigh, and then offering jelly beans or caramels to sweeten his tears.

Beyond the central plaza, the street coursed through town like a narrow river between banks of contiguous turquoise, pink, and yellow painted cinder block walls. I shifted down to first where the cobbles ended and the dirt road began, anticipating the ascent into the mountains.

"*¡Don René!*" It was a woman's voice—barely audible above the roar and rattle of the car. She stood framed in the doorway of one of the last houses in the village looking older than her years, like everyone else in Chalatenango who had survived past forty. Her starched apron was so white it reflected the sun.

I turned off the engine.

"Where are you going?" she asked.

"We're going to Ocotal, Doña Graciela," René said. "What can we do for you?" Graciela disappeared and then reappeared dragging a huge *costal,* a bulging flour sack. Angular shapes strained against the fabric. René opened the back doors of the Land Cruiser. As he helped the woman hoist it into the back of the car, he asked, "Do you know if the soldiers are in the hills?"

"I saw them go up yesterday, but they came down this morning," she said. Then she asked René if we could take a girl up with us. René nodded.

"Can you also take a boy?"

The girl, a young woman of about seventeen, was wearing an impractical white skirt and a short sleeve sweater that clung to her small breasts. The boy looked to be about eight. His light brown hair was still damp from a morning bath and I could see the furrows left by his mother's comb. They climbed into the back beside the two boxes of medicine and the *costal.*

I started the car. René yelled to Graciela, "*¡Adios, señora, nos vemos,* see you later!" and jumped in.

To me he said, "We'll drop it at the store in Ocotal."

"What's in it?"

"Just cigarettes, sugar, candy, soap, cooking oil, and the like." There were no real stores in Ocotal. I guessed someone had purchased the merchandise in Dulce Nombre and would sell everything up there for a few centavos profit.

A little way up the road René spotted a woman he knew from Ocotal walking toward the mountains. A large *guacal* covered with a plain white cloth was balanced on her head.

"*Hola, madre*, come on," René said as he got out to help her with the plastic basin that held whatever she had walked all the way to Dulce to purchase. He placed the *guacal* in the back with the medical supplies, the *costal,* and our two passengers and then helped her into the front seat between us. She smelled like garlic and wet earth. There was gentleness in her cloudy gray eyes and when she said, "*Buenos dias, señora,*" the wrinkles around her mouth looked like shirring. One safety pin through a buttonhole held the bodice of her faded green dress together, and the tops of her rubber flip-flops had been replaced by twine. I looked away and pressed down on the accelerator.

The turnoff to Ocotal was only five and a half kilometers from Dulce Nombre but it would take an hour to get there. The road was narrow, unpaved, rutted, and studded with boulders. In dry weather a slippery layer of dust and sand coated the surface; now, in the rainy season, it was mud.

It wasn't the kind of ride that invited small talk. Our three passengers were probably holding their breath for fear of going over the cliff or running into the army. I wondered if the young people in the back were Graciela's children or if they lived in Ocotal. I wouldn't ask. The tacit code in this civil war was "the less information shared, the better."

I concentrated on mustering the strength to hold onto the steering wheel in the hairpin switchbacks. The usual layered vista of hills and valleys had vanished and heavy fog obscured the road. The topmost part of an occasional pine tree appeared silhouetted against a background of emptiness, the rest of it hidden beneath the road. The drop off the right side was too terrible to contemplate. There was no guardrail and the road was not wide enough for cars to pass each other. I took comfort in the scarcity of vehicles in the region.

Forty-five minutes after leaving Dulce Nombre we reached La Hamaca, a high ridge where the road dipped like a hammock between two mountains. I always got out there, as much for the view of the San Salvador volcano to the south and the mountains of Honduras to the north, as to rotate the levers that cranked the front wheel axles into *doble*, four-wheel drive. Several minutes past La Hamaca, before the turn-off to Ocotal, I noticed empty tins in the road.

"Look, René," I said, "the soldiers' leavings. I hope they're from yesterday."

I steered around the next hill. And there they were—twenty, maybe thirty soldiers in green-and-brown camouflage outfits. Perhaps they had been marching up the mountain and were taking a break. Or maybe they had stopped because they heard our car. Whatever they had been doing before we arrived, in spite of the machine guns, helmets, and black boots, they looked as disorganized as a herd of cows grazing in a field. Several soldiers sat on the ground, their backs against the near-vertical rock wall and their helmets on the dirt beside them. The fog was lifting, and I could see clusters of three or four soldiers dotting the road up to the next turn.

Two of them came forward. At ten paces one soldier took his pistol out of its holster and walked to my side of the car.

"*Buenos días, señora.*" At least he was polite. "*Su identi-*

ficación, por favor." I handed him my ID card and the car registration. I had the impression he was wearing a mask until I realized that his head was shaved and I was seeing the sharp contrast between his cream-colored scalp and tanned face. I thought he was too young to look as comfortable as he did with a weapon in his hand. I strove for a relaxed but impatient attitude while he examined the documents. My heart was beating so hard I was afraid he'd notice it pulsing beneath my cotton t-shirt. He put the gun back in the holster, bent down, and peered into the car.

"And *your* papers?" he demanded of René, who already had his cards out. I handed them to the soldier who looked them over while no one in the car made a sound.

"And your *salvoconductos*?" he asked.

We did not have *salvoconductos* because we didn't need safe conduct passes to travel in Chalatenango Province. René was a Salvadoran citizen and my visa was up to date and indicated that my application for residency was in process. Our church IDs verified that we were lay religious workers with the Diocese of Chalatenango.

"We don't have *salvoconductos* because we live and work in Cha—" I started to explain, but he cut me off.

"The car keys! Everyone out of the car!"

I handed over the keys and grabbed my *cesta*. The woven plastic market basket contained my everyday necessities. I took out my water bottle, unscrewed the top and began to drink. I wanted the soldier to think that thirst was the reason I was carrying my *cesta*. In addition to water the basket held my glasses, toilet paper, flashlight, camera, Mexican string hammock compressed into a ball, and most important, my precious notebook and journal.

The fog disappeared altogether and the sun, not quite at its peak, beat down like hot rain. Only the car separated us from the soldiers. We huddled behind it inches from the edge in the meager shade of a lone pine tree. The old woman took out her rosary. With her arm around the boy's shoulders, the young woman said, "Everything will be all right."

René predicted for my ears alone, "We're going to end up in La Cuarta." He sounded matter of fact, but the pupil of his exposed eye jerked right and left. La Cuarta, the Fourth Brigade, also known as El Paraiso, was the main army base in the province. I had been detained there in the hot sun for several hours with my Cambridge, Massachusetts sister city delegation during my first visit to El Salvador in 1986. We were carrying contraband medicine and thought for sure we'd be turned back. The soldier who inspected our bags must have seen the hundreds of little boxes of penicillin packed among our clothing, but he didn't stop us. I suspected he could not read.

"They have no grounds to hold us," I whispered back. René tilted his head, half smiled, and raised the eyebrow over his patch. He is humoring me, I thought. Maybe it's a good sign.

The soldier holding our papers signaled the other guy to search the car and ordered one of the loungers on the road to help. They took a quick look beneath the front seats and then climbed into the back. They checked out the old woman's *guacal,* opened the *costal*, and rifled through the two boxes of medical supplies. When they reported their findings, the soldier with our IDs frowned. He walked over to me and asked, "Where is your *salvoconducto* for the medicine?"

"We don't need a safe conduct pass for medicine," I insisted, but he was adamant. I was about to quote from the Salvadoran constitution when I felt René tap me on my arm, a reminder to be contrite. I tried to look earnest and innocent. René was right to rein in my indignation. I would have overdone it. If the constitution hadn't gotten the desired effect I was ready to refer to the FMLN-Government Accords of San José, signed in Costa Rica almost a year before between the Frente Farabundo Mart' para la Liberación Nacional and the Armed Forces of El Salvador, and if necessary, cite the Geneva Conventions. All three documents guaranteed freedom of movement to civilians as well as access to medical care. But even I knew quoting them would probably have angered the soldier. And he had the gun.

He turned away and sent the fellows who had done the inspection back to the car. They placed the boxes on the ground. While one picked up an item and read the label out loud, the other took notes. When they finished, one of them handed the list to the soldier giving the orders and tossed everything back into the boxes. I felt a little stab of annoyance that we'd have to sort it out in Ocotal. The soldier glanced at the paper, turned toward the steep cliff, found a toehold and scrambled out of sight as effortlessly as if he were running up a flight of stairs. The two who had searched the car retreated into the milling detachment. The boxes sat in the dirt next to the car.

The old woman sighed. She said she'd like to sit down but not in front of the soldiers. So we climbed into the car leaving the rear doors open, hoping for a breeze.

Five minutes later a couple of soldiers drifted over to the car and asked to buy cigarettes. The fellows who had done the search must have told them about the *costal*.

"Do you know how much cigarettes cost?" The young woman directed the question to René and me. Neither of us smoked. The only thing I knew about cigarettes was that they were sold by the piece, not the pack.

"Try twenty-five centavos, " René replied.

The soldiers were amenable. They left, and two others appeared. During the next hour, at least fifteen soldiers purchased cigarettes and matches, gum and candy, small packets of coffee, sugar, and salt. One guy asked for toothpaste. I wondered if they really wanted the stuff or if they were flirting with our attractive shopkeeper. She played her part with conviction—ticking off our made-up prices with authority, doling out goods and taking in coins like an experienced sales clerk.

I figured that whoever was in command of the detachment must be stationed out of sight on top of the cliff, and it was he who would pass judgment on us. Maybe he had radio contact with the Estado Mayor, the military high command in San Salvador.

The stream of customers eventually stopped. The soldiers donned their helmets, formed a line and filed up the road.

"I hope we get our IDs and keys back," I mumbled.

"Maybe they're just going to eat lunch," the old woman said. *Lunch.* It was getting on toward noon. But why are they going away just to eat their army rations, I thought. René and I had shared my little bit of whole wheat bread, peanut butter, honey, and an orange before we left the city at six A.M., and my stomach had been rumbling for the last hour. We planned to eat lunch in Ocotal where a group of women cooked meals for our meetings.

The last soldier disappeared around a turn.

We were alone. A little blue car perched on the narrow shelf of a road chiseled out of a mountain, caught between the edge of a precipice and a sheer wall of dirt and rock. From a distance we were a blue dot suspended in the middle of a vertical wall, an incongruous blot on the vista of green valleys and rugged mountains. For the first time that day, I noticed tiny yellow wildflowers peeking out of crags in the wall. A sweet perfume floated on the air. Birdcalls echoed between the hills, and up close I heard the low hum of insects. Something about the sun and stillness called up lazy summer afternoons in my childhood.

A blast shattered my daydream. I jumped.

Bullets, mortars, and other flying objects hissed by. More explosions and gunfire followed. The mountain shuddered. I felt my heart beating all over my body. An acrid odor caught in my throat and made my eyes tear. All of us dropped to the ground except the old woman who slid to the floor of the car fingering her beads. I saw her lips moving.

My ears hurt. Across the valley, a row of small fires sprang up along the mountain ridge. Thin funnels of smoke curled through pine branches.

"Can bullets go through the car? Can they go through tires?" The young woman's voice was weak. She huddled next to René behind the rear wheel. I crouched behind the front wheel shielding the boy. René said he was pretty sure bullets could penetrate both the car and the tires. The young woman started to shake.

The soldiers were shooting at the *compas*, the FMLN, who had fired on them from the valley below, and possibly from the mountain across the valley. The army was launching mortars and shooting from the plateau above us, where I had imagined the commander reviewing our case. We were stranded in the middle. A bullet, grenade, or mortar might blow us apart at any moment.

The car door hung open on the driver's side. The old woman had shifted her body away from the assault and her head was wedged beneath the steering wheel. Clouded or not, her eyes were shining with terror. She still clutched the beads.

I was surprised I did not panic. I was afraid, but it was rational to be afraid, I reasoned. And that was the odd part: to feel fear and still be able to think. I felt like I was observing the scene from a distance, methodically examining possible routes of escape and coming up with none. Still, I marveled at my rationality. Then time stopped, and in that faraway place I began to listen for the pauses between the volleys. For what seemed like a long time, but was probably no more than fifteen minutes, I concentrated on the silence and not the bursts of fire. All the while I could see my fear. It looked like a depressed hollow in the center of my heart. In the hollow was a field with fertile soil. Fear sprouted and blossomed there, then dropped its seeds. I watched fresh sprouts appear. I was fascinated with the image. But I was not taken in. I stayed focused on the spaces, willing them to expand. And they did. An eerie quiet enveloped us.

It was broken by a voice shouting from above, "Turn the car around!"

I yelled back, "You have the keys!" I wondered if the battle was over.

A soldier picked his way down the cliff, tossed the car keys to me and scampered back. I measured the car with my eyes. It seemed longer than the road was wide. It was not possible to turn the car around.

"I can't do this," I said to René. He took the keys and without thinking, the rest of us climbed in. René, with that one eye, backed the car down the winding, narrow, slippery path until, at a particularly treacherous ledge where the road bowed out barely a few extra inches, he began the delicate maneuver. I held my breath and controlled the urge to jump out. Shifting back and forth between first and reverse, leaning hard left on the steering wheel, then sharp right, advancing and retreating, inches forward, inches back, slowly, patiently, René turned the car around.

As soon as we were facing back toward Dulce Nombre de Mar'a, I let my breath out. I thought we would soon be away from these guys.

But a soldier stood in our path. He must have descended while we were preoccupied with surviving the turnaround. His arm was thrust forward, the flat of his hand toward us, an exaggerated imitation of a traffic cop. He commanded us to wait for someone who would accompany us to the Fourth Brigade. I looked at René. A little bulge in his cheek indicated a clenched jaw. It was the only sign that he was not pleased about having been right.

Our passengers climbed out of the car. The soldier did nothing to stop them. René and I were the ones they wanted.

"Gracias a Dios," the old woman said when her feet touched the ground. "Thank God we are alive. But I am afraid for you."

The young woman helped her place the *guacal* on her head, took the boy's hand, and looked down at her feet. As they started walking up the road the old woman glanced back and said, "God protect you."

I watched the three of them until they disappeared around the next bend. I wondered how far ahead of them the soldiers were. I wondered if it was irresponsible to per-mit the kid to go with them. I wondered if they would get to Ocotal. Then they were gone, and I still did not know their names, nor if they were related to each other.

A soldier in blue jeans, t-shirt, and tennis shoes approached us carrying a small shoulder bag that I hoped contained our ID cards. The sunlight flashed off the pistol in his hand. He stuffed it in his belt to lift the boxes of med-icine into the back of the car and hoisted himself in after them. The other soldier closed the doors behind him. René remained in the driver's seat, and we both turned to look at the soldier. He pointed the gun at René and motioned with it for him to get going. I sucked in my breath. Would he shoot? If he shot René on that road it would be suicide as well as double murder. What about me? The soldier who had examined my ID had seen I was a U.S. citizen, but did this one?

What was I thinking? The protection of U.S. citizenship was not guaranteed. I had just experienced the possibility of being killed in crossfire. A village could be attacked at any time with me in it. And if I were intentionally targeted, the Salvadoran government would deny it.

No one said a word during the trip down. Three quarters of an hour later we rolled slowly into Dulce Nombre de Mar'a. People in the street stared, but no one yelled to us or waved. Gregarious René looked straight ahead and acknowledged no one.

At the *convento* where we held our health promoter trainings, René pulled over and announced he was taking the *costal* inside. He told me to run to ANTEL, the telephone office two blocks ahead, to call the parish house in Chalate. Was René nuts? What about the soldier, the gun? We got out of the car at the same time. I looked back at the soldier. He had an odd expression. His gun was not visible and he looked bewildered and, yes, afraid. Maybe he thought we were going to get our pals in the FMLN. And that was when I understood the civilian disguise and knew he would not pull the trigger. He did not want to be noticed in what might be enemy territory. Half the time the soldiers were in this part of Chalatenango and the other half it was the guerrillas.

The ANTEL door was open but the place was empty. I lifted the receiver of the nearest phone, heard a dial tone, and placed the call. Blinding sunlight streamed through the open door. On the eleventh ring, Alfredo, one of the younger priests, answered. I had been taught it was important for our safety that someone knew where we were. I really didn't understand how Alfredo's knowing could protect us. Our lifeline felt like a too-short length of frayed twine. But I told him what was happening. I was about to say good-bye when the *carrito azul* appeared at the door.

"Don't hang up, Padre, here's René."

Alfredo told René he would get the Bishop to phone the colonel at the Fourth Brigade. The Bishop's intervention meant they might hassle us at El Paraiso just to make life difficult, but they would probably let us go. It seemed like our troubles would soon be over.

I took the wheel. A half hour later the soldier signaled to the guards in front of the huge iron doors to El Paraiso. They waved us through and directed us deep into the base to a parking area outside a long one-story building. Two more soldiers with machine guns stood nearby.

Our chaperone/guard/captor—I never knew which— jumped out. He entered the building with his hand resting on the shoulder bag. When he had not returned fifteen minutes later, I thought we should go inside and try to get our IDs back from the officials in there and request a *salvoconducto* for the medicine. I didn't want to get stopped again that day. I was also hungry.

"What about food, René? Do you think we could get something to eat in there? And I need a bathroom. I haven't peed all day."

René advised holding on a little longer. He said we should sit and wait. Then he said, "It's the antibiotics and that one little bottle of painkillers that got us in trouble, you know. They're going to accuse us of supplying the guerrillas."

"What's the matter with them? Nobody else is supposed to need painkillers?"

"Shhhh, Susana, *cálmate*, relax. This might take a long time." René used the less formal, friendly form of "you" with me. "Do you have anything that might look suspicious?"

I had my work notebook. I always carried it. I used it for plans and objectives for training sessions and village visits, notes on decisions and results of meetings, and "to do" lists. I didn't want to admit this to René because he had told me never to carry CODIPSA materials with me. Technically, my notebook wasn't CODIPSA material so I decided not to tell him.

I had my personal journal, too. *Oh, no!* I thought. My journal was full of descriptions of people and places. And names—even though I had been warned about this by members of the Town Council of Cambridge's sister city back in 1986. They told us about a European journalist in El Salvador whose tapes, notes, and address book were confiscated. A few days later, the local colonel arrived in the village with a troop of soldiers to haul away the people identified in the journalist's notes and tapes.

I felt sick. When did I stop being careful? During all my visits to El Salvador before working with CODIPSA I had left numbered blanks in my notes where proper names could be copied in at home from a crib list hidden in my bra. The enormity of my transgression took my breath away. I had to force myself to stay focused.

"I can't think of anything, René."

It was another hot thirty minutes before several soldiers sauntered toward the car. They looked disorganized, a bit like the detachment on the road to Ocotal. Our soldier was not among them. He must have been anxious to shed his unpredictable charges and he probably felt lucky as Hell to be safe on the base, away from the fighting in the mountains. I hoped he had remembered to explain to these guys that we were only there because we needed to get permission for the medicine.

When the soldiers stopped behind the car, probably to figure out what they were doing, I remembered that my camera might contain exposed film. I took it out of my *cesta* and opened the case. The counter indicated I had taken ten pictures, but I couldn't remember what they were. I told René I was going to open the camera and destroy the film, but then I decided to re-roll it instead to save the pictures. I pressed the rewind button and cringed at the whirring noise. I stuffed the camera under my shirt to muffle the sound. Then, without moving my upper body, so the soldiers wouldn't see me bending down, I slipped the exposed roll up behind the dashboard and found a snug fit between a couple of wires. I hoped René had noticed my quick thinking. As soon as I straightened up a soldier appeared at my window. He ordered us to empty the car and get out.

René's needs for three days were in a small backpack. Mine filled a large backpack, my *cesta*, and a cotton shoulder bag. I put all of these on the ground while René took out the two boxes of medicine. We were asked to stand to the side while they made a cursory inspection of the car and looked over the display. They hadn't suspected anything hidden in the car and they didn't open our bags. In fact, it seemed like they were just going through the motions. I had the impression it was a game. Soon they would turn to us and say, "We were only fooling. You are free to go."

I realized that was not going to happen when these guys moved out of the way for a no-nonsense looking fellow in his early thirties. He was taller and broader than the others. *Probably well-nourished as a child*, I thought, *and not forcibly recruited from a slum in the capital or a poor village in the countryside*. He did not speak while he strutted around the display. He bent over my *cesta*—he made it look casual—and pulled out my camera. I felt smug about remembering the film. But he stuck two fingers into the little pocket of the camera case and dug out a scrap of yellow paper. I stifled a gasp and avoided looking at René. I had forgotten about that little photo list. I hadn't written on it for weeks. The officer looked at me with a self-satisfied "gotcha" expression on his face.

"Hmmm. What do we have here?" he said.

I tried laughing it off. "That's nothing. It's just the way I keep track of pictures. It isn't important." I reached for it, but he pulled away.

"*Muy interesante,*" he said. He held the tiny note between thumb and forefinger six inches from his face. He raised his free hand and placed it between the paper and the sun to eliminate the glare. Then, squinting, he read aloud in a tone that sounded sarcastic, mocking, "Las Vueltas, Las Flores, Arcatao. Why are you carrying a list of *these* villages?"

He might as well have said, "What are you doing with the *subversivos* in these villages?" The army operated as if the repopulated communities, the ones to which people displaced by the war had returned, were inhabited by guerrillas or their civilian sympathizers, and they made no distinction between the two. In spite of the heat, I felt my face flush.

I said I was part of the health commission, and that they were just some of the communities where I worked.

"Why are their names written here?"

"I took pictures of children during our last immunization campaign and I wanted to remind myself where they lived after the film was developed." It was none of his business. My photos featured health promoters and their children, spouses, and parents. Innocent pictures. But guilt and innocence were irrelevant.

Soon he tired of trying to decipher my scribbles and put the scrap of paper back into the case. It was the medicine that claimed his attention. He probably thought it was a cache of illegal drugs. He called over a medic who counted each pill and compiled a list. I pulled myself together and stood behind the medic to make sure what he wrote was correct. I glanced at René while I took down my own inventory and maybe I imagined it, but I saw a slight upturn at the corners of his mouth when he looked at me.

During our four hours at El Paraiso we were not given food nor the use of a toilet, nor *salvoconductos* for us or the medicine, nor our identification documents. When I pulled the *carrito azul* onto the highway, we had *two* soldiers dressed in civilian clothes in back. I had been ordered to drive us to the headquarters of the Policia de Hacienda, the PH, the Treasury Police, in San Salvador. I was driving us to jail. The PH was the branch of the Army charged with public security at the national level. It was famous for human rights abuses. I drove as slowly as possible—my meek and only act of protest.

Several kilometers down the road we would pass one of the communities where I worked, but I couldn't think of how that could help us. As we approached a dirt field just before the village, I saw a soccer game in progress. Most of the village was out cheering the players on.

"Susana, stop here!" René's voice startled me.

The soldiers jumped up, but René was out and running across the road before they could grab him. I turned toward them and scolded, "He *has* to tell someone what's happening because a lot of people in Chalatenango are probably worried. We were supposed to be back by two o'clock."

I was trying for righteous indignation, but my hands were shaking. The truth was no one expected us to return before Tuesday or Wednesday. Anything could happen to us before then. I was surprised that my outburst seemed to subdue the soldiers.

René was standing on the side of the road with Rosa, a CODIPSA health promoter. When he came back, he said Rosa would get a message to Padre Gabriel, the head of the Social Secretariat of the diocese, who lived in a nearby village. Maybe Rosa would tell Gabriel. Maybe he'd intercede. The Bishop had not.

René's refusal to give up should have inspired me, but as we continued our slow progress toward captivity, the fear and confusion I had repressed all day were threatening to erupt. I contained them by worrying about petty details like having no money or clothes for the city. We arrived at the Policia de Hacienda at six o'clock.

The sign on the door of the room in which we spent the next several hours said "*Control de Reos*," Prisoner Control. I remember the room as white, rectangular, and empty. Except for a mirror, the walls were bare and there was no furniture, although we must have sat on something—perhaps a bench against one of the walls. The room in the PH felt like a way station, an interlude between all that had happened to us that day and what was to come. *Like purgatory*, I thought.

The PH was as efficient as the soldiers on the road and at the Cuarta Brigada had been bumbling. Right away two men carrying clipboards interviewed us. I couldn't hear the exchange between René and his interrogator, but the eyes of the one who sat next to me held steady, and he looked me in the face while he completed the questionnaire. His gentle, almost apologetic, tone of voice made me wonder, for a second, if there were social workers in the Army. I started to relax, but caught myself. Maybe it's a ploy to get me off my guard.

The questions were of the when-did-you-stop-beating-your-wife variety. I answered "yes" to "Was the prisoner captured in the Department of Chalatenango?" but insisted I was detained, not captured. So he wrote *detenida* in parenthesis on the form, although he didn't cross out *capturada*.

Someone brought us each a plate of cold *pupusas*, probably left over from dinner. We finally got to use a toilet. In the bathroom I was astonished that I hadn't urinated in more than twelve hours. When I was a child my father used to tease my mother by calling her a camel because she never seemed to need a public rest room when they were on the road. I almost chuckled out loud thinking that I must have inherited that camel gene.

I was beginning to relax or I would never have allowed my mind to wander like that. It was ironic that the only time I felt safe that day was in the custody of the Policia de Hacienda, the expert and well-known abusers of human rights.

When they asked us to sign off on their inventory of the medicine, I refused because the list was exaggerated and did not match the one I had made at the Fourth Brigade. I noticed the hint of a frown on René's face and wished I hadn't made this an issue. I knew he might be treated worse than I would be. We were in this together, but my North American passport could separate us. I was about to waver when René said he wouldn't sign either. So they took René with them to witness the recount of the medicine.

Alone in that room, I worried that they weren't going over the medicine. Maybe they were torturing René. I should have signed and kept my mouth shut. Why did I keep making mistakes?

But René came back unharmed, and they typed out a new accurate list that we both signed.

An hour later the man who had interviewed me stuck his head in and announced that they had contacted the U.S. Embassy. "Someone is coming for you." *Me or us?* He had used the singular, but maybe that was because René was in the bathroom. I worried it might be just for me. But since the U.S. was funding this war and pulling the strings, I figured they had the authority to help René, too.

At about nine o'clock two neatly dressed clean-cut young people were escorted in. They started speaking to us in English. I interrupted in Spanish, and said, "If you don't mind, I prefer that we conduct our meeting in Spanish so René can participate."

They introduced themselves as Lisa Gamble and Michael Mullins from the U.S. Embassy. We recounted the events of the day, and when they talked about the chances of getting me out, I said I'd be grateful for anything they could do. "But I'm not going anywhere without René. If you can't get us both released, I'm staying with him."

They glanced at each other and went to talk to the PH officials. Although we were alone in the room, René and I didn't say anything to each other. Since they had a two-way mirror—why else would there be a mirror in this otherwise empty room—they probably also had the place bugged. We'd exchanged only a few sentences all day, and almost nothing since being stopped on the road to Ocotal. We were winging it. The only fallback plan wasn't worth the name: making sure other folks knew where we were or where we were supposed to be.

About thirty minutes later, a soldier came in with another paper for us to sign. On top it said, "Charges and release form." Then Lisa and Michael returned, smiling.

The form stated we had been released and all our possessions had been returned to us, identifying the car and the medicine in it. We signed—in duplicate. Someone was called in to sign on behalf of the PH and affix the official PH seal. He kept one copy and handed the other to René.

I realized the document was, in effect, a *salvoconducto* for the medicine. I wanted a copy, too. I thought I might need it after I took René home to his wife in Soyapango, when I would have to make my way across the city alone. By the time they had made one for me, Lisa and Michael had disappeared. Afraid the soldiers might take us back into custody, René and I almost broke into a run the moment I had the paper in my hand.

In the paved parking area of the Policia de Hacienda, two spotlights illuminated our way. Lisa and Michael were waiting in their Embassy car. They must have had the same idea about recapture because their chauffeur gestured for me to drive out in front of them. Two soldiers closed the gate behind us. I drove through and watched the Embassy car in the rearview mirror. We headed off in different directions.

¡Libertad! Sweet freedom! I took a deep breath. The air smelled like rain. The pavement was wet. The streets were dark and deserted. Even in the capital it was dangerous to be out at night, and ours was the only moving vehicle in sight. I wondered what René was thinking while we drove around looking for a public telephone. I had acted independently several times during the day, and we hadn't been able to decide together about a strategy at the PH. I hoped I hadn't made things worse between us.

"There's one," we said in unison as a phone came into view on the opposite side of the street beneath a solitary working streetlight. We looked at each other and started to giggle. As if choreographed, we both put a hand over our mouths, which made us laugh harder. We were giddy, but it wasn't safe to relax.

When we calmed down, René got out of the car. Halfway across the street he stopped, turned, and motioned for me to join him. He called Padre Alfredo in Chalate. I called my friends, Kevin and Ellen, and asked if I could stop by around midnight. I hoped they understood that if I didn't get there, I was in big trouble. I knew not to give detailed information over the phone.

René directed me in a circuitous route to Soyapango, managing to evade army roadblocks. Before we reached the development of row houses where he and his wife lived, he put his hand on my arm and said, "I'm going to get out. I can cut through here. I'll have a better chance of skirting the patrols on foot."

I stopped the car. There were no lights on the street. I saw no houses. On the edge of the illumination of my headlight beams, a dark woodsy area strewn with trash looked ominous. I had no idea where we were except for a faint pinkish tint on the horizon that announced downtown San Salvador. Nor did I know how to get to the neighborhood of San Salvador where Kevin and Ellen lived.

René gave me directions and I wrote them down. His voice was calm, personal, almost intimate. He didn't hurry off, although he must have been anxious to see his wife and get home to relative safety. We sat in silence for about a minute. When it was obvious there was nothing left to stall the inevitable, he said, "*Nos vemos*." After a pause he said, "and you better get rid of the medicine first thing in the morning. Leave it at the Arzo [the office of the Archdiocese]. We'll figure out how to get it later."

I'm sure I appeared composed but I was on the verge of panic. I felt like someone was pushing on my chest. I didn't want René to leave. It would be like losing a vital organ. My life depended on it. But it made no sense to hold him back.

I took his outstretched hand. It was a long handshake. "*Cu'date, Susana*, take care of yourself, be careful."

He got out of the car and came over to my window. He said good-bye, again. Then he turned and I watched him disappear as if absorbed into the night. If there had been time then to examine that moment I might have recognized the shift. At the time I was conscious only of being more alone than I ever wanted to be. Later, I would say that was when René began to trust me.

இ *இ* *இ*

H. Susan Freireich went back to school to study public health after twenty-five years of teaching, community organizing, and political activism. She went to work in the civilian communities caught in El Salvador's civil war and is writing a memoir about the experience. She is the recipient of the 1998 Frances Shaw Fellowship, granted annually by The Ragdale Foundation to a woman who began writing seriously after the age of fifty-five. She has also received support and time for her work from Norcroft, Hedgebrook, Blue Mountain Center, and the Djerassi Resident Artists Program.

A Methodist Prayer Rug

In Turkey, a reluctant shopper succumbs.

"Come in, come in," he beckoned in accented English. "It is my turn to cheat you next."

I looked up, surprised at his honesty amid the fast talking vendors of the Grand Bazaar in Istanbul.

His coal-black eyes locked with mine and he flashed a bright-white smile that shined like a Pepsodent commercial against his tan skin.

"It's O.K. I won't cheat you as much as your president."

I had to laugh with him. It was a line I had never heard before.

"Please. You come in now?" he implored. "We have beautiful carpets."

"Yes, I'll look. But only look." I was firm from the outset.

"O.K. lady, I will sell you carpet. We have fortunate saying. If you look me in the eye, then I have you. You already look at me. You buy a carpet. You see."

What a silly superstition. It wouldn't persuade me, a very savvy shopper, to buy a carpet. I was sure of that.

I sat on a cushioned bench along the wall of his family's carpet shop. Thick, luscious carpets hung on all the walls. I felt like I was in a large, exotic tent, the kind I imagined they must have in Marrakech, where camels might carry carpet rolls across the desert until they set up camp for the night. It felt close and dense and plush. The shop had stacks of carpets on the floor in piles ten, twenty, thirty deep. More were rolled like thick cigars, propped in the corners.

"Some apple tea, you would like?" he asked.

I didn't, but I didn't want to be rude. He clapped his hands and it appeared.

"A sandwich, maybe?" he also asked.

"No, thank you." This was going too far. A glass of hot tea, barely larger than a shot glass was O.K., but a sandwich? When was the last time a salesperson at Macy's offered me a sandwich—for free? I didn't want to feel indebted, but I was hungry. He sensed my hesitation and clapped again.

"Here, for you." He handed me a hamburger bun, dry, with a thin slice of tomato and a slice of cheese.

I didn't feel too indebted.

"What kind of carpet you want to see, lady? Wait," he interrupted before I could even answer. "I think I am being rude. My name is Muso. What is your name?"

"Jeanne," I reluctantly told this stranger.

"Jeanne," he repeated. "That's a very pretty name. Now, Jeanne," he continued, "what type of carpet would you like to see? I have room-size carpets, round carpets, carpet runners. I have wool carpets, I have cotton carpets, I even have silk carpets," he added at the end, almost in a conspiratorial whisper.

"A small carpet, to hang on my wall, like a picture," I said. I had no intention of buying a carpet—a wall hanging, maybe.

"For you, Jeanne, I have just the right thing."

Sure, sure, I thought.

He came forth with an armful of small carpet rolls. Each no larger than the bound samples you find in the carpet store displays—the ones they let you take home and lay all over your house to decide which color works best against your linoleum, or hides the dirt tracked in by your kids and the dog. He unfurled the first one at my feet.

"This is wool," he said. "Every carpet has a different motif. There is a language of motifs. Each carpet means something."

I was impressed. It was beautiful.

"Wait," he said. "I show you more."

He laid another one at my feet. This one was made of cotton, with more knots per square inch in a steepled geometric pattern.

"You can tell this is the top," he told me. "It points to Mecca. It is a prayer rug." He unrolled a larger one, with side-by-side geometric patterns. "This prayer rug is for two people. Is there a Mr. Jeanne?" He didn't wait for a response. "I have for whole family."

He quickly unrolled an even longer carpet with space for four to kneel and pray. It would be an interesting conversation piece, but not very practical for my Methodist upbringing. I shook my head no.

"Wait," he began again. "I have just the thing. This one is silk," he said as he twirled the fringed 18 x 24-inch prayer rug in the air like a pizza.

It fluttered to the ground at my feet. It was exquisite. The colors were iridescent, the knots were meticulously even and tight, and the pattern was a tree of life. My heart leapt.

"This is the one!" he said. "I knew it." His eyes danced.

"How much?" I asked cautiously, not wanting to reveal my excitement, but he knew. I couldn't tear my eyes from the deep navy background, the brilliant burgundy border, or the cream-colored vase from which the intricate tree of flowering blossoms burst forth.

"Jeanne, you have good taste. This is a signed one." He pointed to the foreign script centered on the top and bottom edges. My heart sunk. He saw that, too. "Do not worry, Jeanne. I give you good price."

He paused. I held my breath.

"Seven hundred U.S. dollars," he said.

"No, too much," I said, shaking my head no, but holding out hope.

"Do you not think it is beautiful," he pleaded. "It has 1,200 knots in each square inch. And look," he picked it up and spun it again. This time it landed facing in the other direction. "See how much the colors change?"

He was right! The deep navy and burgundy turned to pitch black and bright red. I stared.

"See, Jeanne. It is like getting two carpets for one price."

"It is beautiful, but it is too much." I held my ground. Besides, I couldn't hang it upside down, just for variety's sake, against its grain, just to show the change in colors. A tree of life must grow up, not down. No two-for-one bargain here.

"How much you pay for it, Jeanne?"

I was ruthless. I cut the price in half. "Three hundred and fifty U.S. dollars," I countered.

"No, no!" he exclaimed. "I cannot do that at all. Just look at this." He flipped the carpet over so I could examine the back of it. "These tiny knots, they are done by hand, not on a machine. This one little carpet takes months to make. Because I know you really like this one, I let you have it for six hundred dollars."

Now I felt guilty. Some poor Turkish woman had hunched over her loom for months to make my carpet, already I was calling it mine, a dangerous sign in the midst of negotiation. I upped the ante fifty bucks. "Four hundred dollars," I told him.

"No, for four hundred dollars I can sell you this beautiful wool rug." He laid it next to my glistening silk carpet with the richest colors and softest nap. The silk felt like velvet as I rubbed my hand along the design. The wool reminded me of my grandparents' carpet, the rough one on the living room floor that I would lie across, on my stomach to watch television when I was a kid. When I'd get up, I'd itch on my elbows and knees.

There was no comparison, but he wasn't coming down. He didn't counter-offer. I'd have to bid against myself. "Four hundred and fifty for the silk," I told him and added, "but no more."

"I'm so sorry, Jeanne. Five hundred dollars is my best price." He began to roll it up.

But I had to have it, I knew it the moment I saw it, he knew it the moment he had locked eyes with me. It now hangs on the wall in the dining room of my Pennsylvania farmhouse. I touch it when I cross the room and rub my hand gently down the soft nap of the tiny silk knots. I am transfixed by the intricacy of the design and the shift in colors as daybreak moves toward sunset across the farmhouse windows. I say my Protestant prayer of thanksgiving and touch the Islamic prayer rug that represents the fortunes in my life—to travel, to experience, and not to have to make 1,200 knots per square inch to survive.

ॐ ॐ ॐ

Jeanne Stark is an avid traveler with the goal of visiting all 700 of UNESCO's World Heritage Sites. Unfortunately the list grows larger each year and at a faster pace than she can travel. Her day job is as the marketing director for her local hospital. She lives in Pennsylvania.

❧ ❧ ❧

My Visa to Spanish Territory

Asia provides the backdrop for her TLA (torrid love affair) with a dark Barcelonan.

M y plan to travel overland from Nepal to India included the seemingly reasonable step of procuring an Indian visa in Kathmandu. In the U.S., one can obtain this visa over the internet. Or in Bangkok, where I had just been a month earlier, any competent travel agent will go to the embassy for you and return with an authorized stamp in a few hours. In Nepal, however, it takes at least nine days, seventy dollars, and four separate, in-person trips to the Indian Embassy, a bureaucratic black hole where dozens of long-lost travelers lie mummified inside a giant cocoon of red tape.

Although I arrived as the embassy opened, a line of thirty people already stretched ahead of me—which may not seem so bad, until you consider that the office is only open for two-and-a-half hours per day. Visa hopefuls who do not make it up to the window within this time frame must return the next business day and queue all over again. And that's just to get the first ball rolling, a telex to your home country requesting your criminal history and psychological profile. Once the telex comes back, you shuffle through the queue again to submit your application and then return a third, teeth-gnashing time to pick up the visa itself. Of course, there is no guarantee you will actually reach the window on any visit, so the process can go on indefinitely.

Knowing none of this on my first go, I went in and attempted to decipher the instructions, which had been painted across one long wall by an illiterate tagger. Failing to comprehend the finer points of the slow-motion Visa Conga, I slid past the line and hovered near the window— merely to ask a question, of course.

"Excuse me, Miss," a polite and beautifully accented voice from behind me intoned, "over here is the end of the line."

For a second I thought I was receiving cosmic interference from Iñigo Montoya, the swashbuckling, dulcet-toned avenger from *The Princess Bride*, one of my all-time favorite movies. I turned around to defend myself and there stood a Spanish boy with curly dark hair, a laughing mouth and skin like melted caramel. Carlos was twenty-six, a fellow Sagittarian, very charming, eloquent, funny, sexy . . . very Spanish. After talking nonstop for two-and-a-half hours in line and then whiling away the afternoon in historic Durbar Square, we launched a Torrid Love Affair.

"You are in Spanish Territory now," he declared on our first night together. "And I'm very sorry, but nobody is allowed to emigrate until they are totally exhausted."

It was an epic TLA—and my standards are quite high. I've spent the past two years happily single, traveling as much as I can while I have the opportunity, and perfecting the TLA as an art form. A time limit, I've learned, is a key ingredient. Nearing the end of his eleventh-month trip around the world, Carlos would leave for India as soon as his visa was ready, spend two weeks there and then fly from Delhi to Barcelona on December 9—which also happens to be my birthday. It was an immovable deadline, at least to a pragmatic Spaniard. So we had nine days, the minimum time it takes to get an Indian visa in Katmandu. Luckily, his practicality seemed limited to travel logistics. In between lovemaking sessions and trips to the Indian Embassy, we ran laughing through the streets of Kathmandu and snuggled together in the cold foggy nights under the long shadows of the Himalayas. The Thamel district swirled around us like a rowdy carnival; the antique city of Bhaktapur provided an enchanted backdrop for our whirlwind romance. Kathmandu pulsed beneath us like a beat, a heady aroma, an exotic and inescapable rhythm. "*La Maja*," my Latin lover whispered, stroking my cheek, "*La Maja*."

On Day Six of the TLA, Carlos very sensibly pointed out that I was going to India anyway, so why should we not go together, at least as far as Varanasi? Nobody seemed to be *totally* exhausted yet; a few more days couldn't hurt . . . and I did try, but flights were limited and the ticket I bought turned out to be for the wrong day, due to a clerical error. Upon further investigation, the air ticket he held was also for the wrong day—a different wrong day, bought from the same incompetent clerk. After a dramatic confrontation at the travel agency, Carlos finagled a spot on the waiting list, but getting two people on the sold-out flight seemed impossible, star-crossed. And he had a timeline to keep. So, I cancelled my useless plane ticket and we parted in Kathmandu, with vague regrets. I didn't say goodbye—I never do. Instead I imparted the classic traveler's send-off, "See you next time," although we made no plans or promises to meet again. He left for the airport, one hand grasping the hapless clerk by the shoulder and the other clutching enough baksheesh to get himself on the flight, come hell or high water. The Spanish are a determined people.

La chica sola once again, I set off by bus to the south of Nepal, where an army of evil protozoa invaded and waylaid me for several days. It's a good thing I didn't go with him, I consoled myself, bedridden and miserable in a jungle infirmary. When I recovered and finally made it to Varanasi almost two weeks later, Carlos was long gone but an email awaited me. "I miss you, you know," he had written. On the supposedly sold-out flight, there had been an empty seat. One. Right next to him. *A sign?* He expressed regrets about not trying harder to take me with him. "But, what's done is done," he conceded, ever practical. He was now on the other side of India and would fly home from Delhi in a few days. He invited me again to visit him in Barcelona; he truly hoped I would keep in touch. I replied affectionately, noncommittally. Overall, I was quite pleased with our encounter, though vaguely dissatisfied with the "practical" ending.

I called my friend Kavita from Varanasi. I planned to visit her at her home in the north, but the journey would take three days and I whined to her, "I don't want to get stuck spending my birthday alone in some godforsaken bus stop." Generously, she offered to meet me halfway. We would celebrate my birthday in Delhi, and then travel to Palumpur together. It wasn't until I confirmed the train ticket that I realized I would be arriving in Delhi on the 8th. I knew Carlos would also be in Delhi on the 8th. It would be his last day in India, the end of his eleven-month voyage around the world. I was sorely tempted to email him—how could I be in the same city on the same day and not tell him? But there was a high chance he wouldn't check email in the next twenty-four hours, and I would not risk casting shadows of regret or guilt across the final day of his journey, no matter how much I wanted to rewrite our ending. What to do? I decided to leave it to fate.

After fourteen hours on the train, I arrived in Delhi, searched out a cheap room in the traveler's ghetto of Paharganj and accepted a friendly cup of *chai* from the old Major who ran the guesthouse. Then I rang Kavita again. She was on her way and would meet me the next morning, on my birthday. Now, sleep-deprived but wide awake, chores accomplished, my thoughts returned to the Spanish boy. I could picture him here perfectly...sitting in a café, perusing his guidebook, and making plans for his momentous last day. He could be here right now, on this very street. Stupid, I chided myself; there are 13 million people in Delhi, not counting tourists and homeless beggars. He could be anywhere. What are the chances, really?

Walking down the crowded Main Bazaar, dodging rickshaws and gingerly stepping over the mounds of cow dung and rotting garbage clogging the street, I paused at a clean, sunny "German" bakery. He likes pastry for breakfast. Out of the corner of my eye, I glimpsed a young man sitting alone in the front window, his back turned toward me. Thick, dark curls hung past his collar. Holding my breath, I turned to look . . . but no, it wasn't him. I went in anyway, sat in the rooftop garden with a coffee and croissant, and considered how to spend my day alone in Delhi. First, I needed to find a replacement AC adaptor; a power surge in Nepal had zapped mine, turning my precious laptop into dead weight. I paid the bill and left my coffee half finished, resolving to head downtown and look for a computer store. Walking back up the alley, I passed another German bakery—ubiquitous in this part of Asia. Unable to help myself, I peeked in. And there in the window, with a cup of *chai* in front of him and his Roman nose buried in his guidebook, was a bent head full of curly dark hair . . . a Spanish boy. MY Spanish boy. I began giggling uncontrollably and had to stand in the street for a full minute to collect myself. Then I walked in and tapped him on the shoulder.

"How did you…what *are* you, some kind of witch?!" he blurted out, the look on his face a mixture of wonder and sheer terror. After recovering from the initial shock, he graciously invited me to spend his last day in India with him. I happily accepted and we picked up right where we left off, with a slightly different Asian capital in the background. A few minutes after midnight, delaying just long enough to give me a birthday kiss, Carlos had to leave for the airport.

"Come to Spain with me!" he begged, only half-joking.

"Run away to Kerala with me!" I countered, half-serious.

We talked about a rendezvous in Spain, perhaps in the spring.

"I hope you will come," he said, "but!" His face became serious, Iñigo-like.

"But what?" I asked.

"Don't come to Spain until you're ready to change your life!" he ordered.

"What? Why?"

"Because when you come to Barcelona, you will fall in love. You will settle down and stop wandering. So do everything you need to do first, then come. Don't come just to break my heart."

As he got into the waiting cab, he worked up the nerve to gulp, "When...?"

"When the time is right, I think we'll see each other again." I predicted with a mysterious smile.

Speechless, the no-longer-sensible Spaniard just nodded.

"Your fate will always find you," I promised him, "if the door is open."

˞ ˞ ˞

Laurie Weed is a freelance writer, a traveler, and a willing slave to Fate.

ℬ ℬ ℬ

The Time of the Three Musketeers

In a Paris neighborhood, the author treads the same streets as her childhood hero.

Modern St.-Germain is lively and prosperous, yet it is the seventeenth century, still strangely present here, that establishes its character, and I find that to understand the way it is now, it's necessary to try to see it as it was four hundred years ago. Since I have come to live on the Rue Bonaparte, the street that lies between Les Deux Magots—Hemingway's hangout—and the church of St.-Germain-des-Prés, I find that, beside the shades of Sartre and Piaf, there is another crowd of resident ghosts who urge themselves forward for recognition through four centuries. They include the Musketeers—d'Artagnan, Aramis,

Athos, and Porthos; four queens—Catherine de Médicis, Marguerite de Valois (or "de Navarre" after her marriage to Henri de Navarre, later King Henri IV), Anne of Austria, and Marie de Médicis; the sinister Cardinals Mazarin and Richelieu; Kings Louis XIII to XVI, many Henris; and numberless other misty figures in plumed hats whose fortunes and passions were enacted among the beautiful, imposing buildings of the seventeenth century still in this neighborhood. Theirs is the spirit that prevails today, and that moves me most.

In a way, I had been prepared for them. My particular connection to this Parisian neighborhood started in childhood, thousands of miles away; I was over thirty before I ever actually saw it, but when I did, I knew it well. Not that I was one of those good little French majors that had grown up dreaming of France, not at all. I am here by accident.

It was a Francophile librarian at the Carnegie Library in my hometown of Moline, Illinois, who placed in my hands, when I was nine or ten, the works of Alexandre Dumas. I read all the ones we had, in translation of course, and that is where Paris and I start, with my childhood reading of *The Count of Monte Cristo*, *La Reine Margot*, and, above all, *The Three Musketeers*. Was it this early passion for Dumas that preordained that I would someday live five minutes' walk from where the real d'Artagnan lived, almost on the spot where the Musketeers fought their duels, and, above all, where the romantic queens of legend, Marguerite de Valois, then Navarre, and Anne of Austria actually trod, four centuries ago?

If only we could recapture how we read when we were children, burning with interest, with breathless excitement, unwilling to put down our book to eat or sleep. Often we can remember the actual circumstances

of where we were sitting, the injunctions of our parents
to come to the table, or go to bed. My memory of my
childhood literary enthusiasms is still vivid. I read *The
Three Musketeers* on a visit to my beloved maiden Aunt
Henrietta, in Watseka, Illinois, the time I nearly died.

I had come down with polio, or at least that's what doctors now say in retrospect it probably was. I don't know
where my parents had gone, or where my little brother
was, and I can't remember if the doctor was called. My
childless aunt had not had much experience with childhood illness so was less, rather than more, concerned than
she probably ought to have been; I had never been so sick
and never have been since, with a raging fever, and a head-
ache so horrible I can almost still feel it, an unusual thing,
for pain is usually impossible to remember.

So my recollection of burning with reading fervor has
a certain explicable component. Literally feverish, I lay
on the sofa in the Victorian parlor or in bed for days with
the enthralling story of d'Artagnan, Athos (my favorite), Porthos, and Aramis. They were alive for me—the
Musketeers, their leader M. de Treville, the wicked Milady,
the handsome Duke of Buckingham, and the beautiful
Anne of Austria, she whose reputation was saved by the
frantic voyage of d'Artagnan to England to replace her
missing diamond studs before her husband Louis XIII
could find out that she had given them to France's enemy,
Buckingham. Would she get them back in time to wear
them to the ball where she had been commanded to appear
in them?

Hindsight changes one's reading of Dumas. I see now
that I must have been given an expurgated children's edition. In Dumas's original versions, both Anne of Austria
and La Reine Margot were free with their favors, but I got
none of those innuendos as a child, and was surprised when

rereading these books as a grown-up to find how rather explicit they are. I had never understood, for instance, that the villainess Milady de Winter seduces d'Artagnan and takes him to bed. Rereading *The Three Musketeers*, it is bound to seem today that the seventeenth-century ideas of masculine behavior—touchy honor, always being insulted, challenging each other and dueling mindlessly, rather like the young bulls in the children's book *Ferdinand the Bull*, seem, in truth, rather silly, and we should hope that men have evolved, mostly, at least in some societies. In many other places, it seems, they are still going through their Musketeer phase. Still, who would change the swash-buckling movie version? Even though I could not accept Gene Kelly in the role of d'Artagnan, (the earlier Douglas Fairbanks was better), Lana Turner entirely suited my view of Milady, and Van Heflin, Keenan Wynn, and Gig Young made a handsome trio of Musketeers. I would see all the films over and over. Meantime, I believe I was saved from serious complications of polio by my determination to remain conscious and finish Dumas's wonderful novel.

How do we account for the curious thrill we feel standing in some ancient space, in the presence of some historical artifact, thinking of all the things that have happened here? It is surely something about immortality, the idea of one's self connected, by being present, to the past and to the ongoing. It was only a few years ago, before we came to live in this apartment on Rue Bonaparte, that one day when I was riding the 69 Bus down the Rue du Bac, I noticed on the building at number one, a plaque that said: "Here stood the house where lived Charles de Batz-Chastelmore d'Artagnan, captain-lieutenant of the Musketeers of Louis XIV, killed at the siege of Maestricht in 1673, immortalized by Alexandre Dumas."

Perhaps that little plaque more than anything else brought home the realization that Dumas's immortal characters had once been living people who may have conducted their sword fights on the very spot where I was standing, in what were then the fields called Prés aux Clercs, a favorite dueling ground lying around the abbey of St.-Germain between our street and the Rue des Sts.-Pères. Of course, I knew there had been a historical d'Artagnan, but I had not until then experienced that particular sense of the reality of past events that sometimes strikes with special force. Would having known when I was a child that I was reading true history have increased my excitement and pleasure at Dumas's tale? Now it was hardly possible to feel any more pleasure and excitement than was mine to have my childhood favorite again before my eyes.

Perhaps not everyone remembers the engaging young d'Artagnan of Dumas's creation. Like the hero of a fairy tale, he sets out from his native province of Gascony for Paris, to make his fortune, with only a few possessions— his father's blessing, a powerful ointment, his sword, and a yellow horse. His naïveté and cheerful, trusting nature endear him to the fierce Musketeers as much as to us. Is it too much to say that an American may find something of ourselves in his wonderment as he confronts the big city for the first time?

We know quite a bit about the historical d'Artagnan. He was born in Bigorre, in southwestern France, became a Musketeer (an elite corps of the king's soldiers) and rose in their ranks, married a rich widow, Charlotte-Anne de Chanlecy Damas de la Claixe (or Clayette), and he himself had become rich, as a captain in the Guards. In 1659 the couple moved to the corner of Rue du Bac and the Quai Voltaire, in what was later called the Hôtel Mailly-Nesle; "hotel," meaning large private house, the word not having at all the connotation of inn or lodging we think of today. Apparently they were not entirely happy, or not happier than most couples.

Something is known of the d'Artagnan household. Charlotte-Anne brought a dowry of 60,000 livres worth of property, 24,000 livres in cash, and furniture worth another 6,000, large figures for today. Their wedding, at the Louvre, was attended by the king and Cardinal Mazarin. D'Artagnan was an important and trusted minion of Louis XIV—entrusted, for instance, with the arrest and delivery of the disgraced minister Fouquet to prison, after Fouquet had had the bad judgment to build a château more beautiful than Louis's.

An inventory of the d'Artagnan property shows them to have had two carriages—one for four people, one for two, the former lined in green velvet with four mirrors and green damask curtains, the latter upholstered in red damask. It was a time when wealth was ostentatiously displayed, and it was important to display it.

They had a servant called Fiacrine Pinou, and a big table and armoire in their kitchen on the ground floor off the court. Upstairs, an antechamber and a big room was hung with tapestries of leaves and flowers—*milles fleurs*, the prettiest ones. These hung also in the bedroom on the second—third, in the American sense—floor. In the bedroom, too, a huge bed hung with striped silk was placed behind a screen, and on the wall a mirror and a portrait of Anne of Austria, the queen who d'Artagnan served so well. There was a lovely view of the Seine. D'Artagnan himself had lace gloves, silk stockings, a bathrobe lined in green satin, two swords, one with a gold handle...

Many buildings like the one the d'Artagnans lived in contained "apartments" from a very early time, that is, apartments in today's sense of an individual habitation consisting of a number of rooms in a larger building containing several such habitations. The d'Artagnans lived in such an apartment. It is also said this style of dwelling—with many families in one building—existed in ancient Rome; anyway, it is still the dominant way of living in Paris. Our building on Rue Bonaparte has four families, counting us.

The French novelist Boris Vian recounts that, in 1765, one William Cole, an Englishman, took lodgings on Rue Bonaparte. His rooms were in what was then called Hôtel d'Orleans "in the Fauxborg [sic] St.-Germain," which was probably across the street from us at number thirteen, looking over the gardens of the Duc de La Rouchefoucauld, descendants of the author of the famous *Maxims*, a hundred years after his death. (The spelling "fauxborg" gives an idea of the original meaning of the modern word "faubourg," false city, or suburb.)

Cole was accompanied by a pushy French servant, for he had found that it was "absolutely necessary to have a French Servant, as [my] own knew not a word of the Language." Unfortunately the fellow was drunk and threw in "impertinent" observations that ruined Cole's experience of going around to look at churches and tourist sights, much as we do today. He was also cheated by his landlady. English mistrust of the French (and vice versa) such as Cole's goes back eternally, or at least to 1066.

Cole described his rooms in some detail, giving a glimpse of what these apartments were like, and though this was a hundred years after d'Artagnan, much would have remained the same:

> "…up two Pair of Stairs; it consisted of a little
> Bedchamber for my Servant in the Passage or little
> Gallery to my own,…a Bureau, half a Dozen elegant &
> sumptuous elbow-Chairs & a Sopha of the same Sort,

of the Tapestry of their own Manufacture." He also
had an "elegant & lofty Crimson Damask Bed…raised
on a Step," and red tiled or oak floors, heavily waxed,
and in general was very comfortable.

For the d'Artagnans all was to end badly; after they had
two sons, d'Artagnan began to stray, Madame to nag, and
then to have him followed. Finally they parted. She went
back to her country place to live, and d'Artagnan went off
on the king's wars. Eventually, he would be killed in battle,
serving his king.

But he lives on. There are descendants today who can
claim him as their ancestor. And most days as I walk up to
the Boulevard St.-Germain past the church, a man is standing, dressed as a Musketeer, perhaps d'Artagnan, with
leather baldric and high-heeled shoes, shoulder-length hair
and wide plumed hat that he is quick to doff while bowing at any queenly figure who comes near enough to toss a
euro in his little cup.

🙢 🙢 🙢

*Diane Johnson is a bestselling novelist, travel writer, and essayist.
She holds a Ph.D. from UCLA and is the author of the National
Book Award-nominated* Lesser Lives *and* Le Divorce, *as well
as the acclaimed novels* Le Mariage *and* L'Affaire. *This excerpt
was drawn from her nonfiction work,* Into a Paris Quartier. *She
currently divides her time between Paris and San Francisco.*

MARIA FINN

ൟ ൟ ൟ

Learning to Dance

A New Yorker in Havana meets a son of Changó.

*J*t's said that the national pastime in Cuba is seduction. Seduction is a language and a way of life on the island. It's in the walk, the scant clothes and sweaty glow in the tropical heat, the waves crashing around the couples kissing on the Malécon at dusk. It's even part of the religion. The Virgin del Caribe del Cobre is Cuba's national patroness, but in the magical Santeria religion, she is Oshún, the Cuban Aphrodite. She's a black, voluptuous, rumba-dancing goddess who can be generous or ruthless. She's no virgin. She has many lovers, and her favorite is Changó—the Santeria *Orisha*—or god—who is a skirt chaser, irresistible to women, his domain virility, passion and dancing. Before I left for Cuba, a *santero* in Brooklyn warned me, "You're going to be swept off your feet by a son of Changó. Be careful."

I left a cold, gray New York, and just four hours later arrived in Havana, where flamboyant trees created umbrel-

222

las of bright orange flowers shading the streets from the sun burning in the open blue sky. Billboards with portraits of a young Che Guevara, the handsome face of the revolution, lined the road that led to the center of the city.

Perhaps because it has been off limits for so long and because of its reputation for vice and revolution, this city is not only decrepitly beautiful, it is also infinitely alluring. Driving through Havana, I didn't see the interiors—the crowding, the frustration and poverty, but rather the gorgeous facades, the orchids dripping from trees, the banana and mango fruit ripening in the side yards. When something is dangerous or sexy, Cubans use the word *candela* to describe it. Literally it means fire, but it's used as a warning, or as a stand-in for a long, low whistle. Havana is *la candela*.

The men in Cuba know a thousand ways to tell a woman she's beautiful. *Rica, guapisima, lindisima, sabrosa*. Delicious, the prettiest, the most beautiful, the tastiest woman in the world. They look you up and down like they are starving. It doesn't matter who they are. Bus drivers, the soldiers on the corner, the man selling oranges, the fish monger, the family man, the professor, the artist, the immigration officers. If you are a woman in Cuba, you are an object of their veneration and desire.

One afternoon, I caught a cab and my driver, a middle-aged woman with sparkly brown eyes asked me where I was from—then paused for a just a moment and asked, "Are you married?"

"No."

"Do you have a boyfriend?"

"No."

"Have you met a Cuban man yet?"

"No."

"¡*No me digas*!" she yelled. (You don't say!) She immediately pulled a U-turn, eyes darting between the road and me in the back seat. She explained that she was taking me to her house to meet her son. She went on to list how handsome, nice, reliable he was. And he can dance. Oh, can he dance.

Startled, but charmed at the same time, I finally talked her out of it, and explained that I was running late to meet friends at Casa de la Música in Miramar to go dancing. Most mothers want grandchildren and a family around them. If they happen to be a pipeline to American dollars, all the better. Unfortunately, the suspicion that a Cuban man's interest might be due to money or a way to the U.S. never really leaves. She eventually agreed to take me to my destination, all the while expounding on her son's virtues.

This music venue, along with the other Casa de la Musica in Centro is considered the best place in Havana to dance to salsa, but at night the prices to enter run between $10 and $20 dollars apiece. Cubans can't afford this, unless they're out with foreigners, so the lines at night look like some bizarre Father's Day outing, as the couples all tend to be young Cuban women and much older European and Canadian men.

But during the afternoons, the crowd was all Cuban, gyrating their hips in the popular dance move known as *la batidora* or the blender, and shimming their shoulders, known as *el tembleque* or the shake. Before the band started, hip-hop music piped through the large hall. Soon the aisles filled with dancers and the musicians had the entire room on their feet. When the band started playing, the whole place swung into motion, the dance floor filled and Cubans jumped up to dance on their chairs. Women jumped on stage and were grinding their hips with the musicians while they played.

I was mesmerized by the frenzy taking place around me.
It was as if in that moment, the last remnants of my repressed
upbringing were mocked, and trampled. I realized that this
unabashed dancing is how life is meant to be lived. Here,
sexual inhibitions, shyness, shame had no place. I excused
myself from the people I had come with and started dancing
with the Cubans, feeling like I had arrived.

The favorite Orishas, those who granted money, love,
power, and wisdom had been painted in bold colors—
cerulean blue, crimson red, sunflower yellow—on the
white-washed alley walls of Callejon de Hamel along
with portraits of poet and revolutionary José Marti. At
the end of the alley a crowd hovered around the rumba
performers. We all strained to see as the musicians played
the drums and gourds, the singers sang songs of the countryside, romance, and the nature gods, and the rumba
dancers started their coquettish movements toward and
away from each other, rolling their shoulders, lowering
their upper bodies down to the ground. A woman glided
away from a man; when he feigned lack of interest, she
moved closer, rolling her shoulders to beckon him, until he
responded and started circling her again. The dance had
all the primitive elements of mating, and the complexities
of seduction.

Along with virility and womanizing, Changó's domain
is dancing. I noticed several men wearing the red and
black beads of Changó and watched them dance, their hips
and shoulders rolling, working up to the crescendo in the
music like a storm brewing.

And in this concentration of men, the *piropos*, or compli-
ments, flew:

"Why are you walking alone when you could be walking with me?"

"If you cook the way you walk, I'll even eat what sticks to the pan."

"If beauty were a crime, you would deserve life in prison."

"There's going to be a lottery tonight and you have all the tickets."

Cuba is a nation of sons of Changó.

I had first learned to dance salsa in New York at Angel Navarro's Mambo Unico. Early on, attempting to follow the instructor's directions and trying to move my hips and shoulders at the same time made me look like I had some sort of nerve disorder. I stood behind the other dancers, avoiding the mirror while concentrating on the instructor's feet, and counting to myself, "One, two, three, pause, five six, seven, pause." Eventually I added a styling class where our instructor showed us exactly how to extend our fingers, shift weight from one hip to the other for a hip roll, and then hold our arms stiff and shake one shoulder and then the other into a shimmy.

The instructor's steps, her grace and utter control were not so much taught to us, as would be the case with trained dancers, but rather we imitated them, standing behind her in rows, counting, repeating, mimicking over and over. With time, my dancing became a little more certain, a little smoother. I realized, each time I learned one of these provocative moves—a hip roll, a shimmy, a body roll, I was shedding some of the shame I had acquired growing up in my Catholic community, where women's sexuality was not celebrated—quite the opposite. I learned from the women who danced salsa a new kind of sexy—not a size four, but a showing what you got, of being seen and loving the eyes on you, of wearing tighter clothes regardless of your size, and knowing that dancing well is the most seductive thing in the world.

Out at the salsa clubs in New York, every dance with a partner was like a twelve-minute relationship, and you can tell a lot about a man from one dance—whether he watches out for the other couples on the floor and doesn't spin you into people, if he makes you feel good, touches your back in a way that is respectful, but firm, so you know to trust your lead. An excellent lead can make you feel so good—beautiful, desired, protected, important—that you forget it's merely an activity, a metaphor at best, two people creating an illusion. Sometimes I wanted this feeling so badly, I pursued it off the dance floor, and into places much less safe.

While open to having fun in Cuba, I was determined not to fall in love. I had a bad habit of getting involved in complicated, long-distance relationships, or choosing men who weren't fully available in one way or another—those in love with their art, their expeditions, their ex-girlfriends, their own pain. The last thing I needed, I reminded myself, was a relationship with a Cuban, and to have Fidel Castro, the U.S. government, and Miami's exile community between us. I wasn't going to do it. Maybe some dancing, but really, I was just going to have fun.

Then I met Rafael. He drove a taxi *particulare*, a black-market car that helped supplement the meager rations and pay he got for his official job as an industrial mechanic. When I first met him, he ushered me towards his blue Lada with a cracked windshield.

We haggled over the price for a ride. He started at five dollars, but I countered with three. I hadn't been able to find a book of matches or a lighter since arriving in Cuba, so we agreed on four bucks and he'd throw in a box of matches. I had plans to meet people from school at a concert of *trovadores*, scheduled to play that night. I had it in my head that they were performing at La Casa de las Trova, in Centro Havana.

In illegal taxis, the rider always has to sit in the front seat, apparently so the police won't know we're a fare. I always chatted with my cab drivers, but with the young men who gave me rides from my neighborhood, this seating arrangement always made the ride feel like a date. Rafael and I made polite conversation. He asked, in rapid, blurred Spanish, where I was from. I told him New York, and I was teaching a class in Cuba for three weeks. He looked young, so I asked if he was a student.

"*Ya*," he answered with a wave of his arm.

This meant he had finished school already. Potholes in Havana are formidable, and I sucked my breath in a few times as he jerked the steering wheel to miss them.

"*Tranquilo*," he said. "I'm a good driver."

He spoke Spanish so difficult to follow that I had to ask him to repeat things a few times, and then just gave up and pretended that I understood what he was saying. He told me that he had a very intelligent dog, and when I asked why he thought the dog intelligent, he explained, but I couldn't follow his Spanish and ended up just nodding. He seemed to be making sideways glances at me on occasion, which also somehow made him seem young, particularly in a country where men will stare you down in the most shameless manner.

Rafael stopped to ask directions several times, and I got the sense that he had no idea where we were going.

"Do you have a map?" I asked him.

He clutched his steering wheel. "There are no maps in Cuba," he said. "*Tranquilo*."

We finally found the club down a dark cobblestone street. The locked door and silent block made me apprehensive. It appeared closed and I didn't want to get left there alone. I didn't know what to do.

Rafael got out of the car and knocked on the door for me. He yelled to see if anyone was inside. No one answered, so he asked if I needed to go back.

I shrugged and said, "I guess so. How much?" I hoped the ride back would be free.

"Four dollars," he answered. He opened the passenger door for me.

I looked down the empty, dark street. I had lost all negotiating power.

Rafael drove me back to my apartment, pointing out that I didn't have to walk up the hill, implying this was some sort of bonus.

He stopped in front of my house and as I prepared to get out of the car, he asked, "You want to go dancing tomorrow night?"

He seemed shy and confident, young and worldly at the same time. He didn't have the aggressive swagger and stare many Cuban men use on women as a form of seduction. He was also gorgeous. Over six feet tall, broad shoulders and light brown skin, a chiseled handsome face with a child's easy smile. I would come to learn that he had Chinese, African, and Spanish ancestors. He had a gentle courtesy about him, a casual way of opening doors. He was sexy, but also safe, I thought. And he'd probably make a good dance partner.

"Sure," I said.

"What's your name?" he asked.

"Maria."

"That's a beautiful name. It's my favorite," he said. "It's my mom's name."

Later, when I looked at my calendar, I saw I had been supposed to meet people at The National Theater the night of that cab ride with Rafael. Since they were a group of *tro-vadores*, I assumed the venue to be Casa de la Trova. At first I just thought this an unfortunate mix-up on my part, but later I came to think of it as serendipitous—or fate.

The next night I was nervous heading off into the night with a cab driver. I wondered if it was safe, and I suspected he was just inviting me so that I'd pay his way into an expensive disco. If things went bad, he knew where I lived; he could stalk me. But motivated by the thought of a great night of dancing, I took a deep breath, put on a sundress and dancing heels, and walked down the hillside to his blue Lada.

We drove down the main artery, calle 23, where the young people cruised and transvestites in tight skirts and high heels kissed the cheeks of gorgeous young mulattas, then through Centro Havana, where salsa and rumba spilled from the apartments, over balconies down to the streets where children played baseball with rocks and men gathered around dominoes. Then finally we drove along the Malecón, tasting sprays of salt water as they crashed against the seawall and splashed through the car's windows. Couples lounged here at dusk—some sat next to each other looking out over the water, others faced traffic, holding hands and staring in silence, some lay on their sides, heads up on elbows, almost touching.

We finally arrived at a beautiful spot just below the old Spanish fort, El Morro, that sits on the bluff across the bay from the port of Havana. The beam from the lighthouse reflected off the ocean, and waves splashed the old cannons still standing guard over the city. Inside the small, cement bar, Cubans danced to salsa, hip-hop, reggae, and American pop. We found a table in the corner and Rafael wiped off a seat for me to sit on, then went and bought a few rum and sodas. I tried to give him money, but he refused it. This made me feel a little guilty about my earlier worries, but it also made me less suspicious of him.

I watched the dancers gyrate, mesmerized by the way they moved: they could isolate two different body parts and move them both differently—one to the clave, the other to the drums, carrying on two conversations at once, as if their bones were fluid. Partner dancing here was not about counting steps and executing complicated turns. A woman wedged between two men, butt thrust out, was grinding, simultaneously, with both; one woman balanced herself over a man in a chair, performing something akin to a lap dance; I saw a man swivel down to the ground, his head level with the crotch of his partner.

We sat at the table sipping our rum and colas, the music too loud to talk much. I tapped my foot and swayed a little to the music, sending off the signal that I would like to be asked to dance. I had a feeling he worried about my dancing. Here, as in New York, having an inept dance partner made you look bad, and nobody likes that on the dance floor. I could almost sense him mulling this over. Foreigners dancing in Cuba aren't a pretty sight. There's usually this sort of bouncing we do that has no connection whatsoever with the music.

When Rafael finally asked me to dance, in a smooth maneuver he tucked us into a corner where we wouldn't be noticed. We started dancing, a little awkwardly at first, then found the music.

"You can dance," Rafael said, and we moved to the center of the dance floor. "*Que rica.*"

He smelled nice, like soap and aftershave. He put a hand in the small of my back, and we joined our other hands. He was a perfect lead. Gentle yet in control. He had an excellent sense of rhythm; he kept the beat, and wasn't boring. He changed from stepping to turn patterns in response to the music. He maintained a polite distance and at first, it was just about the dancing.

We danced the *casino* to Cuban *son*, then a merengue, and as the night wore on we were less reserved. The DJ switched to *reggaton*, and we started grinding our hips like the rest of the bar, my back to him, his hands on my hips, then facing each other; then we were back to more demure stepping and turning in sync with one another from a distance.

We danced on, a film of sweat covering both of us, stopping just to swallow mouthfuls of sweet rum and cola. Cuba's sexual freedom was exhilarating. And while our verbal conversations had been difficult due to language, this one was perfect. We had our own private conversation, humorous, amorous, bold, and then timid, expressed with our hips, shoulders, and feet.

At 4 A.M., the bartenders herded us out onto the old stone patio, where the spray from the sea cooled us and the few lights still glowing in Old Havana sparkled in the distance. Leaning against the damp rock wall, under the rustling palm trees and starry skies we kissed for the first time.

꿏 꿏 꿏

Maria Finn has written for a number of publications, including The New York Times, The Los Angeles Times, Audubon Magazine, Saveur, Metropolis, Forbes FYI, *and* Gastronomica. *She has edited two literary anthologies,* Cuba in Mind *and* Mexico in Mind *and is working on a memoir about learning to dance and how this led her to Cuba where she fell in love and married her cab driver, Rafael. She has lived and worked in Alaska, Guatemala, Spain, Cuba, and has traveled extensively in Latin America. She now lives in New York City.*

KATHLEEN SPIVACK

From the Window

Adrift in the City of Light, at least they had each other—sort of.

I am sitting here, ready to start my next project. Something to do with love, the endless subject. Is there any other? Refugee love.

Yes, I'll write about love tonight, although love itself hides in the night, a gray ghost, aching a little at its own longings and memories. I'll write about love while a woman sits up in bed, pressing a thin cambric nightgown against her breast, her hands fluttering aimlessly, wondering what happened and where it all went. And will it always be like this, her tight throat, and it will, it must, its vacancy etching itself into her body forever. Refugee love, always adrift, looking for a home that in the end turns out to be merely temporary, a nonexistent resting place, forever lost.

Love sifts itself through the stubbed out ashes and the whiskey glass; that void that maybe only a mother

234

filled—and that was long ago. There is no end to it, this wanting.

My friend Leonard and I had escaped from home. Home was mundane, everything we wished to forget. But as yet we had found nothing else to replace it. We had come to Paris in search of exotic love. Now we were spending the afternoon together, disappointed.

We were sitting in Raspail Vert, a cafe in the angle of the Boulevards Raspail and Edgar Quinet, right around the corner from the cemetery of Montparnasse, where Sartre and Simone de Beauvoir lie buried in state, side by side, surrounded by their lovers. It was *our* cafe, our usual Saturday afternoon meeting place. Leonard was, as usual, complaining, expecting me to be rapt with attentiveness. He was complaining of his lack of sleep.

"I hear them, I hear them every night." Leonard reached out and touched my arm for emphasis. He wanted to make sure I realized the gravity of his complaint. "They just carry on. For hours. Do you think I'm mad?" This was obviously a rhetorical question.

"Every night!" Leonard exclaimed with more fervor. "They always start just after I've finally managed to fall asleep." His lips pouted in an aggrieved expression. "It's not as if I'm a prude or anything."

It was hard not to laugh. I tightened my mouth and looked deliberately straight ahead, assuming what I hoped would appear to be a neutral listening posture.

We were both trying to scrape a mossy living from the underside of Paris, and we met every couple of weeks or so to compare notes on home and how it was going for us here.

Leonard came from my own hometown, a small New England village, once a mill town, where there's nothing to do since the mills closed down except scrape a rocking chair back and forth across a sagging front porch.

We'd never go back there. There was nothing to go back for. *A Hundred Years of Boredom*, in grainy black and white. *Peyton Place* and worse. An anywhere deserted mill town at its worst.

One might think that we left this rundown village, with its empty red brick buildings brooding along a polluted river, long ago. We'd certainly tried. Leonard majored in French at Middlebury College, so strong was his longing to change his cultural identity.

He wanted to travel as far away as he could from his dad's furniture refinishing business, where he spent every summer during high school and college dipping bureau drawers into five different types of acid baths, then pocking them with a little BB gun sort of thing to make them look "antique." In the middle of the endless din Leonard and a few other lucky souls produced what looked like worm holes, which supposedly upped the value of the maple-veneered furniture. Leonard spent his free hours standing there, while he patiently rubbed the layers of chemical varnishes onto the pocked wood surfaces, as if rubbing green sheen onto the dollar bills that would pay his Middlebury college tuition.

Leonard dreamed himself down and out in Paris but he was forced to stand, dripping with sweat in the middle of his father's factory, the boss's son, contemplating his future and being told he was lucky to have one after all. Each summer while he worked, wrinkling his nose against the greenish odor, his mouth moved silently, shaping itself around the refined syllables of French.

"Authentic," was the word his father used, imagining that what was "authentic" could be acquired just by knowing how many layers of oil and varnish to apply.

Leonard and I longed to be "authentic" but no matter how many layers we painstakingly applied to ourselves the rough edges refused to be concealed. We rubbed and rubbed against the curly finishing edges of a scornful Paris, but it did not take: we carried on us the ever-present oil of our despairing origins. So here we were, making do, trying to plaster on a bit of "artifice" instead.

The product of too much reading—as much of it on the job as possible—Leonard had come to Paris wanting to wear ruffled sleeves, appreciate beauty, and sip fine wines. He enrolled in the Sorbonne. He spoke French daintily and carefully, rolling each syllable as if it tasted creamy as the creamiest French brie, coating his mouth with it and swirling it around with his tongue before allowing the sounds to leave. He affected an exaggerated nasality to the language: I, who spoke less well, timid and stumbling, found it extremely aggravating to listen to him. Braying, I called it to myself, "The man is positively braying."

Leonard, like myself, was no more authentic than his dad's doctored Maine furniture, or rather, he was, no matter how hard he tried not to be, an authentically American not too bright young man looking for French love to transport him to another plane.

His French was too loud. He had long blue-jeaned legs, curly blond hair, and a naive open American look. He did not have working papers, which would allow him at least to work in the country. He did not have charm. He took course after course, taught English to refugees more lost than himself, and prowled the quays and the English language-speaking Shakespeare and Company bookshop in search of nothing. He wrote his parents that he had decided never to come home.

But now, sitting in the cafe, it seemed that what he had come to want, more than anything, was an uninterrupted night of sleep.

"I can feel it, when they're about to start, you know, a feeling in the air. It wakes me up, even before they've done anything."

Leonard lived in an undistinguished narrow street, one of the many dark and charmless streets behind the Gare St. Lazare. The idea of travel permeated the neighborhood. The ungainly train station, the metro, the pushy buses: everyone was hurrying somewhere in Paris looking busy, going to meet friends, and going to other more intimate assignations.

But Leonard and I, on our two separate sides of Paris, me, near the Gare Montparnasse, the train station that served the vibrant south, and Leonard, behind squat St. Lazare which brooded northward, seemed to be going nowhere fast.

You can gather I did not exactly take to Leonard. So why did I agree to meet him? Desperate me, I simply could not face another lonely moment, skulking by my concierge, asking permission to use the shower. I felt myself become a cringing shadow of the boisterous girl I was, temporarily permitted to look at glamour in French, but through a window only. While the Parisian women flitted by, sure of themselves and light and slim and sexy, I slunk along the streets, went to futile job interviews, and avoided people's eyes while at the same time wanting desperately to be noticed. "Ah, Mademoiselle. . . ." But that never happened. Hence Leonard.

Now, for want of anything better to do, I sat across a table from Leonard in a smoky cafe and listened to him carry on. My mother would have been happy. For we had more in common than we liked to admit.

In our Paris, the City of Light, we huddled, each in our small dark old *chambre de bonne* for which, as Americans, we were exorbitantly charged. We longed at night for something to happen to us here, something of a transforming nature, something that would justify our separation from language, home, and family. We longed to be lifted out of and saved from ourselves. Meanwhile, we wrote faithful optimistic lying postcards home to our families.

"Do you ever think about going home?" I asked him, as I always did during our inevitable Saturday afternoon get together. As always, we had tried not to meet, pretending we might have other plans until the very last minute, when it was obvious we did not. Self-scrutiny was the malady we shared, more sickly and more secretive than any other addiction that could bind us.

"Never," Leonard insisted.

"Always," I said. "All the time. Anytime anything goes wrong." My parents were constantly writing me, wondering when I was going to come home. Had I found a job? And what was I looking for anyway? And did I know that my sister, their favorite, the more compliant one, had just become engaged?

"Don't look back," Leonard advised. "It won't do you any good." His parents were writing him too, I knew, as well as telephoning my parents across town anxiously with subtle unspoken questions.

"Typically insensitive," I thought of Leonard's pragmatic statements. As if one could just shut off a nonproductive thought. I stuck the end of my tongue into a wobbly filling, testing it. It twinged as it trembled a bit. "Don't you ever think of just going home? Giving it up here?"

"Well," Leonard amended, softening. "Sometimes I do. I really do."

I thought fleetingly of what would happen if I had to deal with a dentist's visit in a language I hardly knew. We were both silent, contemplating the endless gray rain that fell like a curtain beyond the triangle of wet wool and dampness where we sat in front of small overpriced bitter

cups of coffee while the *chink-chink* of kids playing pin-ball
not far from our small round table grilled our nerves. We'd
soon be out in that rain, huddling against it as we beat our
way back to our own lonely rooms.

Leonard leaned forward, expecting me to tune out
everything else and focus only on him. He demanded my
attention. He always seemed both sophisticated and impossible to me. My jaw was sore; a toothache coming on, I was
now sure of it.

"That horrible couple. I can't bear them," Leonard complained. "Just knowing they're there." Miserably he looked
out at the rain. "My window's too close to theirs. I never see
them, you know. I just hear them going at it. Howling, moaning. Sometimes it starts at one A.M. Sometimes at four in the
morning. Sometimes they do it both times. Or more. Just
when I've managed to fall back asleep again. I just dread going
home," he concluded drearily, expecting me to be fascinated,
sympathetic, and horrified at the same time. He watched my
reactions with a little triumphant gleam in his eyes.

There was silence as my tongue found the filling again,
and Leonard and I both contemplated our own loveless-
ness. My filling was definitely wiggling. "Howling!" I
thought. "Moaning!" My heart quickened at the thought
of such expressed passion, but I tried not to show it on my
face. I envied the couple their unrestrained joy. Like cats
in heat, yowling, or like the raccoons that screamed with
their mating all through our spring New England nights,
screeching and clawing in the mysterious tree crooks of our
moon speckled back yard at home. "Howling!"

I thought of times I too had howled with passion—only
one whole aching year ago. And the pain of that remembered twining took my breath away. That cavity, that
exposed nerve, the shaky patch-up job. I tried to talk to
myself to get my head on straight again. There are some

things that are better left unproved. But words like *rutting*, *passion*, even *love*, as in *Our Love Story*, and the dark stone of the words "It's Finished" set up a clanging in my head.

"We're finished. It's over. It's your fault. It's my fault." These words began to pound like a heap of stones roiled by dangerous waves against a black shore. "Over and done with. Finished." I felt faint.

"Yes, howling," Leonard said, apparently not noticing my reactions. He was too caught up in his own. His hands were twisting on the table, his knuckles sharp against the marble top. "Finally they quiet down and I fall asleep again, but then it starts all over again. In the early morning. It's just too much! I've thought of writing them a note."

"Writing a note?" I tried to follow him.

"Maybe you think I'm crazy." He leaned forward, pursing his lips again. "But I'm sure they're trying to drive me crazy." He didn't speak of what he meant by this, but suddenly, abruptly, drove his disobedient hands farther into his pockets. He leaned forward, almost hissing at me. "There have been mornings I've just stood outside the door of their building, waiting to see who comes out. Sometimes I stand there for hours. Each couple that comes out the door makes me wonder, is that them? Could they be the ones? But I've never found the courage to actually speak to anybody."

The cafe was hot, stuffy, and suffocating. I didn't want to hear any more, but Leonard could not stop. He shrugged his shoulders, hunching closer to me. Spittle was forming at the edges of his mouth, and he licked his lips quickly. "You see, its the fact that their window happens to be close to mine. Why the hell can't they shut their window, for God's sake?" He writhed in irritation, his hands twisting in their pockets, and he crossed his legs, drawing into himself farther in the small corner in which we sat hemmed in by the table.

"Well," I suggested, "why don't you shut your window then?"

"No!" he answered sharply. His voice was petulant, aggrieved. "Why should I be deprived of air just because some French people don't have the courtesy to shut their window? Why can't they be more considerate? If they want to make love that's their business, but why should I be forced to listen to them? Sometimes I think they are doing it deliberately, putting on a big show just to wake me up."

Once every two weeks or so was more than often enough to get together with Leonard, this boy my mother was so eager for me to date some fifteen years ago. In our town his family, as owners of the furniture factory, were considered practically aristocratic. I thought morosely about how much I disliked him. My tooth hurt, but he wasn't the least bit interested in hearing about anything except his own stupid obsessions.

"I really want to say something to them," Leonard continued. He was white with agitation. "Something like 'Monsieur, Madame, please *s'il vous plait*, do you realize you are disturbing others: *me* for instance.'" He continued in this vein in his mellifluous French, relishing each sword-thrust word with a courtier's pleasure. "I implore you, you are deranging me with your extreme manifestations of passion. You are disturbing the peace and tranquility of our ancient quarter. Please, Madame, Monsieur, take your ecstatic pleasures elsewhere." Smiling maliciously, he went on like this for quite a while, clearly enjoying an uninhibited French rant.

I was too weak-willed, too lonely, too pathetic, too depressed, to get up and leave, which, I was aware, would have been the normal response. France, as well as a disastrous love affair, had destroyed all my initiative. Wasn't that why I had come to France in the first place? Now

I would pay for it, sitting in dreary corners with dreary people like Leonard. Forever. A forgotten old maid.

When Leonard finished he was winded but triumphant, having managed a whole theatrical speech, just like the ones we so often strained to hear from the top-most balcony of the Comedie Francaise. Perfect eighteenth century French learned from textbooks and novels. French never to be heard nowadays in the actual modern day beleaguered country of France, where they cursed in incomprehensible argot, and spoke a kind of backward slang-language as fast as possible.

Leonard stopped and looked at me. He had tears in his eyes and a vein of frustration bulged in his forehead. "Goddammit," he panted, still irritated.

"What good would it do anyway." I felt comfort was what was wanted, and reached across the table to take his hand, which he reluctantly snailed out of his pocket.

I thought of a couple I once knew in Paris; I saw them as if from faraway. After lovemaking, after the dark shuddering cries that rose, inevitable as if from somewhere beyond the two entwined bodies, the man went to the open window, looked out, lit a cigarette. Later, after he had stayed there looking out at the darkness for a long, long time, as long as he could manage, he came back to bed again, lay down, sighed, and turned his back on the woman waiting beside him. Nevertheless, toward morning, as if despite themselves, their passion crept up and engulfed them once more.

Love. Loss. *Loss* entwined itself around the *Love* word like a vine about a tree, like two inseparable parasitic concepts.

"Why don't you move, then, find another flat?" I suggested, knowing that it was impossible. I was getting more than fed up with Leonard and occupied my tongue by probing the back hinge of my jaw again. That tooth was throbbing awfully.

"Don't be ridiculous," Leonard answered. "I intend to stay right where I am and teach them a lesson." Aha! At this thought Leonard looked hopeful. "I intend to confront them." His New England Puritan sermonizing background was rising instantly and hopefully to the challenge. "It would teach them to be more considerate." Cotton Mather meets Hester Prynne.

Leonard pounced on this new idea in a prissy schoolteacherish way. He was pleased with himself now, at least for the moment, as pleased as if he had actually told off the invisible lovers. He had forgotten we were in France, the land of ostentatious making-out. Whatever the French do behind closed doors, public spaces such as streets, metros, restaurants, etc. are their real theater and a good show is properly appreciated. No better public theater than a bourgeois quartier in the middle of the night.

Tonight, awakened by the vociferous lovers, Leonard would grind his teeth in quiet rage again. "So what, Leonard, your time will come," I started to say, answering his unspoken desperation. Then, "Never mind," I added, as he looked at me a bit too intensely.

"We will never be French," I wanted to say. "And we will never love each other, no, never like that."

"Like what?" he asked, his pupils flickering as if startled. His hands were quiet now, his crossed legs at peace.

It was dusk and still raining. Did we expect anything else? A darkness overcame me as I feared that in fact I would never love anyone again as deeply as I once loved Pierre. I could never explain this to Leonard, and he was silent as if locked in with his own memories and fears as well. Why were we hanging on, both of us, loveless in this strange country?

"Come on, tell me," Leonard said, "Do you think something's wrong with me to be so upset about this?"

"I don't know," I evaded his eyes, eyes that were zooming in on me in fixed recognition.

Together we looked for the waiter who had been hovering somewhere in the dingy reaches of the cafe near the darkening bar, wiping dishes with a soft stained cloth.

"The bill please," we called, like any Americans anxious to be overcharged, to pay nervously with money we still didn't really understand, to say "thank you" obsequiously in a strange language.

The rain was pelting down outside and the street gleamed with wetness as in a dark French film. We'd all seen those films where the Gestapo rounds up all remaining suspects, and in which the hero and heroine turn round a corner, surprised to find themselves alone together and stare into each others' eyes, panting with the chase. Those heart-stopping films where suddenly, impulsively, the protagonists decide to run away together forever, linking their futures. They push their collars up and duck their heads under the unforgiving downpour. The clatter of pursuing footsteps fades. Everything is understood. It has all happened in an instant, it has already taken place in their charged mutually hypnotized stares; trapped animals, held in the searchlight of obsessive love. Yet in the midst of this, in the film they somehow find the time to stop and share a cigarette. The rain is still coming down like blazes, poured by some second assistant flunky from a bucket at the corner of the set. But the heroine looks dewy and beautiful nevertheless. Her marcelled hair is perfect. There is a pregnant silence, She turns her eyes toward him and waits, her eyebrows perfectly arched, because it appears he has something important to say to her. Something he has been carrying inside him for a long time. He turns up his collar and takes a manly breath.

But between Leonard and me there would be no intensity when we parted, each to go in separate directions, outside the Raspail Vert. There would be no panting breathless moment, with desire moaning just below the surface. No hotel, with its understanding concierge looking indulgently at the entering young couple, no waiting softly lit room, no inviting bed in black and white, no window overlooking the sleeping city, with only the glowing tip of a cigarette to silhouette the darkness. We were too irritated with each other for reasons we would never be able to articulate.

I was worried about finding a dentist, and how I was going to be able to manage such an ordeal in French. Leonard hurrying homeward would still be twitching with suppressed frustration, to be rekindled when night fell. As we parted, between us the cold unpleasant rain clanged down like a heavy velvet curtain. The words "The End" scrolled slowly over our unrealized hopes. Paris fluttered like a tipsy backdrop. Having already come so far from home, we would always remain strangers, especially to each other.

❧ ❧ ❧

Kathleen Spivack is the author of The Break-Up Variations; The Beds We Lie In *(nominated for a Pulitzer Prize);* The Honeymoon; Swimmer in the Spreading Dawn; The Jane Poems; Flying Inland; Robert Lowell, A Personal Memoir; *and a novel,* Unspeakable Things *(the latter two are currently with an agent). Published in more than three hundred magazines and anthologies, her work has also been translated into French. She reads her work throughout Europe and the United States, and gives theater performances and master classes. In Boston, she directs the Advanced Writing Workshop, an intensive coaching program for advanced writers. For the past sixteen years she has been Visiting Professor of Creative Writing/American Literature at the University of Paris.*

❧ ❧ ❧

Climbing Back to Childhood

Be it in the Philippines or New Hampshire, you'll find her perched high on a limb.

"Lucía Misa, get off that tree right now!" About forty feet below stood a screaming Sister Divina Gracia, arms flailing, fists clutched, her white robe flapping wildly like a scarecrow's. The sultry tropical wind lifted and erased some of the syllables of her frantic hollering. Pretending not to hear at all, I climbed the coconut tree higher and higher, my breath meeting the open sky. At last, as my foot found the last step nailed by the locals to harvest the ripe and scrumptious coconuts, I savored the scene from my tower, my arms wrapped around the rough trunk as it swayed gently. Peering through the palm leaves, I could see the whole island—the vast ocean dotted by fishermen's home-made *bancas*, with their bamboo outriggers looking like summer dragonflies, a kaleidoscope of thatched roofs, grass huts, children playing *piko* (hopscotch), local lasses flirting with some fishermen, women hanging laundry by the well. Inland, a group of water buffalos stood half-submerged in the muddy lagoon of the inlet, and a field of bright green rice stalks glowed, where four farmers were sowing a new batch of seedlings. Across the Pacific, on the horizon, lay a group of hazy blue mountains bearing the familiar faces of fertility goddesses.

"Yes, sister, I'm coming down now," I yelled back.

Trees were a large part of my childhood in the Philippines. I can still see the giant mango tree in our family's front yard, which I loved to harvest. Occasionally I would have to shoo away Paeng, our neighborhood Tom Sawyer, on the ground looking up, trying to catch a peep of my underwear. And then, years later, there was this grand matriarch fig tree I discovered in the isolated woods of Harbin Springs, California. A group of lovely blue jays and I feasted on a whole bunch of its luscious figs that day. However, it was in the smooth wide arms of the colossal *balete* (rubber tree) that I indulged in the most daydreaming, cuddled up in her bosom.

It is no wonder then that both my children turned out to be natural climbers. Cristina climbed out of her crib when she was nine months old. As she grew older, I would find her on top of the kitchen counters, balancing on the edges of stairways, challenging me in every conceivable precarious situation. She was obsessed with monkey bars, and she would run up and balance herself, hands free, in every park we ever visited. My friends marveled how I stayed calm and confident, and never held her back. But years later, as she left her tomboy ways behind to blossom into a true lady, her climbing days were left behind.

I first handed this legacy of serious tree climbing to my son Eric when he was a robust five-year-old. We used to spend weekends and summers in the wilds of Long Pond, New Hampshire. The kids were barefoot and free—scampering up and down the boulders of the lake's many small islands, swimming alongside a family of loons, or building hideouts in the woods.

Coming back from windsurfing one brisk blustery almost autumn day, I found Eric in the middle of the lawn, looking quite forlorn.

"What's the matter, honey? What happened?"

"My kite just flew off—look, Ma, that great big pine tree ate it!" He was fighting back the tears.

"Don't worry, honey, we can go get it, let's get the canoe!"

His eyes lit up with delight as we paddled backwards against the wind, across the lake. It was his idea that we could get there paddling in the same direction as the strong currents. Parking the canoe, we easily spotted the snarled kite—bright red with its long yellow tail flying wildly from the very tip of the tallest pine on the edge of the lake.

"O.K. Eric, let's go get it. Now I want you to really listen. Here is how to climb a tree." I demonstrated. "Test a branch with one foot, put all your body weight on it, to make sure it can hold you. If it is brittle and weak, it will snap under your foot. So make sure while your weight is on one foot, that both of your arms are holding on to another branch overhead—in case the branch under your foot breaks. Then find another branch to step on with your other foot. Let's do it very slowly, one step at a time."

As it turned out, I did not even have to teach my agile Eric. We found ourselves quite easily on the pine's gnarly, but oh so fragrant, top branches. As I reached out to set the kite free, the wind picked it up and off it landed on to the next pine!

"Oh well, Eric, we have to go down now and you get to climb the other tree. This time, you lead!" He managed to retrieve his kite, and later that night created a beautiful painting of the whole rescue scene.

As he got older, Eric would be more and more daring with heights. I remember Cristina and her father yelling at us, from the handrails of the Grand Canyon. I had followed my son to the very edge of a huge boulder, and sat quietly with him, legs dangling, the two of us mesmerized. Wave after wave of rich red, bright magentas, gold and yellow, and deep purple rays gradually blanketed the awesome mountains. We never said a word. I know the most secret regions of our being met in that sunset.

We went on to climb many mountains around the East Coast. People were always startled to see this boy dancing down the rocks, light-footed and carefree, and his mama tagging at his heels.

Because I was in the import business since the kids were born, I was able to take Eric and Cristina home for our annual Christmas vacation. For many years, Eric and I trekked the many textured mountains of the Philippines, while Cristina preferred to bask in the sun, in the white sands of the beautiful Philippine beaches.

Upon Eric's graduation from high school, it seemed just the perfect time to pursue our common dream: a rock-climbing adventure in Moab, Utah. Three days of private lessons in canyoneering, rappelling, belaying—learning the skills of technical climbing! On the first day, Dave, our good-natured guide, gaped with wonder as my goat ascended higher and higher, as if he had been waiting all his life for this moment. Neither of us needed too many instructions on the basic techniques, but still, there was plenty to learn. With our newly acquired confidence, climbing shoes and harnesses, Eric and I had finally arrived at the real challenge of climbing. It was no wonder that one of the first things he did as a freshman in college was to organize a climbing club.

Recently, I was back in the tropics, once again climbing a coconut tree. I could almost hear Sister Divina Gracia as clearly as on that class excursion to the provinces four decades ago. But this time I was in Boracay Island on a private beach resort, with a couple of friends from Boston.

Eric joined me there for five days, and we hired a *banca* to take us around the islands. Each day found us hanging over the edges of limestone cliffs, peculiar to this pristine part of the Islands. On one of the mountaintops, I brought up a concern that had been tugging at me, carefully questioning Eric about his youthful competitiveness and total daring. "Don't worry, Mom, I am past showing off. I know where to stop." He sounded like a wise old voice from somewhere familiar. An image suddenly came back to me in a flash. Back in the seventies, I was on a midnight hike with a friend in the Cordilleras, said to be the sacred mountains of the Philippines. As we reached the ledge of two connecting mountains, a gigantic, white mountain goat suddenly perched itself on the mountain's highest point. He stood just a few feet from us, blinding us with his brilliance. A few seconds later, he leaped into the abyss, as if flying with his pair of graceful blue horns. I shivered with awe. The next day, when questioned, the locals told us that there were no mountain goats in the area and it was obvious to me that an old spirit had appeared before us.

By the end of March, I was finally home in Long Pond and thinking about climbing. I looked out the window and there stood my majestic white pine. A pillar proudly reaching almost three stories high, its glistening needles in full regalia. Last fall, I had cleared the dense brush to build a Zen garden. And what a king of trees I had found—great for climbing!

With the help of my friend Victor, I secured a rope around its lowest branch. Victor told me to be careful, as he helped me get started up, then drove off on an errand. Wearing my red suede climbing shoes, I started the ascent. First, I had to clean the huge trunk of all the brittle twigs around it. There were just enough large branches for every step up. I held on to the branches overhead, just as I had taught Eric, over a decade ago. Inhaling the perfume of the pine needles as they gently brushed against my cheeks, I was ecstatic. Now I could see rooftops. My house looked like a gray tool shed. Here I was, seeing the eagle's view of the pond, as I reached for the highest branches! It is always on top, I thought, that the world dissolves. Stillness. Immensity always softens, humbles. Here only sounds exist. "*Crack*!—a sunflower seed being split by the feisty chicka-dee-dee. *S-c-r-a-t-c-h,* the bright yellow goldfinch scrapes the fresh lichen off the maple tree next door. "*Uak uak*!" Three black and white hawks, circling the juniper tips. Sharp cries with each smooth glide. "*Trtt-trtt- trttt*" the woodpecker drills away, up and down the trunk of the still leafless silver elm. Beneath all these springtime melodies, the mad roaring of the rain-fed springs playing a steady bass. I was dazzled by the swirling diamonds dancing on the water's surface as the sun shimmered and melted the scattered ice and snow. A glossy black form slithered out of an opening in the snow, an otter enjoying its lunch, its whole body undulating with every gulp. Slap. It slipped back, and the snow closed in to fill the hole. God's chronicle for the day.

Victor was back, digital camera in hand. . . . "*Donde estas, chica*? Where are you?" I pushed apart the pine needles. "Here! I'm here!"

"Wait until Eric sees this," he chuckled. "I'll email him tonight!" That night, I got a call from my son, "Mom, I can't believe you climbed that tree—it's over seventy feet high! Don't you climb that tree again—it's too dangerous! Mom, do you hear me??"

ჯ ჯ ჯ

Lucía "Ciay" Misa, a native of the Philippines, moved to Boston Massachusetts in 1978. She set up an import company with her mother as her supplier and partner. After twenty-four years, she retired from her business, and divides the year between her lake home in New Hampshire, and her yoga retreat center on Palawan Island, Philippines. She has two children, Cristina and Eric. Visit her website at www.talikwas.com.

JENNIFER SIEG

ℬ ℬ ℬ

The Cuy of Cooking

One country's pet "Ginger" may be
another's culinary delicacy.

*I*n the main cathedral in Cuzco, the Inca capital of
Peru, hangs Marcos Zapata's richly painted mural
of The Last Supper. True to the biblical story, Christ,
surrounded by his devoted disciples, is sharing the bread and
wine of his last earthly feast. And there, in the middle of the
table, in the traditional place of honor for the main course of
such a significant meal, lies a guinea pig—whole, skinned,
and waiting to be devoured.

Guinea pig, or *cuy*, is a delicacy in Peru, attentively raised
in the mud houses of Peruvian families and reserved for special occasions. I first heard about it from my sister-in-law, a
first generation Peruvian-American, who related the story of
visiting a pet store as a young girl and being mortally embarrassed by her mother's lip-smacking amidst the cedared

aroma of the "Small Household Pets" aisle. Intrigued, but not quite convinced that Jenny's story was entirely true, I decided to find out for myself on a recent trip to Peru.

The day before I left New York for Lima, I called my best friend Christine for a quick bon voyage chat. Christine and I had known each other since we were seven, when she would put Ginger, her beloved pet guinea pig, in a pink "Let's Go Barbie!" convertible and take her for walks around the neighborhood. Over the next several years, Christine would raise and breed at least a half dozen generations of guinea pigs, until a one-eyed mutant appeared, convincing her that too much inbreeding had weakened her prized pigs' genetic lineage. The cyclops and his brothers and sisters were abruptly whisked off to the nearest Petland, but Christine has never given up her devotion to guinea pigs. It goes without saying that she was horrified when I told her of my quest to locate my own Ginger, or at least her distant cousins, in the culinary halls of Peru.

Sure enough, there it was on nearly every menu I surveyed: oven-roasted *cuy*, baked *cuy*, and the ambiguous "Peruvian-style" *cuy*. My traveling companion Carolyn, who sported what can only be described as a stomach of iron and a palate of steel, couldn't wait to get her hands on some. I was a bit more hesitant.

Two days before our brief visit was set to conclude, Carolyn and I found ourselves seated at an outdoor café in Aguas Calientes, a small, seedy village nestled in the shadows of Machu Picchu. Carolyn didn't even need to look at a menu. Without a moment's hesitation, she happily ordered her *cuy* and waited expectantly for me to do the same. I couldn't. The thought of eating something that closely resembled a sewer rat made my stomach turn, and I wondered if I would even be able to look at the thing when it reached the table. Disappointed by my lack of adventure, I meekly ordered the *ceviche* and waited apprehensively for our food to arrive.

Forty minutes later, Carolyn and I were still nursing our Cusqueña beers, waiting for the waitress to appear with lunch. I couldn't help but wonder what was taking so long. I couldn't erase the mental picture of the chef retreating to a living room above the restaurant, selecting a squeaking guinea pig from a cage packed with his brothers and sisters, bashing him over the head with an iron skillet, and skinning him even as he eked out one final squeal. My stomach tumbled again and I quickly excused myself and darted toward the bathroom, carefully averting my eyes as I passed the open kitchen door.

Shortly after I returned to the table—only slightly less green—the waitress arrived carrying our lunch. When she laid the *cuy* on the table, Carolyn's smile quickly melted to a grimace. There, staring back at us from his bed of limp lettuce, was a charred, furless guinea pig. My own sheer misfortune caused the waitress to set Carolyn's plate with the poor animal's head facing me, and I found myself looking past huge, razor-sharp teeth into the dulled eyes of the dead animal.

"You have to take off its head!" Carolyn shrieked.

Through my own stupor of mortification, I felt slightly confused. Hadn't she seen the mural? Didn't she know this was what it was going to look like? Then I realized I had the luxury of being rational—I wasn't faced with a plateful of dead rodent for lunch.

I had to hand it to her, though; Carolyn was a trooper. She bravely picked up her knife and fork and began sawing away at the overcooked little body. My *ceviche* sat untouched as I studied her in awe.

"How do you eat these little suckers?" She muttered to herself as she hacked away at a hind leg. When she finally wrestled a morsel free, she popped it in her mouth with nary a second thought.

"So?" I asked.

"I'm not sure. I can't get enough meat to distinguish its taste."

My stomach flipped again. I looked down at my plate of food and thought how nice it could have been, knowing full well I'd never get a forkful anywhere near my mouth under the current circumstances.

"They have to take off its head!" Carolyn pushed her chair back from the table, knocking a skeletal yellow cat off the empty chair next to her as she scrambled out of her corner seat. "How do you say 'head' in Spanish?" she shot over her shoulder as she headed toward the kitchen.

"*Cabeza*," I answered softly, preoccupied with the thought of how beheading the little beast was going to make it any more appetizing at this stage.

Carolyn returned to the table a few moments later, head-less guinea pig in tow. The chef had even been kind enough to hack it up into more manageable pieces, no doubt inwardly laughing at the culinary naiveté of this blond gringa. She again took up her rigorous sawing, trying desperately to carve free an edible chunk of the dark purple meat. But her efforts were futile; the guinea pig seemed to be all bones. In my mind's eye, I was blinded by a ghostly vision of its enormous front teeth and its lifeless eyes staring up at me from the table. Carolyn, too, must have been suffering some post-traumatic stress from the initial sight of the poor thing, for she finally dropped her knife and fork in exasperation and hastily excused herself to the bathroom.

When she came back to the table, my friend was a sickly shade of olive. On her way to the bathroom, she had had the misfortune to catch a glimpse of our waitress gnawing on the abandoned head of Carolyn's lunch.

"See, this is how you eat it!" the waitress exclaimed as she took a colossal bite out of the guinea pig's cheek, making sure not to miss out on its succulent right eye.

Carolyn's decision had been made. Realizing she had neither the patience nor the inclination to make a meal out of the charred rodent, she deserted the carnage on her own plate, picked up her fork, and reached across the table for mine.

ૐ ૐ ૐ

Jennifer Sieg's travels have taken her around the globe, where she has come face-to-snout with some the the world's most exotic culinary delights. As in Peru, she generally relies on her traveling companions to serve as gastronomical guinea pigs.

LONIA WINCHESTER

꙾ ꙾ ꙾

The Truth About Eyes

Travel takes many forms, travelers many paths—some
more difficult than others.

*T*he way I walked saved my life. I held my head straight,
never looking over my shoulder. I took confident steps,
never stopping to ask directions. My pace was even and my
face was happy, even laughing. For nearly five years of my life
I walked as though I belonged, and so I moved freely among
people who wanted to kill me.

During the Nazi occupation of Poland I was a Jewish
girl in my early twenties who could and did pass as a Pole.
I spoke Polish without Yiddish inflections and, most important, I was lucky enough to be born with the typical Polish
blond hair and blue eyes. In fact, I thought of myself as not
only a Pole but a Polish patriot. However, in the eyes of
Catholic Poles I was a Jew, not because of a belief in the doc-
trines of the Jewish religion, which I had not, but because
of having been born into a Jewish family and having an

258

identification with the Jewish culture in which I was raised. This was enough to assure my death if I was found out. And my danger was less from the Germans than from the Poles I considered my people.

It was September 1, 1939 and the mechanized German army with its powerful air force invaded Poland, which implausibly threw cavalry against the Nazi tanks. Two days after the fighting began, the polish government ordered all able-bodied men to leave Lodz, the textile manufacturing city where my family lived at the time. It was said that the Germans were expected to be there in a few days and would probably take away all the men they could find. Eleven of my family—brothers-in-law, uncles, and cousins—heeded the order and went to Warsaw, presumably to join the army. For two days Lodz was almost empty and without a city government.

In Lodz, conditions for Jews were bad from the start of the occupation. A large part of the population was either German-born or descended from Germans and many of them were Nazis even before the war. When the war began, they carried out sabotage and subversion against the Polish authorities. When the German army came, they openly sided with the invaders and were given positions administering the city. They petitioned Hitler to annex Lodz to Germany and he lost no time doing that. They called the city Litzmannstadt, after a German general from World War I. The German soldiers drove around the city in open cars looking for orthodox Jews. When they saw one they would cut—or more often tear—off their beards. Many Jews were expelled, sent out of the city in open railroad carriages during a winter that was the harshest in living memory. Those Jews who were allowed to remain, as well as many from the surrounding towns, were driven into a ghetto, the first one created in Nazi-occupied territories.

It took the Nazis only two short weeks to overwhelm the obsolete Polish military. The swift defeat came before my relatives could be inducted and given uniforms and arms. So they, and some other men they knew, began to walk home from Warsaw to Lodz, eighty miles to the southwest. Too tired to walk all the way, they stopped in Brzeziny, a village about seven miles short of the city and sent a young boy ahead to hire a horse and wagon to carry them the rest of the way home.

While they waited for the boy to come back, someone in the village shot through a window and wounded a German soldier. Immediately the Germans surrounded the village and herded together everyone they could find—men, women, children, Jews and Gentiles—including the eleven men of my family and their companions. They forced the terrified people into a large barn and barricaded the door. Then they set fire to the barn. The German soldiers stood outside and shot anyone who managed to escape the burning building. There were no survivors, but an account of the events came to us from the boy who was sent for the horse and wagon. He had returned a little while later, while the fire was still burning, and learned from one of the soldiers what has happened.

The boy, who had worked in my sister Bronia's knitting factory, came to her house in Lodz and told her of the massacre. The news sent our family into a state of shock. Mercifully, my mother was spared the pain of this tragedy (and almost certain death in the concentration camp), having died three years before. Bronia and a friend traveled as quickly as they could to the village where the atrocity took place to try to find the remains of her husband. They searched through what was left of the barn. Among the remains, Bronia found a photo of her four-year-old son Kuba, one of her husband's documents, and some charred fragments of the sweater she had given him for the journey. She collapsed in a faint, overcome with grief and shock.

Bronia and I had had some difficulty understanding each other, but when her husband was killed we drew closer together through our common concern for her son. Two days after the massacre she asked me to take Kuba to Warsaw, saying she would follow in a few days, and then, after tending to some business, go with me to stay in Nowy Korczyn, the small town 120 miles southeast of Lodz where we had grown up. I readily agreed to do this, being glad for a reason to leave Lodz—where there were already a great many German soldiers. At that time, almost everyone in Poland expected the war to last only a few weeks, after which it was supposed the soldiers would leave. But, as a Jew, I instinctively preferred to be as far away from the Nazis as possible. Yes, I wanted very much to leave Lodz.

The bus trip from Lodz to Warsaw was a nightmare. Ours was the last bus to make the trip before the Lodz ghetto was closed, and it carried twice as many people as its normal capacity. Bronia had to bribe the driver to let Kuba and me get on. Most of the passengers were returning to Warsaw after having fled from there only days before with their vital household goods. Now they were carrying back the same suitcases, bedding, and cooking utensils, jamming as much as possible into the overcrowded vehicle.

In Warsaw, Kuba and I stayed in the large apartment of the in-laws of my younger brother, Fischl. This family had become very rich supplying yarn to the many knitting factories in Poland. By the time we got to Warsaw it had been bombed and looted by the Germans. The shops were out of bread—the staple food of eastern Europeans—and people were dying of hunger in the streets. But, while most of the population had nothing, those with money, like our hosts, had everything they desired. For Jews, however, this comfortable living would not last long.

Four days after Kuba and I arrived in Warsaw Bronia came, and three days later she and I left for Nowy Korczyn, leaving Kuba temporarily in the care of Fischl's wife Frania. Bronia had arranged for the three of us to stay in Nowy Korczyn in the home of her in-laws, but since they hardly knew me, she thought it best to take me there herself and get us settled before bringing Kuba. By this time, all of our family had left Lodz to return to Nowy Korczyn. Jews all over Poland were leaving the cities for small towns, where there were no ghettos, more food was available, and where they thought they would be relatively safe. Too late they learned that the Nazi tactic was to drive the Jews from the villages into towns, pick up the Jews living there, and move all of them to cities for transportation to the death camps.

I became restless because I was anxious to do something against the Nazis. I made enquiries among my friends and learned that there was an underground resistance group in Nowy Korczyn that consisted of politically involved young people who hated the occupation. I joined the group with enthusiasm. There were fifteen of us, eleven boys and two girls from middle-class Jewish families, some of whom I knew from my childhood, and two Gentile Poles. While there were many underground resistance groups throughout Poland, as far as I know, ours was the only one with Jewish members. Our group included mostly idealistic leftists who put their principles above cultural distinctions, personal safety, or gain.

The older members of the group impressed on us that the most important thing was to be able to trust each other without reservations. Nevertheless, we took the precaution of meeting in cells of four or five members, each time in a different location, and with each cell not knowing about the activities of the others. We used assumed names and never mentioned our correct ones. We discussed ways of escape in case of discovery, and each one was assigned a place outside of town to stay overnight if necessary. To increase security, these arrangements were changed from time to time.

I couldn't help feeling a thrill of excitement about being a part of this clandestine activity, but after my experience in Lodz and Warsaw, I knew that even in a small town not yet closely regulated by the Germans it was a deadly dangerous game. Anyone in the group could have denounced the rest of us for a reward. In fact, when I came back to Nowy Korczyn after the war ended to look for the surviving relatives, I found out that one of our Gentile comrades in the resistance who had given shelter to a Jewish boy later denounced him to the Gestapo. His reward was probably a pint of vodka or a pound of sugar. However, after the terrible murder by burning of eleven men of my family in the village near Lodz, I felt such rage against the Germans I was very willing to risk my life to hurt them.

One of our fellow conspirators was a young Jewish boy named Josef. He was very talented in graphic arts, though he was untrained. He volunteered to forge identity cards—the Kennkarte issued by the German occupation authorities—for the members of our group. His forgeries were excellent, seemingly undetectable. Many people would have been very happy to pay large sums for these vital documents, but Josef never charged his friends anything. I remember the day when each of us in the resistance group was issued our forged Kennkarte, and along with it a small white capsule of cyanide, a substance that was then more cherished than gold. The Kennkarte gave us Polish identities; the cyanide ensured instant death in case we were ever caught by the Germans and tortured for information. It turned out that there weren't enough capsules to go around. I refused my share of the poison since in those days I was young and felt very strong and sure of myself—certain that I wouldn't break under torture if I were captured. Today I have a more realistic view of human nature in general and myself in particular. At least initially, the cyanide capsules served the good purpose of bringing home to our younger members a sharp awareness of the mortal danger they were courting.

The Kennkarte stated that my name was Leokadia Wawrzykowska (my real name was Lea Lukawiec) and that I was a Catholic Pole from Opatowiec. I was sure that I would be able to carry off this false identity because of my knowledge of Catholicism—learned from my childhood friend Stefa—and, most importantly, my traditional Polish looks. Also in favor of my being able to move safely among the Poles was the fact that with my hair in braids and my small size I still looked like a schoolgirl, although I was twenty-one-years old when I joined the resistance.

Getting started in our underground activities was difficult, as we had no money to buy arms and supplies. We couldn't expect to get these from the Polish resistance units and we had no better luck with the Jewish community. The Jews who initially survived the Nazi invasion were generally certain that the war would be over in a short time. Because of this belief, even though they were constantly harassed, they preferred to wait out the war rather than get involved in resistance activities—which were not only highly dangerous but could prolong the military occupation. The Germans encouraged their belief by establishing a Judenrat (a Jewish administration) in each town and city,

through which the occupation authorities could make their
ever-increasing demands on the Jewish population.

No one then could even imagine "The Final Solution,"
and the Jews, especially the wealthy ones, counted on brib-
ing the Germans to ensure their safety. We went ahead
with organizing our group anyway and used whatever
money we could lay our hands on to support our operations.

Josef was not only a generously talented artist, he was
mechanically skilled as well. Out of bits of electrical parts
he had built a shortwave radio that enabled us to listen to
news from abroad.

Every evening, two or three members of our group would
gather in an inside room of an abandoned building to hear
forbidden BBC broadcasts with news of the war. But even
though we were often confused about the facts, what our
hearts felt without question was the change in the announcer's tone as the weeks passed and the German war machine
advanced all over Europe, with one country after another
taken over by the Nazis. There was no need to know the
language to sense the BBC announcer's growing despair.

From the larger resistance groups we got leaflets that
contained information about the German attacks and
explained how to avoid German strategies for discovering resisters. Since my typical Polish looks made me the
least likely of my co-conspirators to be noticed in a crowd,
they picked me to act as the group's courier. My job was to
ride the trains from town to town disseminating information, raising money, and encouraging others to organize
resistance groups of their own. I did this with the leaflets strapped to my belly under my blouse. This meant,
of course, that if I ever aroused enough suspicion to be
stopped by the police or soldiers and searched, I would certainly be tortured for information and then shot. Nor was

my assignment unusual at the time. There were probably hundreds of such couriers working with resistance groups all over Poland.

To give myself the advantage of knowledge in these highly dangerous forays, it was important to have as much information as I could get about the place I was going to visit next. While traveling there on the train I would always try to strike up a conversation with someone from that town—while carefully concealing my purpose and identity. Traveling anywhere was very dangerous; Polish police or the Germans were always checking the documents of people on trains and asking questions. Almost every day some new regulation was passed concerning identification papers, so it was impossible to know for sure if the documents that were O.K. yesterday would be good today. I was lucky—somehow I managed to avoid this kind of trouble.

When I arrived in a new town, my first and most difficult problem was to find accommodations—either no one wanted to risk letting me stay with them or I considered it too risky to stay in places I was offered. Sometimes I had to visit two different towns in one day because I was unable to find a place in the first one where I could avoid the curfew and stay overnight without having to worry.

In the towns I visited I was especially exposed while recruiting. I never knew if the person I was talking to would turn me in to the Germans, but I had to take chances if I was to find other resisters. My "good looks" (not looking Jewish) helped me to play roles and make contacts. For each contact you take on the identity of the person who, you sense, the other person thinks you are. In those nerve-racking times I had to repeatedly invent and "become" a self that would be trusted by each of the people I met. The tension caused by this constant deception, and the high state of alert it required, left me exhausted at the end of the day.

Sometimes, when I lay down to rest in the evening I tried to take in all that had happened during the day, and most times my mind just could not cope with it. I thought about how to explain to myself what I was doing. It seemed to me then, and it still does now, that there are few brave men or women in the sense that they are "fearless." To me a brave person isn't one who's immune to fear. It's one who is afraid and yet manages to control his or her fear, overcome the instinct of self-preservation, and take whatever action that's needed to achieve the goal. If you have to do something risky, you just do it, without thinking about fear.

In most places I found sympathizers who were willing to help me avoid capture. I had many close calls. One time the person in whose apartment I was staying got a phone call telling her that soldiers were on their way to pick me up. I ran out of the apartment and down the stairs as the Germans were coming up in the elevator. I left so quickly I had to abandon whatever clothes I wasn't wearing, including my coat and hat—which was very unfortunate, since it was already winter weather. Winters in Poland are usually very cold, but during the war years they were particularly harsh, or at least it seemed so. Another time, German soldiers came to a house I was visiting moments after I arrived. I managed to race out the back door and hide in the yard while the Germans questioned my hosts at gunpoint. Events like these were typical of what I experienced frequently in my efforts to evade exposure and capture during two years as a resistance courier.

During those years I walked through the streets of unfamiliar villages and towns never looking over my shoulder or asking for directions. I couldn't risk being stopped and questioned because I appeared to be a stranger. Although my Kennkarte looked real, it was untested. I had no idea how it would stand up to the scrutiny of a skeptical German soldier, or worse yet, a Gestapo officer. The document itself appeared authentic enough, but all the information on it was fabricated. Even though I had memorized every letter of my new identity, there was always the chance that in a tense situation I would make a fatal error. And on top of the ever-present possibility of having my identity routinely checked by the authorities, there was the even greater concern that I would run into someone I knew, someone who could and would denounce me as a Jew. And if ever I failed to be mindful of my danger, I was constantly reminded of it by the decrees posted throughout Poland by the occupation authorities, alerting citizens to the extreme penalties awaiting those involved in aiding the enemy, i.e., the resistance.

There were no instruction books on how to handle difficult underground situations successfully—at least I didn't have any. One depended on good instincts, steady nerves, quick wits, and most of all, good luck.

The greatest danger to a Jew trying to get by on false "Aryan" papers wasn't detection by German soldiers, but being unmasked by the Polish police or Polish neighbors. Unlike the Germans, who rarely could tell a Jew from a Christian by sight unless he or she looked like a Nazi caricature, the Poles were expert at identifying Jews who were not very obviously Jewish. There were substantial rewards for turning in a Jew, but some Poles, including some police, made out even better by blackmailing Jews who were passing as Poles. Such extortion could go on profitably for years. There were several methods of identification available to blackmailers: Recognizing characteristic facial features, detecting typical mannerisms and inconsistencies in behavior, recognizing flaws in forged documents, and, in the case of men, the ultimate test—an invitation to the suspect to drop his pants. In the end, it was mainly great good luck that saved me and the other members of our group from capture.

Although being a resistance courier was a very risky job, when I went out as Leokadia Wawrzykowska I was somehow transformed into a more confident person. The fear of being Jewish left me when I disguised myself as a Catholic girl. I felt sure of myself and it showed. This was probably because in my situation such self-assurance was essential to survival. I couldn't afford to be afraid or nervous, I couldn't afford to think I was pretending. My behavior, my appearance, my voice—everything had to say I belonged. The slightest show of uncertainty—a sideways glance or hesitation before making a turn, any indication that I didn't know what I was doing, that I wasn't who I pretended to be—could mean the end of my life. By pretending to be someone who belonged, I temporarily acquired the self-confidence of an insider. I was like an actor who mentally becomes the character being played.

The only thing I really feared was my eyes. They were sad eyes, eyes that held thousands of years of Jewish pain. Even though my face was laughing and my step was light, I feared that my eyes were so sad they would betray me to anyone who looked close enough. In a mirror I could see that my eyes were not like those of typical young Polish girls. Yes, I had their blond hair and their fair complexion, but I didn't have their laughing eyes.

Somehow I survived in spite of my eyes.

It was November 2, 1942, a date I'll remember all my life. I had just returned to Nowy Korczyn from a courier trip and ran into my good friend Stefa on the street. When I told her that I'd just stayed with her sister, Stefa suggested that I spend the night at her house. She said we could drink a little vodka and I could tell her about my visit with Lotka. I was glad to have this invitation. For the past three weeks I'd spent my time almost entirely with strangers in very tense circumstances, so I looked forward to the comfort of being with an old friend. That evening I went to her home on the edge of town. We played for a while with Stefa's little girl and then put her to bed. After a light supper and a glass or two of vodka we talked for several hours and finally went to bed.

In the middle of the night we were abruptly awakened by the sounds of screams and gunshots. Stefa and I looked at each other with terror in our eyes. We knew it was the Germans and that they were searching for Jews with the help of the local police. We could hear them going from house to house, demanding to know the identity of each person. Anyone who was caught hiding a Jew was shot on the spot.

Stefa's mother came running into the bedroom and in a loud whisper gave me an order to stand on a chair she placed in the middle of the room. Standing on another chair set next to mine, she opened a small trapdoor into the attic and pushed me through. She was a tall, heavy woman, but she hoisted herself up after me, breathing hard, and showed me where to hide. I lay down on the wooden floor and she covered me with hay. Then she quickly lowered herself down to the bedroom and closed the trapdoor behind her. From my dark hiding place I could hear the German soldiers when they came to the door shouting "*Juden! Juden!*" Stefa's mother let them in, but neither Stefa nor her mother said a word about their hidden guest.

I stayed in the attic for two days. Three times each day either Stefa or her mother brought food to me and then left, quickly closing the trapdoor—there was always a possibility

that another German patrol would come to the house looking for hidden Jews. Between being half delirious with fever
from a cold I'd caught the day before and suffering from
the shock of my narrow escape, I ate almost nothing during
those days. Nor could I rid my mind of the thought that my
friend Stefa, her mother, and probably the little girl would
have been killed had I been discovered by the Germans.
During the second night, Stefa's mother opened the trapdoor
and helped me down. Words were not sufficient to tell her
and Stefa how grateful I was—hugs, squeezed hands, and
looks were all I could offer, and were all that was needed.

Two days later I had a visit from Janek Rozycki, a Polish
man of my age whom I'd known for a long time and who
I liked very much. On this visit however, Janek brought
news that filled me with horror, grief, and rage. He told
me that during the night of the house-to-house search, as
my life was being saved by my Catholic friends, all the Jews
of the town were rounded up, transported by horse-drawn
wagons to the nearest railroad station, packed into cattle
cars, and sent to the extermination camp of Treblinka.
This included my father, my brother Fischl, my brother
Herman, along with his ex-wife and his mistress (for all
his wealth, he was treated the same as the others), two of
my sisters, and all seven of their children—my entire family, except for Bronia and Kuba, who fortunately had left
Nowy Korczyn a month earlier.

After Bronia's husband was burned alive by the German
soldiers, a Catholic man named Maniek who'd worked in
Bronia's knitting factory in Lodz, told Bronia that he'd
always been in love with her. He said he wanted to help
her and offered to pretend to be her husband, since a legal
marriage was out of the question.

Although Bronia had no feeling of love for Maniek, as the
apparent wife of a Catholic Pole she would have a chance for

survival. For the sake of her son she agreed to the arrangement and the three of them moved to Lisow, a village about
thirty miles from Nowy Korczyn, where Maniek had a close
friend. (On their way to Lisow they passed through Busko
just after all the Jews there had been taken away. I was to
learn much later that among these victims were the mother
and younger brother of my future husband.)

There was no time to mourn the loss of my family or to
organize an attempt to find them. I knew that I must leave
Nowy Korczyn immediately before someone recognized
me and turned me in. Stefa helped me get word to Bronia
that I wanted desperately to leave Nowy Korczyn and
stay with her. I felt so fortunate to have a friend like Stefa.
Since childhood, she had accepted me when other Gentile
children ignored me or worse.

Word came from Bronia that Maniek would come to
Nowy Korczyn to get me. When he arrived, he paid Stefa's
brother to take us in his horse cart to the village where
Maniek and Bronia lived in a rented house. The trip took a
bumpy two hours, but it was well worth the discomfort to
feel the relief of being reunited with Bronia. We had been
separated only a short time, but so much had happened.
Now, not only were her husband and our brothers-in-law,
cousins, and uncles dead, but our father and all our brothers
and sisters and their children were gone. We had a little midday meal and then I lay down to rest and reflect on what had
changed in the terrible days just past.

Although I was shocked and horrified by the savage
murder of the men of the family in that barn near Lodz,
and felt deeply the anguish of my sisters on the loss of their
husbands, and of my nieces and nephews on the loss of
their fathers, the unimaginably awful fate in store for my
immediate family dealt me a blow like no other.

On January 15, 1945, my twenty-seventh birthday, the
Russian army entered Czestochowa. This was the best
birthday present of my life. Actually, when the Russians had
reached Warsaw their offensive against the Germans had
stalled and they stopped there for almost a year before coming to Czestochowa. Ironically, the few Jews remaining in
Warsaw believed that under the Russians they were safe, so
they came out of hiding, only to be killed by the Poles.

For most of two days and two night I stood on the sidewalk outside in freezing cold, watching with melancholy
satisfaction as panicked German soldiers raced to get out
of the city. At one point I was jeering at the Germans and
one of the soldiers aimed his rifle at me. Someone grabbed
me from behind and dragged me out of the way. Later I
watched equally panicky civilians, probably *volksdeutsche* or
collaborators, begging the retreating soldiers who were riding in trucks to give them a lift.

Not long after, I phoned my sister Bronia and arranged
with her for all of us to meet in Lodz at the home of a
friend. Getting from Czestochowa to Lodz was not easy.
With the arrival of the Russians there was a huge movement of people from one place to another. Many like me
were anxious to return to the hometowns from which
they'd been driven by the Germans. Trains were few and
extremely crowded. I waited for two days on the platform
in the station trying to get on a train going to Lodz.

The meeting with Bronia and Kuba in Lodz was very
emotional. Not only were we reunited after a long separation, we were trying to adjust to the realization that while
the war was over for us, we were the only survivors of our
family.

Before we started to search for an apartment I told
Bronia: "Now that I've survived the war, I want to be
myself. I'm walking off the stage and don't want to pre-

tend any longer." After more than five years of living with the stress of pretending to be someone else I was unwilling to continue concealing my identity, whatever the disadvantages. So, even though Bronia was supposedly married to Maniek, a Catholic Pole, we decided to look for an apartment as Jews. There were plenty of empty apartments in the city, but as soon as we said we were Jewish, doors were closed to us. We finally did find an apartment after a long search, and both of us got jobs in the knitting trade we knew so well. We began to think that we could start rebuilding our lives.

I was shocked to discover that after they had endured so much suffering at the hands of the Germans, Jews were still unwelcome in Poland. Little had changed from the war years as far as anti-Semitism was concerned. Many Poles resented the fact that so many Jews survived and were beginning to return to places they had been forced to leave. Some of those Poles were afraid that the returning Jews would demand return of the valuables or the property entrusted to them for safekeeping. Worse yet, many Jews who survived the war were murdered by organized gangs of Polish youths who were hunting them.

Having gotten ourselves settled, and now having some extra money, it was decided that Bronia and I would go to Nowy Korczyn to see if any of our family might have survived and returned there. We had very little hope of finding anyone, but we felt that we had to be sure. This was what most of the few remaining Jews did once the war ended. We left Kuba with Maniek in the apartment.

On our train trip from Lodz, we got off in Busko, the spa town that was the nearest stop to Nowy Korczyn, and walked the rest of the way, about fifteen miles. Once in Nowy Korczyn it took only one day to come to the terrible realization that none of our relatives had survived.

Back in Lodz, Bronia said she wanted to start her life over in a new place. Maniek wanted to go with her, but he was an abusive alcoholic and Bronia decided that she had done her duty as a wife, so she took the opportunity to be rid of him. Like many Polish Jews she wanted to go to Palestine, but she said she wouldn't go without me. But I felt that Poland was my country and, despite the hardships I was sure to encounter as a Jew, I wanted to make my life there. However, it soon became apparent that I would be facing something far more dangerous than mere hardship. A pogrom in Krakow was followed by a worse one in Kielce. Among Poles, rumors again circulated about Jewish people kidnapping Gentile children to use their blood to make matzo. As ridiculous as these stories were, they were widely believed. This old blood libel never died in Poland! Once again, the Poles found self-created justification for killing Jews. I knew that despite my feelings about Poland being my homeland, I had to leave.

When I think back to the German occupation of Poland I can hardly recognize the person I was then—the small Jewish girl who managed to survive so many dangers, surrounded by a hostile people, living with a false identity, subject to being unmasked and killed every moment of the day and night for four and a half years. With the customs and cultures of the Poles and Jews being so different it was impossible to know every detail of the life I pretended to live, and yet one small mistake could mean my death. The strain of those years left an imprint on me that's never been completely erased.

While living through that difficult time I took every opportunity to acquire knowledge that might help me survive. I also reflected on the causes of war and the motiva-

tions of my oppressors. I thought about how people can so
easily be dehumanized and perform inhuman acts, so that
a Jewish policeman in the ghetto could hunt his brothers
as cruelly as the Nazis, or a Pole could turn in a Jew for a
pint of vodka. I read books on Nazi ideology and philosophy to try to understand what could make humans behave
like beasts. I found under the boasting and strutting deep
feelings of inferiority and resentment that irrationally
focused on perceived injustices to themselves, while ignor-
ing the brutalities perpetuated on their innocent victims.
I took from my study of history the lesson that man is his
own worst enemy, destroying others, and in the process
himself.

I have one memento from my pre-war youth—a photograph that I carried throughout my life. It's a photo of
me and a girlfriend climbing up the side of a rocky cliff. It
was taken when I was about sixteen years old. My friend,
a Catholic Pole, had invited me on an excursion to the
mountains. I'm wearing shorts and a sleeveless top and my
hair is pulled back away from my face. We look like two
typical young Polish girls enjoying nature. And that's what
we were—almost.

Being Jewish always reduced me to an "almost" status.
When I was growing up in Nowy Korczyn, Stefa and
another Catholic girlfriend and I spent hours together
playing in the fields and in the woods. I loved nature and
spoke about my feelings. But my friends doubted that a
Jew could really love nature. Jews were supposed to love
only money and playing dirty tricks. But my friends liked
me and offered me their highest compliment. "Lonia, you
are just like one of us, almost."

When opportunities to return to Poland arose later in my
life, I thought about what it might be like to see my homeland again. I'd missed Poland so much when I'd left with

Bronia after the war. In Prague, our first stop after leaving, I walked around the cobblestone streets each day for two weeks searching for a reason not to return to Poland. "What am I doing here?" I asked myself repeatedly. Prague was a beautiful city but it wasn't my home. No other place in the world could be what Poland was to me—my language, my country. Over and over I reviewed in my mind the horrors of the pogroms and I reminded myself that I wasn't wanted in my country, but I wanted so much to return.

If I did return to Poland I knew I would look up Stefa and other people I'd known. I would have gone to places where my family had perished, where my home had been destroyed, and where I'd cried the only tears I'd know. When I thought of such a return all I could imagine was more disappointment and pain. I couldn't bear to face the feelings a trip like that would revive.

Sometimes I wondered if going back to Poland might have a different effect on me. Perhaps facing my fears and losses would help me resolve the phobias that continued to plague me. But I'd lived with these fears for so long and I knew them so well I couldn't risk making them worse by going back to their origins.

In 1978, my husband, Mark (also a Polish Jewish survivor), and I took a vacation with our young son, Gene, to southern Spain, driving unhurriedly from village to village. One day we wandered into a large field much like those in Poland where I'd played with Stefa. This field was filled with vibrant red, yellow, and blue poppies. I picked one and then another—and suddenly I was like a girl again, running happily from flower to flower. Running through the field made me feel free, as though I could get out of myself into a world where the weight was lifted from my life.

Gene understood my transformation and snapped a photo of this rare moment. "Mama, I've never seen you as happy as today!" he said. I immediately felt guilty. I hated myself for not being able to give such happiness to my son every day. I felt that I'd cheated my husband and my children because of the persistent sadness I'd carried with me from the war. But I also knew, deep down, that I'd given all I had to give.

Today when I look into my eyes in a mirror I see the truth about myself. I see that there is some small part of me that will always feel like damaged goods. I can't remember dreams. I can't cry. My phobias leave me scared and depressed. For some reason having to do with my life during the war I have great difficulty remembering numbers. But now I see also that I'm as good as other people, and better than some. I've reclaimed myself and I don't have to pretend anymore.

🙢 🙢 🙢

Lonia Winchester is a writer and artist living in New York City. Now an octogenarian, when she was fifty-three she decided to return to school and get the education she was denied because of the war. After fifteen years of study, she graduated magna cum laude from Fordham University with her B.A. This essay was excerpted from her self-published memoir, The Truth about Eyes.

DIANA COHEN

ℬ ℬ ℬ

Migration and the Sinai Desert

A mother and her children travel beyond
the bounds of maps and guidebooks.

L auren, who turned nine that year, learned to drive on
the long, lonely asphalt scar that connected Tel Aviv
with Sharm-el-Sheik, at the tip of the Sinai Peninsula. Our
old yellow VW Bug came to know that road so well that it
might well have driven itself. Lisa, the oldest, would ride
up front, her beautiful face pinched tight with feelings she
couldn't or wouldn't express. Lauren and her thirteen-year-
old brother, Marshall, would sit in back. When my eyes felt
scorched by the glare of the desert sun, Lauren would lean
over my right shoulder, take the steering wheel in her young
hands, and deftly steer us south. There was something about
the vastness of the landscape that made us fall silent the
farther south we drove. The car was quiet as we stared out

the windows at the enormity of the desert, so impersonal, so timeless.

There were advantages to not having a tent for camping: the stars were the canopy over our heads and we rose and slept by the rhythm of the sun. In the cool mornings we explored rainbow-hued side canyons, and swam and snorkeled in the Red Sea. Once a jeep with two young Israeli soldiers magically appeared from nowhere. *"Giverit, ma po corre po?* Woman, what's going on here?" they demanded. "It's hot, you could get lost, and you and your children could die of thirst," they scolded. But we pointed to our canteens hanging on our belts and I promised that we wouldn't amble up the canyon too far and risk losing our way. Shaking their heads in disapproval but somewhat mollified, they drove away and left us to our explorations.

Throughout the inferno of the afternoons we rested, huddled together in the oval-shaped shade cast by our Beetle. We ate ice cream whenever we had the opportunity and used pita bread as scoops for canned hummus, the mainstay of our diet. In the evenings we would lie on our blankets and watch the sun turn the mountains of Sinai shades of mauve, scarlet, and purple. I would tell the children stories to keep at bay the loneliness that settled around us like the deepening dusk. I'd make a small fire and brew Turkish coffee in a long-handled, royal-blue enameled pot. That old pot, chipped but still sturdy, sits on my kitchen counter in California now, reminding me of how the coffee would foam up in consternation. I'd pull it from the fire, stir in heaping spoonfuls of sugar, then pour its thick sludge into tiny white cups. We'd blow and sip and rock back and forth over our crossed knees from our perches on the still warm sand. We lived that summer much like the Bedouins we would sometimes see tending their goat herds, black slashes on the rocky landscape. We, too, were nomads, peregrinating around Sinai wherever the notion took us.

In those years before tourism, the coral reefs of the Red Sea were pristine and home to some of the richest marine life in the world. Snorkeling in its rich tapestry of colorful corals, brilliant lion fish with neon bright stripes, and graceful anemones that danced with the movement of the water, was like floating in an aquarium. Gorgeous shelled creatures littered the fine ivory sands, while the children's bodies cast flickering shadows on the reefs below. I would look through my mask and see Lisa and Lauren's long hair floating pale-gold and sunlit in the clear, warm waters. One morning we were snorkeling—totally absorbed in the wonders of the sea floor beneath us, floating in a big circle, holding hands—when suddenly we saw a massive dark shape in the distance. Unmistakably, a shark. Frantically scrambling to the safety of the shore was surely the wrong thing to do, but that frightened scramble was done on pure instinct—like gazelles fleeing a predator. Fortunately that one scare couldn't rob us of the joy and mystery of the Red Sea, our playground that whole long summer.

Our fair skin turned a glorious roast-turkey gold from so many hours under the sun. Lisa and Lauren and I wrapped our heads with gauzy cotton scarves, tucking in the ends like a turban. To protect his head, Marshall wore a black and white kaffiyeh—the headscarf worn by Palestinian and Bedouin men that draped flowingly down to his shoulders, secured with a coiled black rope around the crown of his head. The ends of that kaffiyeh floated in the dry air as he walked. Months after we returned to California, I continued to wear one of those scarves on my head, holding on to the spell cast by Sinai, unwilling to lose it so soon.

Midway through telling my story one evening I looked northeast toward Jordan and saw a huge tanker that appeared to be plowing straight toward us across the sand through a clump of mangrove trees. Its lights were blazing in the twilight and it looked as though it would shortly be upon us. Startled, I cried out and we all jumped to our feet, ready to run. Perhaps I had forgotten or didn't even realize how close we had camped to the Gulf of Aqaba, the narrow waterway at the northern end of the Red Sea. Or perhaps a sense of time and space are altered in that strange and ancient place. If it weren't all shifting sand dunes on the other side, we might even have been able to make out lights across the water in Saudi Arabia.

On our first journey into Sinai we met Sara, a ranger with Israel's Nature Reserve Authority. Sara's role in Sinai was to enforce Israel's strict laws protecting the coral reefs and the ancient archaeological sites. As one of the few employees in Sinai, she had been invited by the Bedouins to join a celebration in honor of the circumcision of the chief's thirteen-year-old son. To be invited was a great honor for a woman, and she asked us to join her. Seizing the chance for an adventure in the desert's interior, the three children and I piled into Sara's jeep. As we drove inland, bouncing over corrugated roads, the dust swirled up in clouds around the open jeep. Sara pointed to both sides and beyond the gravel road. "Those areas are full of unexploded land mines," she told us. "They're left over from the 1956 Sinai Campaign and the 1967 war with Egypt. We're safe as long as we stick to the road. When we stop to pee, just stay behind the jeep and don't wander off across the sand."

Darkness came quite suddenly in the desert, but not before we came to Ein Hudra, a paradise of crystal pools and a lush date palm oasis. Sara, who spoke fluent Arabic, introduced the children and me to the Bedouin chief who urged us to join the men gathered around a blazing fire. The celebration supper consisted of paper-thin pita rounds, baked crisp and brown on the top of an old oil drum lid set on stones over the fire. The bread was accompanied by what looked to be chunks of boiled goat, with plenty of hair still attached, and small glasses of strong dark coffee. In the darkness we could just make out figures draped in black, chanting and swaying in rhythm. The women were dancing, aloof and apart from the fire. We rolled into our blankets, listening to the high-pitched trill of their tongues against the roofs of their mouths. It is a sound that expresses excitement and joy and the cama-raderie of women—a wonderful sound to fall asleep to.

In those years Sinai was sparsely populated, and visitors, like us were a rarity and a curiosity. One afternoon a fam-ily of Bedouins invited us to their tent. What I remember most clearly is how carefully they used each precious drop of water. The mother, squatting on her haunches, sprinkled a few drops of moisture into each tiny white cup and wiped each clean with her index finger, before she filled it with thick, sweet coffee and served it to the men and then to us. I remember that the only things that moved with any speed in all that heat were the flies, and they mostly crowded around the mother's lips. Other than the flies' faint hum-ming, the silence in their tent was so intense that it felt like even Planet Earth had stopped spinning on its axis.

Marshall had become fascinated with the way the Bedouin men baked their bread. The smoky crisp bread rounds were rolled and eaten, perhaps dipped in hummus, if such a luxury was available. "Mom," Marshall whispered, his eyes large with excitement, "they're making bread over the fire. Can I go and watch?" The Bedouins, in their long black robes, noticed how taken he was with their bread making. So they scurried around and found another oil drum lid for him, so that he could make his own bread for his family. This obviously gave them a great deal of pleasure judging by their big smiles and flashing white teeth in response to the

clear delight of a thirteen-year-old. Those Bedouin would
have been pleased had they known that when we left Israel,
Marshall carefully carried that old drum lid on the airplane
back to California.

Wanting to explore more, we joined a Nature Reserve
Authority trip for a seven-day excursion into the interior of
the desert. One highlight in a week of highlights was hiking
up biblical Mt. Sinai and exploring the Monastery of Santa
Catarina. That was when the term "charnel house" entered
our lexicon. One room in the monastery contained orderly
rows of skulls, their vacant eye sockets staring straight ahead
at eternity. Another room was filled with femurs, all neatly
stacked like kindling. The Greek Orthodox priests were
shadowy figures, walking silently about in their gray cas-
socks. One had a stringy gray braid trailing down his back
to his buttocks. On more than one of these hikes up Sinai's
mountains, I would look about for Lauren; I could always
spot her long colt-like legs, way up ahead on the trail, as she
chatted away in a mixture of Hebrew and English with our
Israeli guide.

During those months the storks were migrating from
Europe; many would drop exhausted at the Nature
Reserve station at Ras Mohammed, at the very tip of the
Sinai Peninsula. I recall the clattering of their long beaks,
although if from fear or habit, we didn't know. The children and I felt so sad and helpless at not being able to
aid them on their long journey to wherever it was they
were headed. Our little group of four was a bit like those
storks; we'd left our home in Spain and were migrating to
another home, yet we had landed parched and lonely on
the immense drift of the Sinai desert.

Sinai was a lonely place for a seventeen-year-old. Lisa
was often moody and silent and I didn't know how to reach

her. I think that the oldest child of any family has it rough, but it was particularly rough for her as I stumbled along learning how to parent a teenager when I was still growing up myself. At least back in Tel Aviv and Jerusalem there were young men her age, youngsters already doing their military service who carried rifles slung over their shoulders, who were eager to be friends and show off their country. The remarkable thing was that these young men were eager to be friends with our whole family: mom, little sister, and younger brother as well as the seventeen-year-old beauty. But Sinai, for all its enchantment, was particularly empty and lonely for Lisa, so far from all the friends she had left behind in Spain. I'm certain we all suffered from loneliness and a sense of dislocation. After so many years living in a small Spanish town, I had dismantled our life and yanked us out by our roots. And perhaps this sojourn to Israel and the summer wandering in Sinai was my way of delaying the inevitable return to the U.S. Only Lisa would return to Spain, alone, to finish her A-Levels at St. Anthony's College.

Did I not understand how much it had cost my children to follow their mother to this country that they had only heard about from my stories? Did I not feel the pain of my youngest son who had left behind his beloved baby parrot CoCo, not knowing if he would ever see him again? Didn't I see that my meanderings were less an adventure than, what, an avoidance? Of what, the end of a beloved era? A return to a country and a way of life that I ran away from years before? However, being in Sinai, despite my daughter's unhappiness, required keeping my wits about me and being inventive, sort of like being marooned far from civilization. There was time to feel the loneliness yet there was no chance to think about the future. Each day was all there was.

For a few days we were joined by two Israeli brothers from Iraq who spoke Arabic and translated with the
Bedouins who wandered by. And on our last trip into
Sinai, we met up with friends from Tel Aviv, Elli and
Osnat. Together we caravanned around to the west side of
the tip of Sinai where we could look across to the oil stations in Egypt, giant flames licking the oil-laden air. Elli
had heard of a spot—El Tur, known for its deep pool of
hot mineral water. We all sat in that pool looking out at the
lights of Egypt until the mosquitoes drove us to take cover
in our blankets. That was the spot where our little VW
Bug got stuck in the sand and it was "dig out or perish."

On this, our last trip returning from Sinai heading
back to Tel Aviv, we drove until it was well after dark.
Because of the inky darkness I missed the kibbutz where
our friends Elli and Osnat were going to pull off to spend
the night. Instead, I kept right on driving until I couldn't
drive any longer. Finally I pulled the car to the side of the
road, we grabbed our blankets and slid down an incline to
sleep along the edge of a lake that we had seen many times
on our drives past. The lake is memorable as there is an
island in the center with what is thought to be a Crusader
castle on its peak. There we dropped into exhausted sleep
having no notion of the shock that would await us in the
morning.

While we slept our car was robbed. Picked absolutely
clean. Everything gone—even Marshall's dirty socks!
Cameras, undeveloped film, money, clothes, and our passports—all gone! Fortunately I had taken the car key with
me when we hastened off to sleep, otherwise we would have
been stranded and in serious danger in the desert heat.

Replacing passports when you haven't a shred of identification to prove you are who you say you are? In the
Middle East? The situation was especially difficult because

Lisa had a flight back to Spain three days later and one of those days was an Israeli holiday when the whole country shuts down. And, like so much icing on the cake, I slipped on the slick marble floors of the U.S. Embassy in Tel Aviv when they opened it especially for us the afternoon before her flight. Not only did they have this rag-tag, sunburnt mother and her three children, none of whom had any identification, but there was the mother, knocked for a loop, lying in the middle of their polished floors! Never, in all our adventures over all the years, have I literally been knocked down so painfully. That shocking collision with the marble floors was a mirror image of the shocking assault of the robbery. And what did I do? I did what I've always done when life flattened me. I planned another adventure.

≈ ≈ ≈

Diana Cohen lived for many years in southern Spain, working as a potter, riding beautiful horses, and studying the rejoneo, *the art of the bullfight from horseback. She wrote for* Lookout, *an English language magazine published in Spain. A 1983 Coro Fellow in Public Affairs, she lives in San Francisco and is finishing a memoir on raising a family during the last years of Francisco Franco's fascist regime in Spain.*

୬ ୬ ୬

A Tale of Two Turkeys

What's an American backpacker in China to do at Thanksgiving?

Even though it was speaking English, I wanted the voice in my head to go away.

"You're forgetting something," it murmured as I stepped off the train in Shijiazhuang. "Didn't you have another bag?" it asked, more insistently, as I dodged touts and money-changers on my way to the bus stop outside the station. By the time I was boarding the local bus that would take me to my friend Sarah's apartment, the voice was bellowing like a Red Guard. "Hey, you left something on the train!"

Halfway to the teachers' college where Sarah taught English, 175 miles southwest of Beijing, my day flashed before my eyes with sudden clarity. I remembered waking up in the women's dorm room at the Qiao Yuan youth hostel in Beijing. The long room full of closely spaced cots had all the ambiance of an orphanage. The beds' occupants weren't real charity cases, though, just frugal European and American backpackers like myself, new university graduates taking a travel deferment on adulthood.

I remembered taking a bus to Tiananmen Square. The Beijing bus had been so packed that sardined riders in front passed their one-mao bills hand-over-hand to the fare collector perched in the back.

I remembered walking from the square to the friendship store on Jianguomenwai Boulevard. There had been crunching locust-tree leaves underfoot, and the crisp air smelled like coal dust and candied crab apples.

I remembered picking up a box of Australian chocolate cookies and an overpriced, underfed frozen turkey from Hong Kong. I remembered tucking the bird under my arm like a clammy football and trotting off to the central station, where I just made my train.

I remembered getting on the local bus in Shijiazhuang, feeling strangely light in spite of the frame pack on my back and the daypack slung across my chest. It was then that I understood what the nagging voice in my head was talking about: Out there in the darkness, chugging through the Chinese countryside, nestled cozily in the overhead storage area where I'd stashed it so a conductor could sweep up sunflower-seed shells and cigarette butts, was my Thanksgiving dinner.

Brandishing the cookie box before me like a protective shield, I knocked on Sarah's door. "Hi, I brought cookies!" I yelped, hoping this would make my friend forget our deal: Sarah had promised that if I found a turkey, she would find a way to cook it.

Sarah considered my maniacally proffered gift. She also eyed my suspiciously light baggage. "You forgot something, didn't you?" she asked. I replied the way anyone who'd just ruined her first Thanksgiving away from home would have: I burst into tears. Sarah responded by doing the very last thing I expected: she laughed until she needed to sit down.

As soon as we both could speak, we agreed that it was too late to do anything that night. Sarah, in fact, seemed to feel that although we'd lost a turkey, we'd gained a great holiday-gone-wrong story that shouldn't be spoiled with a happy ending. I however, tossed and turned on the couch for hours feeling like the world's biggest turkey myself. I'd spoiled Thanksgiving. I'd wasted a piece of meat that had cost more than most backpackers spent in a month on food. If I ever returned home my mother and grandmother, who between them effortlessly orchestrated a ten-dish dinner every Thanksgiving, would undoubtedly disown me. And that's assuming I was even allowed back into my home state of Massachusetts. I slept fitfully that night, haunted by visions of puritanical authorities in buckled shoes sentencing me to wear a scarlet letter for the sin of Absent-mindedness.

Early the next morning I set off on a borrowed bicycle, armed with directions to the train station and a command of Mandarin about as reliable as the local electricity.

Conversational circuits blew almost immediately at the station information booth. "You left what on the train?" the attendant asked incredulously, "You'll have to go talk to security," she snapped, and slammed the window shut. The brownout continued at security. "Did anyone turn in a frozen turkey?" I asked the matron at the desk. She sighed and rummaged half-heartedly through a box of thermoses, ceramic mugs, and other train detritus. "No, no turkeys here," she said. "Try the information booth."

I pedaled dejectedly back to Sarah's, trying to cheer myself up by imagining my dinner being discovered by one of the starving Chinese children American mothers like to invoke, but it didn't help.

Sarah seemed almost relieved that the bird had not come home to roost. But because I felt so terrible, she volunteered her semi-bilingual neighbor, Mr. Yan, to help me talk turkey with security.

Talking about turkeys, incidentally, has not always been possible in China. Mandarin has a well-established word for chicken: *ji*. But the more recent introduction of turkeys required a new word, and the neologism chosen was *huo ji*, meaning, literally, "fire chicken."

My understanding is that the "fire" part is meant to convey something like the English prefix "mega," or "deluxe." All I have ever been able to picture, however, when I hear the phrase is a rocket-powered Henny Penny doing screaming barrel rolls over her henhouse, shooting flames from her tail like a MiG.

For this reason, the conversation with security quickly became one of the most surreal I've ever had in my life. "Can you describe the fire chicken?" asked the first security officer, who looked like he ate railroad stowaways for breakfast. "She says the fire chicken weighs about five kilos," translated Mr. Yan. The corners of his mouth twitched, but he kept it together. "Where did you last see the fire chicken?" asked the second officer, almost completely successfully swallowing a smile. "She left it in an overhead rack in a hard-seat car on Tuesday night...right?" Mr. Yan said, glancing at me for confirmation. "Yes, *ta shuo de dui*," I nodded, as solemnly as I could, desperately fighting back an attack of the giggles.

The men soldiered through the rest of their discussion. I struggled to keep up, biting my tongue every time the words "fire chicken" jumped out at me. Afterward, Mr. Yan explained to me that he'd learned that the train I'd been on had changed course at Shijiazhuang and was now bound for the province of Inner Mongolia. My backward bird looked to be heading north for the winter. "I'm sorry," Mr. Yan said as kindly as he could while trying not to laugh. "I don't think they're going to find your fire chicken."

Thanksgiving day passed with no sign of the wayward bird. I moped through Friday and most of Saturday until finally the god of feathery edibles decided I'd suffered enough. Returning from an errand, Sarah and I skidded our bikes to a stop in the dusty, brick-strewn courtyard in front of her building and saw Mr. Yan beaming in the doorway. "Guess who called," he said, trying to sound casual. "The train station. They found your fire chicken."

An hour later I was holding my well-traveled turkey in my arms. It was still frozen. By the next morning, the prodigal little bird was thawed, stuffed, trussed, and wedged into a portable oven that Sarah had somehow gotten her hands on. The giant egg-shaped device looked more like a beauty-parlor hair drier than an oven, but it did the trick, and several hours later, Sarah and Mr. Yan and I sat down to an inexpertly carved but perfectly cooked Thanksgiving turkey. We served it doused in lumpy giblet gravy, accompanied by powdery rolls, banana bread, gluey mashed potatoes, and litchi-fruit salad. We washed it down with Sprite. It was the most modest Thanksgiving I'd ever been part of, but I can't think of a single meal I've ever been more purely thankful for.

A lot has changed in the years since that Thanksgiving. Sarah got married and moved to New Zealand. (She also became a vegetarian—our ultra free-range turkey turned out to be the last one she ever tasted.) Sarah goes back to China periodically and reports that the Middle Kingdom we remember of bike lanes and old women tottering on bound feet has taken such a great leap forward that I wouldn't recognize it. Certainly China wouldn't recognize me, more amply padded than in my backpacking days, and showing some gray in the blond hair that Chinese children used to dare each other to touch.

Even our idea of Thanksgiving has changed. The cozy story I was raised with in Massachusetts, the one with the friendly natives and grateful pilgrims, has been supplanted—in progressive circles, at least—by a more complicated tale of mutual distrust and limited contact. I accept this revised version, but it has always seemed to me a shame that that first Plymouth Thanksgiving didn't work out better. Because as I learned in China, it could have. Every part of the story—the bumbling new arrivals, the face-saving locals, the improvised feast, the sharing of unfamiliar foods, the gratitude—it all could all have happened. I know because it all happened to me.

♫ ♫ ♫

Nicole Clausing has been leaving belongings in strange places since losing a security blanket in Orlando at the age of three. Her favorite place to lose things is Denmark, because misplaced objects always turn up right where you left them. (Admittedly, "The Tale of the Camera That Was Still on the Restaurant Table the Next Morning" wasn't a very exciting adventure.) If you should be passing through Florida, and you find a tattered blanket lying around, please alert the author immediately. She's in the Oakland, California phone book.

✿ ✿ ✿

10,000 Miles, 24 Water Parks, 10 Stitches to the Head, and 3 Bathing Suits Later

A mother-daughter tale of shared obsession.

We toured the United States by water park, my ten-year-old daughter and I. We set off on a wild ride to slide our way across America. So, people ask, just how does a family decide to spend a summer crossing the U.S. by water park? In Alaska, where we live, nobody would blink if we decided to kayak across the Bering Strait, but water parks? Did we decide to visit water parks first or were the water parks just the excuse for traveling cross-country? I mean, were the water parks the *reason*?

Obviously, they don't know water parks. To know a water

park is to be first in line at 9:30 A.M., last out of the water at 8 P.M., and to be incredibly irritated if they're only open till 6. It's to save showering for home later so it doesn't subtract from your available water park time. It's to find, at the end of the day, that the crowds have thinned out and you can run up the stairs and jump on the slide right away—no line. So you do it over and over again. Zip up the stairs and whirl down; zip up, whirl down.

Which is how this particular story gets started. Sophie and I are in Florida on our first big marathon of the trip: seven water parks in seven days. We have ditched my mother with Aunt Selma and Uncle Howie in West Palm Beach, and we have finished Water Park #6 (Coconut Cove) and Water Park #7 (Rapids). This is now serious water parking. No more Colonial Williamsburg, no more butterfly conservatories. We have many water parks and many miles to go.

We drive to Orlando and make it to Wet 'n' Wild just in time for the discounted evening hours. Now it's the big time. Disney. Typhoon Lagoon. Blizzard Beach. We have traveled all the way from Alaska—sweated through forty more degrees of temperature than anyone should ever need—to get to Blizzard Beach. We have heard of the Typhoon Lagoon wave pool: twenty-foot-high walls of water. We're warned to hold hands.

But the Typhoon Lagoon parking lot is already closed! Apparently other people think 100 degrees is a good reason to head for a water park. But we can't just come back another day, we have slides to run, parks to visit.

"If I sneak in and find a spot, does that mean we can stay?" I ask the man.

"Sure, you're welcome to try," and in we go. Sophie moves aside some cones, we turn left here and there, and we find a spot. Somewhere in the vast Disney World land of parked cars, we have found a spot. We will never find it again.

There's a giant sign at the entrance, listing the rides. Right off the bat, looking at the picture, we eliminate the "Humunga Kowabunga" speed slides from consideration. Sophie and I are not brave and daring. I throw up on merry-go-rounds and she has asked for rides at the state fair to be stopped so she can get off. Neither of us likes amusement parks. We like water parks. Not water trauma, water terror, or water nightmares.

We do the "family" raft ride, which is code for "won't scare you." We put on snorkels and travel "Shark Reef." We ride Castaway Creek and try to remember the cute typhoony names for all the entrances. The place is so clean we are positive they wash their sand. Then we discover the Storm Slides.

The Storm Slides are three body slides that start from one landing. To get to the landing, you travel hill and dale through the South Pacific. There's foliage and wooden bridges, stairs up and stairs down. It is a nature trail jaunt to the landing, and then you make your choice: Jib Jammer, Rudder Buster, or…Stern-something. I can never remember the name of that third one.

You sit down at the head of the water, in a little bubbling pool for your butt. You wait till the red light switches to green, signaling that it's safe to go, and you push off, lying down. You zig left and right, gain speed, move up the side wall of the slide. Now there's a section of tunnel, now an open part. You're whizzing past trees, people, ricocheting from side to side, splashing and holding your breath. Maybe you close your eyes, maybe you don't. It is all very fast, very zingy. Whoosh, whooosh, whoosh, and you're in the splash pool at the end. The splash pool faces a cozy set of bleachers where the other parents—the parents who are not zinging and whoosh-ing—wait for their kids.

This is where we're spending the tail end, line-less part of the day. We are flying up the stairs, dropping our limp dead bodies down on the slides. Sometimes we know which of the three is the better ride, but by now we are so addled and our legs so noodley that we just flop into the most convenient one. Climb, flop, slide, whizz. Again.

I don't know why we are so tired. The stairs can't be that bad. There are only six or ten going up at any given sec-tion. At Splish Splash on Long Island, we zipped through 83 steps five times in the last fifteen minutes of the day. At Rapids, I climbed 120 steps to go down Pirates Plunge, which I will never do ever again in my whole life.

So Sophie and I decide to count the stairs for the Storm Slides. Another Disney phenomenon: there are 153 steps, 110 going up and 43 going down, and we didn't even notice. No wonder our legs are like jelly.

Sophie decides we need to do a scientific experiment to see if the green lights at the top are synchronized. I am supposed to raise my hand in the air when my light turns green so she can see if it matches her light. (We are water park experts; we require empirical evidence.) So I push my body up 153 steps, plant my butt in a start zone, and watch the light. It turns green. I raise my hand.

Ugh, Sophie can't see my hand over the dividers between the slides. My light has already been green for a while. Something vaguely registers that my data is no longer timely, but I stand up and wave to Sophie anyway. As I stand, I feel the tiny bubbles in the start zone jiggle my feet. I trip over the bubbles. Or my feet. Hard to tell.

Next thing I know, I'm flat out on the concrete, my head cracked on the landing zone. My skull and brain are screaming. It is the most incredible pain, and I roll into the fetal position. Which is, of course, just enough roll to start me down the slide.

"Don't lose consciousness!" my brain screams. "You'll submerge at the end and drown." I go down that stupid slide with a cracked head. Oh, the pain! I zing and whoosh—more like flop and drag—and then I'm at the end. I stand up, face the lifeguard and the bleachers, and cross my eyes. There is blood everywhere. I am a blood fire hydrant.

Sophie, horrified, screams, "Mommy, all your hair dye has come out all at once!"

I reach my hand up to my head and blood drips everywhere. I tell the lifeguard I need a towel.

But this is Disney, so within a minute, I am in a wheelchair flying to First Aid. The man asks me how I am and I say fine. He asks Sophie, and she cries. I look at her. Her face looks exactly like the face she was born in, all purple and wrinkly. Her face mesmerizes me.

The nurse asks where we're staying. Hmmm, that's a good question. And which ride did it happen on? That takes some thought. I had a hard time remembering that before. I know I was on the one to the right. Was that the Jib Jammer or the Stern-something? Things just…elude me.

"Well, you better start remembering or your trip to the hospital will be overnight," says the nurse.

"Mommy, Knights Inn. Knights Inn," Sophie whispers.

"Knights Inn," I say.

"Jib Jammer," she says. She is obviously counting her immediately available parents.

"Jib Jammer," I say. I think this will work out just fine. I ask the nurse if she has a butterfly Band-Aid that will stick my head back together. She keeps talking about stitches.

Then Sophie is back. Was she gone? Yes, she had to take the men back to get our belongings. She has a stuffed animal and an extra-large Sprite, too.

"Where did you get all that?" I ask.

"They got it for me," she says.

"You're not allowed to have soda," I remind her.

"They really wanted to get it for me," she says. "It made them feel better."

We change out of our bathing suits in the bathroom. My blue bathing suit is purple now, but that's nothing compared to my rust-colored skin. I look in the mirror and can't get over the quantity of dried blood everywhere. My hair is crusty with blood, plastered with blood in all sorts of loops and curls. I smell of blood.

So they take us off to a clinic in a van. The waiting room is full. I discover the cell phone in my fanny pack. Tim had insisted we get a cell phone for this trip.

"Daddy, guess what? Mommy cracked her head open and there is blood everywhere. We're in the hospital and she's going to get stitches." It occurs to me that these cell phone conversations are punctuating our trip: "Daddy, guess what? We got robbed and you need to send us travelers' checks by Federal Express." The waiting room is laughing out loud. Sophie must be a treat on the phone.

"No," Sophie says. "It's you and the nurses. When they were telling you to keep your head dry for three days."

"Three days?!? We are on a national water park tour! We can't wait three days. We're in Orlando. We still have Tampa Bay. We can't miss those water parks." Which I guess some people thought was funny. But they also wondered where Disney put my blood. I mean, didn't they have to close the ride because of AIDS? Did the blood come down the slide before me? I wonder how I could know.

The bottom line: ten stitches to my head and pain only when I smile, frown, or wiggle my ears. They shave my hair and everything. I finally get the doctor down to only one day out of water, and by now, I can independently remember the name of our hotel. The van comes back for us. Oh, God, I'll never find the car.

But it is 11 P.M., and my car is the only one in the parking lot, the only one with Alaska plates. Acres of Disney World parking spaces—and my car. Tucked into the wipers, there is a note on Mickey Mouse stationery. Scott, the Disney guy, wants to know if I am all right, could I call him so he wouldn't worry. Would Sophie and I accept free tickets to Blizzard Beach? Turned out he'd been checking the lot all night to make sure we'd returned from the clinic.

"Oh," Sophie says. "They are so nice. I had to hug them goodbye because they were so nice."

"Well, some people might say it's their job…."

"I know," she says. "But they were nicer than they had to be for their job." I think so, too.

Which left me with only one problem: how to get the stitches out. The doctor told me a week or ten days, no longer or the skin would grow over them. Oh, yuck. But after Blizzard Beach, after Texas, after rejoining with Tim, we were on to Colorado, Water World, and his family. That would be more like two weeks.

Tim's sister Holly is a nurse. Or rather, was a nurse. Sort of a skeleton in the closet that no one talks about. But this wasn't brain surgery, it's just snipping stitches out, right? I wanted to show some confidence in her skills.

Our sister-in-law Linda said, "Outside. Do it outside. I don't want any blood in here." We went out on the porch with the new manicure set from my mother. There was nothing to worry about after all.

"Only time I've done this," said Holly, "was on a goat."

⁂

Barbara Brown and her ten-year-old daughter spent one summer crossing America ... by water park, beginning from their home in Anchorage, Alaska. While on the National Waterpark Tour, Barbara broadcast regularly from public radio stations around the country. These broadcasts can be heard at www.barbarabrown. alaskawriters.com.

Up Close and Personal in Frankfurt

It wasn't a bird.

"Did you see that?" I asked my husband, my eyes wide.

"Was it a redbird or something?" he replied, craning his neck. "I saw it disappear into those bushes."

Spring had begun in earnest, and I gloried in our daily walks to work through Grueneburg Park in the middle of Frankfurt, Germany. Every leaf was gold-green in the sunlight; the air was filled with the rich scents of warming earth and blooming flowers; and after the long cold, the park had begun to fill with people. Freed at last from the confines of winter, men, women, and children began streaming into the park.

That's when we had our first sighting. But it wasn't a bird.

"Is that a wig?" my husband asked with wonder, as the subject of our discussion re-emerged from the bushes.

"It's very red, isn't it?" my voice was unnaturally high-pitched in my efforts to sound completely natural. Completely normal. As if I saw a naked man in a red curly wig sunbathing in public every day of my life.

"Where do you suppose he found a wig that color?" my husband asked. His voice peaked an octave above normal.

After that, there didn't seem to be much else to say to each other and we finished our walk in awed silence.

We saw Red Wig—and his numerous companions— many times that spring and summer. They were impossible to avoid, as their favorite sunning spot was right next to the main path. As near as we could tell, their group assembled every morning by seven-thirty and didn't dissipate until well after dark.

But they were nothing compared to what the other side of the park had to offer.

The morning of our second sighting, we were again on our way to work. The weather was cool and damp, every blade of grass, every leaf, every flower sparkled with dew like diamonds. A light mist overlay the park and added a reverent hush to the world. An unfamiliar chuffing noise approaching rapidly from behind was the only sound in the vast stillness of the park.

Curious, I stopped and looked back. The mists parted and a figure emerged, coming at us from across the jewel-strewn grass. A very large man, clothed only in a very small and insufficient undergarment made his way across the meadow towards us. Arms akimbo and flapping like giant wings, knees brought to chest height with every step, feet set down in an exaggerated giant step; he was breathing like a steam engine and covered a surprising amount of ground in very little time.

He emerged, wraithlike from the mist, passed a few feet from our dumbstruck visages, and faded away before us, the mist closing behind him as if he'd never been. Only his footprints in the dew remained to mark his passing.

After a few moments of reverential silence—and to give him time to get well ahead of us—we resumed our stroll, too shocked to comment on what we'd just seen.

Finally, as we reached the edge of the park, my husband found the words to express our deep feelings.

"With all that exercise, he ought to be in better shape than that."

I nodded mutely, afraid to trust my own voice.

All through that year, Grueneburg beckoned to us, and Birdman and Red Wig became permanent fixtures in our lives. We silently rejoiced with Birdman as his girth slowly shrank (although his undergarment never seemed to cover any more than before). We smiled and nodded at newcomers to Red Wig's group of companions, and we slowly grew wiser in the ways of the Germans, until I thought I was prepared for anything. But I was wrong.

It was late summer, and I was riding my bike through the park to an early-morning appointment. Head down, intent on speed, I pedaled furiously, looking up only as I approached the pedestrian footbridge leading out of the park.

And there he was. Not Red Wig, not Birdman, but surely their close cousin. This man was jogging.

I swerved wildly, nearly sending myself into a tailspin on some loose gravel; I braked just in time to avoid going over the railing. As soon as I had regained my balance, I turned and gaped.

This intrepid exerciser, this bold body-builder was wearing a t-shirt. And pantyhose. And nothing else.

As summer rolled into fall, the weather cooled and our sightings grew less and less frequent. We no longer looked forward quite so much to our rambles through the park; our friends had gone, and were now swathed in coats and hats, indistinguishable from the rest of us mortals until spring should bring the sun again.

To console ourselves in our loneliness, my husband and I headed south of Frankfurt to Sachsenhausen, a district renowned for its restaurants and bars. We sought comfort in the food and warmth of a Spanish restaurant.

As we made our way along the narrow street, we passed a brightly lit sausage-vendor's cart. My chin was sunk into my coat in a vain attempt to keep out the freezing November wind that blew relentlessly around us. My husband interrupted my shivering by nudging me gently, a look of delight on his face.

"Look!"

And there he was, buying a sausage.

Wearing only a set of headphones.

A long-lost cousin to our friends in the park! My heart soared at the sight, as if I had caught a glimpse of home from far away. How he came to be so far from friend and home we will never know. Had he missed some vital cue to retreat indoors or into muffling coat? Or was he a rebel, a black sheep of the family, who refused to bow to convention even in sub-zero weather?

Should I approach him, I wondered, and offer him directions to his friends in Grueneburg? Or congratulate him on his single-minded adherence to his beliefs and preferences?

But something checked me, and I refrained. The German people are too reserved; he would not wish me, a stranger and a foreigner, to intrude on something so private.

So I merely gazed in wonder and appreciation at this relic from warmer days, other places.

The stranger completed his purchase, took his sausage, and strode away into the darkness.

And once again it was my husband who expressed the deep feelings of our hearts and gave voice to the question that plagues all of us at one time or another:

"Where does he keep his change?"

⁂

Kelly Schierman currently lives with her husband and three sons in Croatia where she works part-time as a freelance journalist and full-time as a mom. She has recently traded in her frightening encounters with German joggers for even more terrifying encounters with Croatian motorists. However, in spite of the roads, which defy the laws of physics, and the drivers, who defy the laws of man, she is already in love with her new home.

No Place

At a Mexican orphanage, a volunteer
learns the meaning of choice.

We found Ruben hiding by a makeshift toy horse—a barrel covered in a shabby blanket. He looked up when we approached but quickly looked down again, his eyes fixing on a clump of dried grass. "Rubencito, *chiquito, papacito,*" Juana exclaimed, throwing her arms around him. "Why are you here, beautiful?" she continued in Spanish. "We were worried about you, precious."

I looked on in awe. I couldn't believe that Juana—barely sixteen—already talked like a Mexican mama. The sugar words rolled off her tongue. And I couldn't believe that I, too, was being the perfect stereotype. She's from such an icy place, I could almost hear Juana say, that she can't kiss the cheek of someone she just met that day, not even the cheek of a child.

Thank God Juana's here with me, I thought. Imagine if I'd come with someone like myself. Someone else who only stood to the side, pressing down her sundress with sweaty palms. And it wasn't even hot. The sun had slipped behind the mountains an hour ago and now—with the wind blowing the dust into testy whirls—there was a chill in the air. No, I shouldn't have come. I should've known I'd make a mess of things.

I'd come to the orphanage with my neighbour, Juana, to drop off some donations and to celebrate Mexico's Children's Day. I'd never before been to any orphanage anywhere but Juana had been to this one several times. So, knowing exactly where to go when we arrived, Juana led me into the play-room. Then she sat down on a faded floral armchair and I perched on the edge of the one beside her. Donated furniture, I thought, as the springs groaned. Just like the television in the corner. Just like the toys in clusters on the floor.

We rustled our own bags of donations and a small crowd gathered. Juana pulled out a Barbie in a frothy white gown and gave it to a girl with black pigtails. "Isn't she gorgeous?" Juana squealed and the girl nodded. "Not as gorgeous as you, though," I added and the girl looked at me dubiously. Her shoes too big, her t-shirt splattered with lunch. Then she plunked herself on Juana's lap. Damn, I thought, she was gorgeous but it seems I shouldn't have said so. I never knew what to say to kids and here I was more lost than ever. I just couldn't stop imagining how terrible life would be without a family.

I handed out the rest of the goodies, then escaped to the kitchen to help Jenny and Karen (the orphanage's foreign volunteers) make sandwiches. By chance I'd met them recently while doing errands but there hadn't been time to talk—just a minute to stare at each other, dumbfounded.

Besides the people I worked with at the local university's English department, I never saw foreigners in Huajuapan— the small town in Oaxaca state where I lived. I'd had no idea there were volunteers in town and after so long away from my northern home, their brilliant blondness seemed blinding.

"We came three months ago through our church in the States," Karen said. "Donations from the congregation pay for stuff the orphanage needs. Like a new fridge," she continued, pointing with a slice of white bread to the old one. "With fifteen kids, that's useless. We end up leaving food on the counter."

The fridge was indeed small, a skinny rectangle that came up to my chest. But like everything in the kitchen— from the white tiled floor to the white walls—it was clean. "So what exactly do you do here?" I asked, guessing they were responsible for the tidy shine.

"Everything," Karen answered. "We even teach, and that's tough because we don't speak Spanish. So we learn our colors or whatever and then we teach them."

I'd found a rhythm halving sandwiches but what Karen said stopped me cold, mid-slice. "Why don't the kids go to school?" I asked.

"The government won't let children without birth certificates attend," Karen answered, now wrapping sandwiches in pink paper napkins, her stubby fingers surprisingly quick. "And some of the children were abandoned without them."

"But that's not fair," I protested.

Karen's lips formed a grim line. "Lots of things aren't fair here. I was going to stay a year," Karen continued, her blue eyes suddenly filling, "but I'm going home next week instead. I miss my family. I've never been away before and though I pray for strength, I can't hack it here. And I feel horrible, really selfish. I'm going home—I can choose to go home—but these kids…they don't have that choice."

A clown swept through the building and herded everyone outside for the activities, including a magician. Various families from the community had arrived and the Children's Day celebration was beginning. I found Juana and we sat down next to each other on fold-up chairs. The sound system whined; the sun glared. "Welcome," a woman said into the mike. "To start, I'd like the children to line up here.

"Now," she continued. "I'd like our guests to choose a child to be partners with for this afternoon's activities." Various people walked to the front and chose the smaller children, leaving the older gangly ones to look on awkwardly.

"Let's get a kid," Juana said, dragging me by the arm. And so we did—one of the last left in that stricken looking line—Ruben with his brooding eyes and slightly crooked teeth. And as we led him to our seats, Juana hugged him and I smiled, wanting him to feel comfortable. But of course I was worried. I didn't know what to say to an orphan girl, let alone a boy. A man should've taken him, I thought. A man would've known what to do.

Though perhaps not the magician, who was now in the circle of brown grass serving as the stage. We, the audience, weren't sure what the magician had been trying to do, but this obviously wasn't it—his face contorting, his hands squirming under a cloth.

"Now," the magician finally said to his assistant, directing him to reveal his arms. And the cloth came off with a flourish but nothing had changed—his hands were still tied.

"Amazing!" boomed the assistant, trying to explain away the failure, trying to loosen the knots.

"This is stupid," Ruben said and Juana laughed like he'd told a joke.

"Come on, gorgeous," she said, pulling him to his feet. "The games are starting. What'll we play?"

We circled the yard. "How about bowling?" I asked but Ruben's lips curled like there was something repulsive about plastic pins. "Perhaps bingo?" I continued to the same effect. "Or that game with the toy horse?" I was getting desperate. Apparently the orphanage had made Ruben grow up fast and at nine, he was already a bored teenager. Then Juana cut-in.

"Dice?" she asked and this time Ruben nodded.

The woman working that table handed Ruben a plastic cup in which he plunked the two dice and rattled them around, hoping to roll higher than his competitors. Ruben tipped the cup and the dice spilled out, making seven. A mid-range score, but still possible to win on as the girl who'd rolled first had gotten a four. But the final player took his turn and rolled an eight. "So close!" Juana exclaimed, as the woman handed the winner three bills of play money. "Want to try again?"

Ruben won the next two rounds and a smile twitched in the corners of his mouth—a smile he tried to squash even as he received his winnings. Then on the fourth round the cup spit out a two and he lost. And, having lost with the lowest of rolls, he didn't want to play again. So after that we went to the dart table, but the luck of his snake eyes slithered after us and Ruben's darts missed every balloon. With kids on either side popping the pink and yellow globes, I suddenly thought of my own childhood and the uncomfortable rub of my shorts in gym class, of the fact that the only goal I ever made was one I kicked into my own team's net. And something about Ruben told me he wasn't made for competition either, that he took it too hard and that unless something changed, Ruben might just snap.

We continued circling the yard with Ruben unsuccessfully playing games. Then, one by one, volunteers folded up the tables and put away the darts and dice until only the race track was left and everyone was crowded around it.

Ruben waited in line to participate, but a kid butted in front and he lost his spot. Then the race started so soon after that, that there was nothing Juana or I could do. The audience shouted and clapped for the winner while Ruben kicked the ground, his brow furrowed.

Ruben didn't look at me, not even a sideways glance. But I stared at him, with the sun—now sinking fast—casting an angry red light on his skin. "Don't worry," I said. "You'll race next." He has to, I thought—believing the day would be salvaged if people just clapped for him.

"This is a special race," the MC boomed as Juana pushed Ruben to the start line. "Being the last," the MC continued, "the winner will receive a bonus of 300 pesos, making the prize a whopping 500 pesos!" Obviously she meant play money, but everyone in the audience hooted and hollered. "Runners," she asked, "are you ready?"

"Yes!" shouted the kids.

"All right then, on your marks…get set…GO!" The smaller kids stood there, looking confused. But Ruben and two others took off. Really, the race was between those three and it was close. So close, it was only Ruben's toes that crossed the finish line first. In victory Juana raised his arms and she and the MC chanted his name. The crowd joined in, then erupted into applause—giving Ruben an unfettered grin, making me so happy, so relieved that I was the last person left clapping. Everything, I was sure, would be O.K. now.

Juana counted the money. When the games began, each team had received 400 pesos and we had 75 of ours left. Plus we had the 500 Ruben had just won. So we had 575 pesos in total. This was important because it was time for the auction. The community had donated a mountain of toys and the adult participants, by making bids, were to buy things for the children.

"What would you like?" I asked.

"The green truck," Ruben decided.

"But choose something else as well," said Juana. "Somebody might out-bid us on the truck." So Ruben chose a blue truck as an alternative; however, I was sure it wouldn't come to that—the MC was already plucking toys off the heap and they were selling for about 300 pesos. "We've plenty of money," I said and then drifted off to talk to Karen. She was sitting on a nearby stone wall, a Down's syndrome baby on her hip.

"How long has Ruben been at the orphanage?" I asked.

"He was abandoned here a year ago."

"Does he go to school?"

"Yes, but he hates it. He didn't start school when he should have, so he's behind—he can't read or write."

"Jesus," I said, sucking my teeth, wondering what would happen if he never managed to learn.

"He'll probably go into construction," Karen said as if reading my mind. "Construction workers sometimes come here and Ruben helps them. He doesn't get paid—he just thinks it's fun, but he works hard.

"Gosh," Karen said, interrupting herself. "People are going crazy for the toys." I whirled around and saw she was right. "This beautiful doll," the MC was saying, "goes to the woman in blue for 600 pesos!" Shit, I thought, heading back to Juana and Ruben. We might not have enough money after all.

The MC lifted up the green truck. "Two hundred pesos," Juana shouted. "Three hundred," shouted someone else and on and on the price leapt up until it was over 575 pesos, bursting Ruben's light mood. "There's still the blue truck," I assured him. "And look—it's up now!"

Again Juana bid until the price left us behind and this time, Ruben was crushed. "We'll get another truck," Juana said, trying to comfort him. "There're still lots."

"Whatever," Ruben said, walking away.

"O.K., you go play and we'll get a truck for you."

Ruben didn't answer or even look back and I kicked myself for asking what toy he'd wanted. Why hadn't I left it to Juana? She would have just gotten him something without setting up expectations.

Minutes later Juana was holding a truck—orange though otherwise like the others. "Where's Ruben?" she asked, but I had no idea. Not imagining that he would have gone into the now pitch-black yard, we looked through the building. Then unable to find him, I asked Karen if she'd seen him. "I think he's down by the toy horse," she said. And indeed, that's where he was and this time—I'd learned my lesson—I let Juana talk.

"Isn't it a great truck, baby?" But Ruben didn't look at it, so Juana tried to push it into his hands. "Come on, treasure," she urged. "Take it." Ruben clenched his fists until his thumbs and index fingers formed tight spirals like hard snail shells and finally Juana gave up and put the truck on the ground, close to Ruben's knee.

Trying a different tactic, she stroked his face. "Ruben, poor thing, what's wrong?" Ruben, of course, didn't answer. But one thing I was sure of was that the problem went deeper than not getting the truck he wanted. So much deeper than not rolling a twelve or bursting any balloons. Yes, Ruben at age nine had such staggering problems that—as I felt the tip of them—I could barely breathe. No, there were no quick fix solutions like a party or a little applause.

"Come on, dear," Juana cooed. "The other children are eating. Let's get your dinner." Ruben's jaw remained hard, unflinching, and impatience flashed in Juana's eyes. She wrapped her arms around him in a smothering hug and then tried to force him to his feet. For a moment I watched their struggle—him bearing down with his entire weight, her yanking at him—and finally I cut in, using the authority of my years over her. "Juana," I said. "Go get Ruben's dinner; I'll stay here with him."

She left and I sat down in the dirt beside Ruben. I looked at the stars, I looked at him and I felt suddenly and oddly comfortable. "It's O.K.," I said, not worrying about saying the wrong thing. "We'll stay here for a while. Sometimes it's nice to be away from people." I wanted to continue—in the same soft voice—and tell him to forget about this day and everything he'd known so far in life. I wanted to tell him that when he grew up he'd have his happy ending. But I swallowed those words and instead smiled quietly and held his hand. This was real life and I knew I couldn't promise him an *Anne of Green Gables* ending. Life, I realized, would probably continue to be tough on Ruben and maybe all he had to look forward to was a few peaceful minutes looking at the stars.

That night when I left the orphanage, tears streamed down my face. I was remembering what a teacher had once told me—that in a good story, there is always an important change. And I was thinking that if my day had been fiction, it hadn't changed in any satisfying way. In the end, as in the beginning, only some of us have the choice to go home.

≈ ≈ ≈

Canadian-born Andrea Miller has been living in Mexico for more than three years, but she has also lived in Japan, Korea, France, Spain and England. Look for other examples of her writing in various anthologies, including The Best Women's Travel Writing 2005 *and* Tales of Travelrotica for Lesbians.

SUZANNE KRATZIG

꿈 꿈 꿈

Getting There

A bush taxi ride in West Africa offers
lessons in being "there."

As soon as I slid across the seat of the rusty five-seater
and spotted the goat calmly sitting on the floor-
board where my feet should have gone, I knew it would be
one of those trips. This little goat was lucky in comparison
to his brothers and sisters who were stuffed in the trunk
or strapped on top of the car with a bunch of roosters. The
goats' bleating cries sounded like the battery-operated baby
dolls of my childhood: *waaa, waaa, waaa.* The roosters were
mostly silent.

My two friends crowded in after me. Colette was a
petite midwife with hands smaller than her smile, which
stretched across her face in a sea of sparkling teeth and
dimples. She was a transplant from the big city in the south
and one of the few women I knew who would drink beer
in a *buvette* at night. Pauline was a nurse who blushed and

covered her mouth when she talked about a man who'd
caught her eye. Her bulk spilled over into Colette's lap. I
prayed that the chauffeur would not find a fourth to shove
in the back seat with us.

Just after I'd managed to settle myself comfortably, with
my bags on my lap and the furry animal at my feet, the
door on my left opened, revealing a wrinkled, leathery
woman draped in a gauzy headscarf and a sarong. She
shoved herself in, crunching my hip and pinning my arms.
And then she noticed me. "Ooooooh, *Bature!*" she cried,
calling me the word for white person in Bariba, the local
language of which I only knew basic greetings. Her eyes
widened, and she began jabbering away. I caught the word
duro, which means husband, as she gestured towards the
chauffeur and then back at me.

A man who shared the front seat with a market woman
explained the exchange in French. He clutched his briefcase
under his arm and waved the other one around to point at
me and the driver. "She wants you to marry the chauffeur,"
he said. He and the driver laughed. I smiled weakly. This
was not the first time I had been promised to a man without
my consent. I probably had more than 350 fiances scattered
throughout the country.

The chauffeur pointed to his head and circled his finger
around. "She is not all there," he said. "*Elle est folle!*" She
is a crazy old woman.

I just nodded my head. I turned to look at Colette, who
rolled her eyes. The old woman elbowed me in the ribs as
she adjusted her veil and gave me a toothless smile before
continuing to bellow at the taxi driver over the rattling
engine. I sighed and closed my eyes, taking in the heat, the
stench of goat mixed with exhaust and diesel fuel. I wished
I could free my arm long enough to take a book from my
bag and tune out of the ride.

The scenery on this taxi ride was familiar to me now. I regularly traveled from N'Dali, Benin, the small northern town where I lived and worked as a Peace Corps volunteer, to Parakou, the regional capital that was sixty kilometers to the south. The African villages we passed through had long since been scenes of wonder to be gawked at like the Eiffel Tower or Gaud"s cathedral. Now, they were markers: Bahounkpo was the first real town we passed through; Sirarou was the half-way marker; Boko meant we were almost there. Some taxi rides passed by more quickly than others. Despite the company of friends this time around, I knew that this trip would be a long one, especially when I heard sighs coming from Colette and Pauline, who had been traveling in taxis like these long before I arrived.

On my first trip up north nearly one and a half years before, I had climbed into a nine-seater Peugot station wagon taxi with my fellow trainees and their Beninese counterparts. We were halfway through our three months of training, and this was our first trip to our posts, where we would spend the next two years. Early that Saturday morning, our bags were light, but our hearts and minds were overflowing with expectation and excitement. We nervously chattered and laughed as the metal beast clanked and chugged through the southern landscape of palm fronds and pineapple fields.

The expectation and excitement didn't last too long, though. Our driver, first to our amusement and later to our dismay, stopped constantly. He backed down the busy road, horn blasting, for the sole purpose of greeting another taxi driver with the customary finger-snap hand-shake and questions about family, work, village, health, and, my favorite, presence. *"Bonsoir! Tu es la?"* Are you there? *"Oui, je suis la."* Yes, I'm there! "And your family?" "Thanks be to God, they are there!"

Our driver detoured through the busy administrative capital of Cotonou stopping at market after market to load our already weighty car with gifts and goods for northern friends and merchants. In Sehoué, we stopped to buy pineapples and tomatoes. We entered another village in which the road was lined with tables holding bags upon bags of white *gari*, the dried manioc that is used to make porridge. Each village had its specialty, and we collected them all like Happy Meal prizes. What should have been an eight- to nine-hour voyage had already surpassed twelve. Despite the inaction of sitting in a car all day, my friends and I were exhausted. We finally pulled into my village at one in the morning and, thankfully, managed to find someone who could lead us to the compound that would eventually become my home.

After dumping my bags inside, I waved goodbye to my friends who still had a few more hours to travel, and ventured back into my house, exploring its cement walls with the beam of my flashlight. That night I lay awake, listening to the sounds that ruptured the darkness: fluttering and scurrying bats and insects, banging pots and crying babies, distant drum beats. Each creaking door in my neighbors' houses sounded like my own door opening, and I remembered my father walking around our house with a shotgun any time our alarm went off. I prayed that no one had heard my rustling and was coming to investigate, to protect his family. I got up and found a hammer in my living room and placed it next to my pillow. A part of me wished I were still crunched in the taxi with my friends, eagerly awaiting their destinations, but I had already arrived at mine.

Now, nearly two years later, I no longer slept with a hammer next to my pillow. Instead I lay awake and breathed softly, allowing the sounds of a West African night to rock me to sleep like a mama's lullaby. But the uncomfortable taxi rides had become a necessary evil. Had a hammer been able to ease me through each journey, I would have gladly packed one in my bag, right there next to my water bottle.

We had barely left the town when the old Bariba woman yelled out for the driver to stop. She and the chauffeur hopped out, slamming their doors behind them. With the car stopped, the pungent air inside settled upon us like an itchy blanket. I felt like a hanging slab of meat collecting flies. My stomach juices churned in protest to the cauldron of the car. "Why is the window shut?" My head screamed as I cranked it open. A rooster flopped down next to my head, squawking and flapping, and I jumped. Colette and Pauline laughed, as I cursed. I debated over whether or not I should shut the window. If I shut the window, I would begin to bake. If I left it open, I might get pecked in the face by an angry rooster. I looked down at my very first scar between my thumb and finger on my right hand. While gathering eggs on my grandfather's Texas ranch, I had made the mistake of reaching into a chicken coop before the hen had exited. The mark she gave me was a tiny triangle, barely noticeable, and the memory of it was somewhat laughable. Still, I was not eager to repeat the experience. I grudgingly shut the window.

The man with the briefcase in the front seat tapped his hand on the windowsill. Colette and Pauline occasionally clicked their throats or muttered "*vraiment!*" which was the Beninese equivalent of, really, come *on*! Finally, the woman and the driver climbed back into the car, and we started off again.

Not ten minutes later we entered a small town, and again, the old woman adjusted the folds of pink cloth around her head and knocked into me as she indicated a place for the chauffeur to stop. We pulled over next to a mosque. It was ten minutes before the two o'clock prayer was supposed to begin. The chauffeur showed us his five fingers. "*Cinq minutes!*" He said. He and the woman wandered over to wash their feet, face, mouth, and hands with water from plastic teapots and join dozens of other devout Muslims who already kneeled on prayer mats. The rest of us sat in the simmering brew of goat, roosters, exhaust, and sweat. Colette sucked through her teeth and fanned herself with her tiny hand.

The five minutes stretched into ten, and finally, the man in the front seat threw open his door and planted his feet on the dirt. Frustration gathered in him, creeping up his pacing legs, deepening in his clenched fists like a cartoon character who eventually spouts steam from his ears. He was a volcano on the verge of eruption. He had places to be and people to see. He wore a fancy Western suit and complained that he was late for an important meeting. This Beninese man was one of the first I had encountered in my year and a half who had a schedule for which he could actually be late.

Schedules were irrelevant most of the time in Benin, but for the Beninese road, the concept may as well have never been invented. The taxis travel at paces set by the whim of their drivers, passengers, and engines. Sometimes they sped like NASCAR racers, and I closed my eyes and held onto whatever I could with white knuckles. Other times they motored along slowly as the engine struggled up each hill, and I drowsily watched each pebble through the hole in the car by my feet. Sometimes taxis stopped for what seemed like hours, to load mangoes or livestock, to fix a flat tire, to hand deliver a message. Sometimes they wouldn't stop for anything. Chauffeurs kept their hand on the horn as their

cars blew through the village like a fierce *harmatan* wind
from the Sahara. Passengers would simply grit their teeth
and pray for safe and swift delivery.

When the driver and woman finally finished their
prayers, the scheduled man let loose. "You could have at
least politely made your excuses and told us you were going
to stop when we were on the road!" he shouted at the chauffeur, slamming his door. "*Vraiment!* It's incredible!" The
man and the chauffeur hollered at one another in French.
Pauline leaned forward to join the action. Another language, Fon, flew out of her mouth in a high-pitched stream
of dipthongs. The old woman jabbed me in the side as she
joined in with guttural Bariba. The goats banged around in
the trunk. Taxis swerved around us as we all careened down
the skinny, black road. The five-seater had reached its boil-
ing point in a cacophony of tones and gestures and smells. I
desperately had an urge to cover my ears, my nose, but my
hands were crushed between the wrinkly woman and my
friend Colette. I pushed my body forward and wrenched
my arms free.

"*Laisse-le!*" I cried out. "*Laisse-le!*" Leave it! Everyone in
the taxi turned to look at me, this white woman unafraid
to join the action, and their grumbling and snappish comments slowed. After about ten minutes, there was a tense
silence. Even the goats in the trunk seemed to settle in for
the ride.

I turned to look at my friend Colette. She looked miserable, and I knew I must look the same way. Pouting and
uncomfortable. I thought of long car trips with my family,
the invisible lines my sister and I would draw on the seat
between us to separate my side from hers. Suddenly, I
couldn't contain myself any longer. A girlish laugh escaped
from my mouth like an uncontrollable fart. Colette looked

at me with a crease between her eyebrows and a frown on her lips. I quickly shut my mouth, but inside, I was bubbling over with giggles. There were no sides in West African taxis, no space for invisible lines. I couldn't block out the trip no matter how hard I tried. And now. Now that my arms were free, I could reach for my forgotten book if I wanted to, but I didn't.

Instead, I looked at the man in the front seat who didn't take the chance to stretch his legs and forget his schedules for five minutes because his religion doesn't require five prayers a day. I thought about all the yoga classes and meditation groups, gyms and incense candles I'd left behind in the States, all of those actions performed, those items purchased to remind us to stop time and be present. And I thought about the Beninese who always ask, "*Tu es la?*" Are you there?

I let out one more laugh, and then, I closed my lips in a smile. And I stopped to notice it. All of it. The pain in the left side of my back. The goat at my feet beginning to move around and bump the back of my legs. The rooster's head hanging down outside the window. The thumping goats in the trunk. The leathery elbow in my ribs. The taxi bottom scraping the road as we bounced over another pothole. My breath rose and fell in sync with the two women pressed to either side of me. We were all in this together, this stuffy, stinky trip from N'Dali to Parakou, and now, I wouldn't have had it any other way. I would never have traded this trip for a spot in one of the shiny, white Land Cruisers that sped past with international workers inside. They were the ones missing out on the best scenery.

I watched the colors of the landscape flash by me. I smelled the cooking fires as we drove through villages. We stopped once again in a village I regularly visited to do some work with a women's group. The old woman next to me got out for the last time, and we all waited as the driver unloaded her goats. Then I smiled as I remembered a previous taxi ride. We had stopped in the same town, Warikpa, and one of the old Bariba women there recognized me. She had hobbled over to the side of the road. As the driver had gotten back in and started the car, the stooped-over old woman had straightened her shoulders, lifted her face, and called out my Bariba name, Baké. Her eyes had sparkled in the sunlight. She had held her hands out towards me like an offering and begun to chant a *griot's* song. I had asked the man in front what the woman was saying. He had said she was wishing me a safe journey.

I thought about her now and wondered where she was. I imagined she was still singing me a safe journey, and my heart filled. We still had a ways to go to get to Parakou, but in my mind, I had already arrived. *"Tu es la?" "Oui, je suis la."*

❧ ❧ ❧

Suzanne Kratzig has not squeezed herself in a bush taxi since the end of her days as a Peace Corps volunteer in Benin, West Africa, in August 2005, but she intends to go back to explore more of the continent as soon as possible. Her travels have taken her across Europe, West Africa, and the USA. She currently works in Boston, Massachusetts.

ACKNOWLEDGMENTS

Many people's labor, time, and care went into putting this anthology together—hour upon hour of reading, selecting, editing, designing, formatting, copyediting, proofreading, and seeking permission to use the stories. Thank you for all the labors of love provided by Travelers' Tales founding editors and my mentors over the last decade, Larry Habegger and James O'Reilly. Thanks goes as well to Sean O'Reilly for superb editorial help and contributions, and to Melanie Haage for her design and typesetting. Heartfelt thanks to Susan Brady, Travelers' Tales' editor and production manager extraordinaire, for her consistently excellent rendering of every aspect of these books from start to finish. Many thanks also to Amy Krynak, who volunteered her time and talent to work with me as an intern and contributed to the resulting book you hold in your hands.

I want to extend very special thanks and appreciation to my husband Charles Bambach and my dear friend Tehila Lieberman, both of whom also have been my best editors for many years now, and on whose careful eyes and writing judgment I regularly rely.

About the Editor

Lucy McCauley's travel essays have appeared in such publications as *The Atlantic Monthly, The Los Angeles Times, Fast Company Magazine, Harvard Review, Science & Spirit*, and Salon.com. She is series editor of the annual *Best Women's Travel Writing*, and editor of three other Travelers' Tales anthologies—*Spain* (1995), *Women in the Wild* (1998), and *A Woman's Path* (2000), all of which have been reissued in the last few years. In addition, she has written case studies in Latin America for Harvard's Kennedy School of Government, and now works as a developmental editor for publishers such as Harvard Business School Press.